CRADLE OF VALOR

CRADLE OF VALOR

The Intimate Letters of a

Plebe at West Point

Between the Two World Wars

BY DALE O. SMITH

Major General, U.S. Air Force (Ret.)

With an Introduction by John Eisenhower

ALGONQUIN BOOKS OF CHAPEL HILL 1988

Published by
Algonquin Books of Chapel Hill
Post Office Box 2225
Chapel Hill, North Carolina 27515-2225

in association with
Taylor Publishing Company
1550 West Mockingbird Lane
Dallas, Texas 75235

Design by Molly Renda.

Library of Congress Cataloging-in-Publication Data
Smith, Dale O.
    Cradle of valor: the intimate letters of a plebe
at West Point between the two World Wars / by
Dale O. Smith: with an introduction by John
Eisenhower.
    ISBN 0-912697-80-6
    1. United States Military Academy—
Description.   2. Smith, Dale O.—
Correspondence.   3. United States Military
Academy—Biography.   4. Soldiers—United
States—Biography.   I. Title.
U410.P1S54 1988
355'.007'1173—dc19   87-30426
                                       CIP

FIRST EDITION

To the United States Military Academy Class of 1934—
   a band of brothers

CONTENTS

List of Illustrations   [ix]

Introduction by John Eisenhower   [xi]

Preface   [xvii]

Acknowledgments   [xix]

1. Beast Barracks   [1]

2. The Drill Begins   [17]

3. Gaining Polish   [36]

4. We Join the Corps   [54]

5. Academics   [69]

6. Plebe Football   [82]

7. Football Trips   [100]

8. The Cuba Game   [114]

9. The Navy Game   [129]

10. The Gloom Period   [143]

11. Choir Trip   [160]

12. Plebe Boxing   [174]

13. Spring Comes   [185]

14. Dad Gets a Job   [201]

15. Second Choir Trip and Track   [215]

16. Recognition   [232]

17. Where Are They Now?   [245]

Appendix I: Glossary of 1930 Cadet Slang   [256]

Appendix II: "Poison Ivy and Highways,"
   The Pointer, 1930   [258]

Appendix III: Roster of the Graduating
   Class of 1934, USMA   [262]

LIST OF ILLUSTRATIONS

Editorial: "To the Plebes"   [2]
"Brace!"   [4]
Alden K. Sibley   [11]
Cartoon: "Mr. Smith Sees His Grades"   [23]
Do cadets still take fleeting glances?   [47]
Taking break during hike   [66]
James Walsh   [67]

BETWEEN PAGES 76 AND 77

Entering plebe Smith being measured
Smith family
John Lawlor
Ruth Marschalk
Beast Barracks montage from *Howitzer*
Commandant inspecting A Company
Plebe football squad, 1930
Getting the word: 1976
Getting the word: 1930
Color Guard
Dining hall, West Point, from *Howitzer*
Drew Smith, 1930–31
Drew Smith, 1943
Jean and Mother with Viking automobile
"Recognition"
Cast of Hundredth Night Show, 1931
Albert Wilson and John Lawlor
A Company friends in summer camp

Cartoon: "Point Periodicals"   [84]
Cartoon: social life, Annapolis vs. West Point   [131]
Christmas dinner menu   [140]

"On the cuff" Hop Card   [145]
Hop medallion   [148]
Cartoon: military history   [179]
Cartoon: "Dill, Skill & Quill, Chill"   [187]
Joseph Cleary   [195]

BETWEEN PAGES 204 AND 205

On boxing team, 1934
Yearling furlo, summer 1932
Studying in room
Summer camp
Yearling year
Family visitors
Marching to chapel
Hop, Cullum Hall
A Company firstclassmen, 1934
Boxing squad, 1934
With Chinese pilot on Taiwan, 1959
Lt. Drew Smith gets his wings
Plebes reporting, 1970s
Dale Smith, Okinawa, 1958
Dale Smith on retirement, Pentagon, 1964
June Week parades: 1933, and 1975

Summer camp: horse cavalry   [217]
Cartoon: "At last, Lew, we're recognized!"   [239]
George B. Dany   [252]

INTRODUCTION BY JOHN EISENHOWER

The United States Military Academy, at West Point, New York, is a time-honored institution. For nearly two centuries it has provided leadership to the United States Army and Air Force through seven major wars, not to mention countless small wars with the Indians. Its name is familiar to all educated Americans, and its role in defending our country is universally acknowledged. And yet few, if any, of our institutions are less understood. Indeed, most of our citizens regard West Point, as it is commonly called, as the embodiment of a harsh, alien environment, something the average citizen has little desire to understand, much less to become too closely involved in.

The psychological abyss that lies between West Point and the public in general is not difficult to explain, as West Point has, indeed, spawned a culture outside the mainstream of American society. This condition, I might add, has been encouraged rather than dispelled by most graduates. For West Pointers admittedly tend to consider themselves a breed apart; they are remarkably inarticulate in expressing their feelings about the place, feelings that in many cases are decidedly mixed. Perhaps the West Point experience was too traumatic to be readily shared; perhaps intense loyalty precludes objective discussion of its strengths and weaknesses with outsiders. In any case, West Point's graduates have done little to explain their alma mater to the electorate that supports it.

Part of the West Pointer's feeling of being "different" can be attributed to the majestic scenery in the midst of which he strives so hard: the broad vista of the Hudson River from Trophy Point up toward Newburgh, Storm King Mountain scowling down from above. Such surroundings tend to instill a feeling of separateness from the common, workaday world. But also important is the strange position that West Point has found itself in, an undergraduate academic institution that exists only for a single purpose, judged only for its effectiveness in accomplishing that purpose. This in contrast to Harvard, Yale, or any other civilian university in which education is an end in itself. And as a tax-supported institution, West Point is the ward of a jealous and suspicious Congress, sensitive to public opinion. The Academy is chronically the target of ultra-liberal groups who dislike the fact that the military cannot be run as a democracy. These attitudes tend to make the products of West Point somewhat defensive when discussing it with civilians.

When one beholds the seemingly indestructible granite walls of today's West Point, he seldom realizes how humble were the school's beginnings and how precarious, at first, was its existence. From the beginning of our Republic, many saw a need for some sort of military academy, and George Washington, remembering vividly the agonizing weaknesses of his Revolutionary Army, made its establishment a major issue. However, so opposed to any standing army were most of our citizenry that even Washington's prestige could not bring about legislation to that effect during his whole eight years in office. Ironically it fell to Thomas Jefferson, the great foe of standing armies, to make the Academy a reality. In 1802, furthering his idea of a national and scientific university—and hoping to combat a trend toward Federalist conservatism in the Army's ranks—Jefferson managed to secure enactment of a law establishing such a school. West Point, an Army post steeped in the dramatic history of the American Revolution, was chosen as the site.

The Military Academy started out in an unpromising manner. Devoted mostly to the study of engineering—the first engineering school in the United States, incidentally—it had at the outset no set curriculum and no set residence requirements. The first class consisted of two cadets, who graduated the same year they entered. Cadets were treated as "gentlemen," with all the privileges pertaining thereto, and their numbers were small. By the end of 1808, West Point had graduated only forty-five cadets.

West Point looks upon Sylvanus Thayer, a graduate who took over as superintendent in 1808, as the real founder of the Military Academy as we know it, though in official sequence he was the fourth. Based on a study of conventional military academies in Europe, Thayer revamped the curriculum from the ground up, given support, no doubt, by public realization of the poor performance of our troops during the War of 1812 with Britain. The result was a disciplined Corps of Cadets, personified humorously in the motto, "No horse; no mustache; no wife." As the spiritual founder of the Military Academy, Thayer has been deified at West Point, and during his lifetime was given many kudos for this and other public service accomplishments.

Through the years West Point grew, expanding in numbers and broadening its interests from pure engineering to all the combat arms. With its major contribution to the success of our arms in the war with Mexico (1846–48), it became recognized universally as an indispensable national asset. At the same time, it emphasized military professionalism, which implied aloofness from other affairs of the nation and, as an inevitable offshoot of that professionalism, fostered elitism. West Point's atmosphere remained monastic, eventually coming to resemble less and less the real Army it was designed to serve, providing only the ideal military example to be emulated after graduation. Thus the Military Academy became, through the years, an institution far different from the one that Thomas Jefferson had envisioned.

Has all this separateness been necessary? Most of it, probably, as any successful military society must be run with a degree of authority unacceptable to many. But the distance between West Point and the society that supports it has been reduced, if not dispelled, and it could be further reduced if more really authentic accounts about it could be written.

Unfortunately, most accounts of West Point fall into two categories: straight-out histories, and novels. Neither has done particularly well. The histories have tended to glamorize, to romanticize the atmosphere and to dwell on the spectacular accomplishments of those graduates whose names have become household words to the American public. Dwelling on these superstars, who have included most of the Army high command in every war in this century, has caused most histories to neglect the role the Academy has played in developing its vital "other" graduates, the men who have commanded regiments, divisions, air wings. And if the histories have been wanting, the novels have been worse, sensational and utterly foreign to the truth.

Dale O. Smith, Major General, USAF (Ret.), has, in *Cradle of Valor*, performed a distinct service in portraying West Point as seen through the eyes of a cadet back in the 1930s, the years of the Great Depression. He has accurately described that "old" West Point, the school that foaled the high commands of our armies from 1865 to 1987. This he has done by producing selected letters between himself as a cadet and his family at home, generously explained by long and revealing editorial comment.

Not many people could do such a thing. Few families correspond so freely and so frankly; and few display their feelings so openly. For here we see West Point as the cadet saw it at the time—not as sentimental "old grads" recall it in later years. Here patriotism is freely expressed, joshing goes both ways between son and family, and pathos lurks in the backdrop of the Smith family's desperate financial straits. This book is, in fact, a piece of history in itself.

It is a cheerful book, drawn from the letters of a buoyant, outgoing young man and his devoted family, who seem to live his experiences with him, who lend him encouragement and extravagant admiration. Smith appears to have had a somewhat easier time of plebe year than many; his towering height may have made him somewhat of a novelty to the upperclassmen, and his unabashed friendliness no doubt shone through the barriers of the "plebe system." And he knew he was lucky to be a cadet, to have a stable job during a period when many young men like him were out of work. His compassion for his underemployed father was great; his tenderness toward his family was unmistakable; never once in these pages did he question whether he belonged anywhere other than at West Point. These qualities undoubtedly served him well in his later career in the Air Force.

I am able to associate closely to the pages of General Smith's book, as I have much in common with the story they tell. Graduating exactly ten years (1944) after him, I saw a West Point in 1941 that had changed not one iota—down to the grey riding breeches and campaign hats we wore on the last plebe maneuvers before Pearl Harbor. Smith's younger brother Drew, to whom he refers so fondly, was a member of that same class, and I knew him as a friend. Our routine was the same, and even that outlandish lingo called "cadet slang" was unaltered. (Such an expression as "The tac gigged the cow for tying up the subdiver's poop-sheets" does not appear in these pages, but Smith would find the saying unproblematical.) True, our experience with the "old" West Point came to an abrupt halt with Pearl Harbor, but for a year my classmates and I lived in Dale O. Smith's West Point.

Since those days, the Military Academy has undergone great changes, not so much from the effects of World War II as from subsequent new attitudes in our society as a whole. Permissiveness has grown, and unquestioning obedience to authority has vanished from the scene. In that era, West Point, though attempting to hold on to its old customs, has changed somewhat to conform to the outside. Many of its cherished traditions such as an Honor System administered solely by the cadets—harshly, I might add—have been revised and formalized, now administered by the authorities to an extent bewildering to cadets of another era. The introduction of women as cadets, unwelcome as it was to graduates at the time, has been accepted (with some civilizing effect). New privileges and liberties have been granted to the cadets, but at the same time the curriculum, I am told, has been made more demanding. It would seem that West Point today is losing some of its distinctiveness from other undergraduate institutions.

Here General Smith is taking on a fearsome task in his editorial comments, attempting to draw some parallels and more contrasts between the West Point of 1934 and that of 1987. I would never undertake that challenge myself, but Smith has done so courageously.

Times have changed, but the old West Point of Grant, Lee, Pershing, MacArthur, Arnold, Eisenhower, Patton, Vandenburg, and Bradley—to name only a few familiar graduates—is worth understanding in itself. If one has that yen, then he will find *Cradle of Valor* rewarding indeed.

This is a story of my life as a plebe at West Point over a half-century ago, together with notes which compare cadet life then with life at the United States Military Academy today. Letters exchanged with my close-knit family in Reno share dreams, loves, beliefs, fears, and joys. Thus the story is not entirely a military one. It also tells how an American family coped with misfortune and austerity during the calamitous Great Depression. Above all it is a story of warm family devotion, particularly of the profound mutual affection and respect between my father and myself.

Thumbnail biographies of cadets mentioned in the letters appear in footnotes. This random sample reveals how they have repaid America for their education, and tends to validate my father's comment that West Point was the cradle of valor and patriotism.

The class of 1934 had seven years of active service when war erupted: we were too young for high-level command assignments that would put us in the history books. But we provided the country with many experienced colonels and a few brigadier generals, all of whom were desperately needed to fill the ranks at a time of great national peril.

The story may enlighten those who wonder how fundamental principles and doctrines are infused into our military establishment. First-year training is similar at all of our national service academies: here we see the very beginnings of that unique spirit, unswerving courage, and sense of duty that have made American armed forces indomitable.

To say that the military profession was not revered in the 1920s and 1930s would be an understatement. War was in ill repute, along with those who were charged with waging it. Congress had held sensational hearings in an effort to uncover graft during World War One. "Silent"

President Calvin Coolidge had responded to requests for new military aircraft with the reputed remark, "Why not buy just one new airplane and let all the officers fly it?"

A strong pacifist movement prevailed. Its sermon was that the recently won World War was a tragic mistake caused by greedy profiteers, and should never happen again. A woman expounding this doctrine spoke to the assembled students at Reno High School in Nevada and asked us all to sign a pledge that we would *never* take up arms. My roommate's baseball coach at Harvard attempted to dissuade him from trying for West Point. "It's a dog's life," he said. And my basketball coach at Reno High held a similar view.

But, oddly, the Academies were not often associated with war. In spite of my coach's sentiments, in our small city the Academies were considered the ultimate in higher education. Family, teachers, and friends encouraged me to try for one. Romantic novels and movies promised high adventure there. Cadets and midshipmen in glamorous uniforms appeared on magazine covers. Above all, for me, West Point or Annapolis offered the best route to a career in aviation. The glories of flight held the national interest then even more than space travel does today. Incomparable were the daring undertakings of Billy Mitchell, Richard Byrd, and Charles Lindbergh. These heroes were the role models of my youth.

Although nowadays the Corps of Cadets at West Point is over three times as large as in 1930, has added women, has a much more varied and comprehensive program of training and education, and has eliminated some of the more draconian regulations and customs of my day, the fundamental philosophies for training and indoctrination remain unchanged. "Duty, Honor, Country," the cadet creed, is paramount.

I hope this effort will interest and guide those young people aspiring to one of America's service academies, and that the general public will gain from this story a deeper understanding of the doctrines and esprit de corps governing our armed forces.

Reno, Nevada   Dale O. Smith
September 1, 1987

ACKNOWLEDGMENTS

When I was attempting to put my files in some sort of order a few years ago, I ran across these letters, and my wife Virginia suggested that they might make an interesting book. With her encouragement and editorial assistance I went to work. So it was Virginia's inspiration that made this book possible, and I thank her for her patience as I glued myself for many months to the computer.

Another who spurred me on was Colonel Russell P. "Red" Reeder, USA (Ret.), whose many books about West Point have inspired a whole generation of cadets. To update my knowledge of the Academy I made two trips to West Point and received inestimable help from several cadets, among them Eric S. Williams, Timothy A. Lucas, Eric A. Madoff, and Albert T. Wilson, IV.

Also at West Point, the Public Affairs Officer, Colonel John P. Yeagley, USA, and the President of the Association of Graduates, General Michael S. Davison, USA (Ret.), provided encouragement and assistance. Mrs. Marie Capps of the West Point Library urged me to pursue the project and provided sound advice and help with period illustrations.

When the first draft was completed I sent a copy to my former roommate, Brigadier General John D. Lawlor, USA (Ret.), who went over the manuscript in detail, as did his wife Mary. Another copy went to classmate Colonel Thomas C. Foote, USA (Ret.), who likewise thoroughly reviewed the work, along with his brother-in-law Colonel Charles M. Peeke, USA (Ret.), class of 1935. A third copy went to my sister Jean (Mrs. James K. Dobey). For the valuable advice and editing by all these people I am deeply in their debt.

In the formative stages of the task I profited from reading the letters classmate Ralph E. Bucknam, Jr., wrote to his mother during plebe year, and I thank him for this opportunity. Another classmate, Colonel John E. Diefendorf, USA (Ret.), kindly provided me with a number of anecdotes that had escaped my memory. I also thank classmates Lieutenant General Austin W. Betts, USA (Ret.), Colonel John P. Buehler, USA (Ret.), Major General George B. Dany, USAF (Ret.), and Major General John W. White, USAF (Ret.), for providing memorabilia, as well as Major General Alden K. Sibley, USA (Ret.), class of 1933. A Reno author and high school friend, Sessions S. Wheeler, reviewed portions of the manuscript and gave me valuable guidance.

Finally, I am extremely grateful to John Eisenhower and to Louis D. Rubin, Jr., for their invaluable help in putting the book in finished form.

CHAPTER 1 BEAST BARRACKS

I reported to an immaculate yearling in snow-white trousers with a knife-edge crease. He wore a high-necked grey wool dress coat with a band of black braid down the front. A grey black-billed cap sat squarely on his close-cropped head. I could almost see my face in the gloss of his shoes.

He tiptoed to yell in my ear. "Mister Dumbjohn, this is no summer vacation. And it's no college. This is the United States Military Academy, commonly known as Hell-on-the-Hudson. And you're a *plebe*. Get it? The lowest scum of the universe. Wipe that smile off your puss! You're worse than a plebe if that's possible. You're a *beast*. For the next seven weeks you're a beast in Beast Barracks. Get it?"

He stepped back and regarded me from head to toe with an expression of stern disapproval, his white-gloved hands firmly at his sides. I soon was to learn that there were no pockets in West Point uniforms. Cadets had to stand with arms hanging, thumbs touching the seams of their trousers. I also was to learn rather pointedly that cadets did not wear pants, but trousers. "Girls wear pants!"

The ordeal of Beast Barracks caught me by surprise. Nothing had prepared me for this agonizing breaking-in period of incessant drill, repeatedly barked commands, and seemingly endless trivial duties that left me no time even to contemplate my new fate. It took me no time at all to realize why we were called "beasts" because our treatment seemed more appropriate to the training of animals than to future officers and gentlemen. And it was obviously a testing period to see who among us could "take it" and who couldn't.

Today this program is officially referred to as Cadet Basic Training or CBT and is somewhat similar to that found at boot camps of all the

To the Plebes

Y OU PLEBES may not like West Point very well. As a matter of fact, the Beast Detail hasn't done its duty if you do. West Point is hard—it's supposed to be hard. You can't raise good, hard callouses on your hands by tickling the palms with feathers. Better times are in the offing, as the financial writers used to say. The football games for one thing—trips to distant fields of battle. Christmas, then another, with subsequent hops and femmes. June and Recognition aren't so terribly far away.

Some of you have been to college. The majority of you haven't. Don't, for Pete's sake, regard yourselves as college men. You're not—you're far above that—you're West Pointers. Neither are you freshmen —you're plebes. Nine out of ten of you hate the plebe system. A few short months and ten out of ten of you will revere it as part of the life and making of a West Pointer.

The tactical department is trying to make soldiers out of you—not women. The academic department is trying to give you a soldier's and a gentleman's education—not trying to turn out by mass production merely a superior mechanic or clerk or bookkeeper—or snob.

Don't try to be collegiate. The pay you draw each month is for soldiering. You can't get away with that collegiate stuff anyway. A battered hat and a ramshackle Lizzy both are excellent material for a cartoon, but who wants to be a cartoon? A cut class makes good subject matter for a joke, but Life is far from being a joke, despite any attempt to make it so. Life, especially Army life, is a serious job, requiring far more effort than does the nonchalant life of the short-story type of collegian. And anyway, when you've finished here, you won't be going out in the world to sell bonds, you're going out to be one of Uncle Sam's right-hand men.

It isn't conceit to be proud of your cadetship. You don't have to go around telling the civilian population how good you are. But you have a perfect right to pat yourself on the back and be proud you're here. The POINTER criticizes no college or group of college men. We are part of the younger generation ourselves. But in some quarters this generation of ours seems to be going to hell a lot quicker than our dad's did.

Don't let them kid you about the alleged sameness of all West Pointers. West Pointers are alike mainly in exterior appearance. There is no system in the world that can change your innermost soul, or which can change you into what the cits so scornfully call a "wooden soldier". This appellation is largely due to the fact that we are taught to live up to an exceptionally high standard, one which is for the ultimate good of all of us, one which has stood the test of time, and has not been found lacking. On the outside these college men who kid you, or did before you entered, use the same slang, the same line, and dress the same. Most of their original thoughts are from Life or Judge.

The college people that you see in the movies (and in real life) are wisecracking, pretty boys, who siMPLY SLAY the woMEN mY DEar. But when they date them or drag them to dances they pay for it out of the old pocketbook. We don't pay out anything, but we draw a pretty neat set of femmes.

Cribbing, which happens to be a polite word for stealing and cheating, is winked at in some schools. You know what that means here. No need to mention it further.

The average collegian thinks his college year is a success if the "final" dances are good. If you wait that long to see if the year is a success or not, you won't be here for our "Finals," which happens to be Graduation Hop.

College has been defined as a four-year loaf. Well, dad might stand for a lot of deadbeating and softsoaping, but your Uncle Sam won't.

—FWE.

Editorial in *The Pointer* addressed to new plebes in 1930.

armed services, although at West Point much of the yelling of commands has been eliminated. The first purpose of CBT is to make soldiers of the New Cadets, able to obey commands, perform basic military skills, march, be prompt, alert, clean and neat.

More emphasis is placed on physical conditioning than in my day. Scientific programs and obstacle courses have been developed to foster self-confidence, toughness, courage, and the will to win.

A third objective at West Point, and the drill began immediately for us, was to impart mental attitudes, habits, and manners which would mark us as members of the United States Corps of Cadets: absolute honesty, candor, selflessness, attention to duty, pride in the Corps, correct posture and deportment.

In 1930 the initial reception was somewhat different from what it is today but the objectives were much the same.

"Now stand at attention!" my yearling instructor snapped. "Chest up!

Shoulders back! Way back! Wipe that sickly smile off your face, *d'ya hear me!* Heels together. *Pull your chin in!* And you better take this serious, Mister Dumbjohn, because it's about the most serious thing that's ever going to happen to you. (He was *so* right.) Where ya from?"

"Nevada," I mumbled, suppressing my grin.

"Nevada, *Sir!* And speak up, loud and clear."

"Nevada *Sir!*" I yelled.

"Don't forget that 'sir,' Mister Dumbjohn. Suck up that ponderous gut! *More!* What's your name?

"Dale Smith, Sir."

"The answer to that question is 'New Cadet Smith' and you will be New Cadet Smith until you join the Corps at the end of the summer, if you last that long. Understand?"

"Yes, Sir."

"If anyone wants your initials he'll say, 'Mister Smith how many?' Okay, Mister Dumbjohn, Mister Smith how many?"

"D. O., Sir."

Another beast, Urquhart Pullen Williams from Tennessee—that's right, Urquhart Pullen—was similarly instructed and sang out so that everyone in the Area of Central Barracks heard him:

"U. P., Sir!"

There was a moment of stunned silence before the new plebes throughout the Area burst into laughter. Then the yearling instructors broke into broad grins which they quickly swallowed.

"Up" Williams* pulled this stunt many times during that year and no one could figure out a way to reprimand him.

"Okay, Mister Dumbjohn," my yearling warned, "you've had your fun. Now wipe that grin off your ugly puss and take on a brace. Come on, pop up that puny chest and pull in that ugly gut. *Did you hear me, Mister Dumbjohn? Well, do it!* Now roll your hips forward and get that girlish sway out of your back. Try It! Make a nasty motion. Now you're getting it, but keep those shoulders back all the time and your chin well in. *Pull it in!*"

An order to pull in one's chin was used as an admonishment in my

---

*U. P. Williams ranked high in our class and wore a cadet lieutenant's chevrons in first class year. Joining the Field Artillery, Up saw action in Europe during the Second World War as a battalion commander, winning a Silver Star and a Bronze Star. After the war he copped two Commendation Medals for outstanding service.

"Brace!" From 1934 *Howitzer*.

day for any infraction of regulations or customs no matter how insignif-
icant. Consequently plebes went around with their chins almost tucked
into their high collars. This was considered to be good military posture,
possibly a hangover from a century earlier when high-necked leather
collars prohibited a cadet from tilting his head back to laugh. It was said
that George E. Pickett (of the fatal charge up Cemetery Hill at Gettys-
burg) refused to wear the stiff collar and almost got kicked out of the
Point.

Recently medical officers have convinced authorities that circulation
to the head might be impaired by this exaggerated posture. (Could this
be why I'm so forgetful?) Moreover, in the decade following the Second
World War, the Master of the Sword, now called the Director of Physical
Education, was an innovator named Francis M. Green, class of 1922.
He believed the traditional West Point brace did more harm than good
to a cadet's posture, claiming that excessive forcing back of the shoulders caused a shortening of the trapezius muscle (whatever that is)
which later resulted in chins being moved forward. Considering the excellent posture of most earlier graduated cadets such as General John J.
Pershing, this is hard to believe, but Colonel Greene's ideas caught on,
and one rarely hears "Pull your chin in! Throw your shoulders back!" at

West Point today. Instead, one hears the command to "Push up the top of your head!" Some plebes might find this a bit difficult.

In walking around West Point today I miss the erect, eye-stopping posture of earlier cadets. Could the elimination of bracing have been a backward step? In earlier days it was almost possible to recognize a cadet by his posture even when he was out of uniform.

And so on that hot July 1, I was introduced to "The Rock Pile" on the Hudson River about fifty miles north of New York City. The intervening half century or so has changed a plebe's welcome somewhat. Instead of yearlings or thirdclassmen the plebes are greeted by firstclassmen or "firsties"—seniors in universities. And the firsties are dressed not in white trousers and high-necked wool dress coats but in freshly pressed grey slacks with black stripes down the legs, and white short-sleeved shirts with open collars and black epaulets. Gleaming white caps have replaced the dress grey but their hair is not noticeably longer. Casual, more comfortable dress has seeped through the stern grey walls.

Here and there one does see hair considerably longer than average and a broad beam that can't be concealed with the trim uniforms. These are the women cadets, now about 10 percent of the Corps, that Congress in its infinite wisdom has approved for training at the country's first military school.

In the interest of uniformity all cadets, male and female, are dressed alike except for off-duty uniforms. This doesn't enhance the female figure and goes far to defeminizing the women. West Point uniforms were not designed with haute couture in mind. Nevertheless one must admit that there is a better than average share of pulchritude among the female cadets. Those who gain appointments are usually top performers and quite attractive. One stopped me on the sidewalk to ask the time and I could hardly read my watch for admiring her deep brown eyes.

There were 313 of us beasts in 1930. In 1986 there were 1,330. Today's plebe class is too large to be received in the Area of Central Barracks. New plebes are first assembled at the Multi-sports Complex on the hill near Michie Stadium. Parents are included and a welcome is given by the Superintendent: "Your young sons and daughters are in good hands!" Then they receive their first packet of clothing, including six athletic T-shirts, two gym shorts, sixteen pairs of long black socks, two jock straps (the women get bras), a copy of *Bugle Notes* commonly known as the Plebe Bible, and a barracks bag.

Finally all don T-shirts and shorts. A long checklist is pinned to their shorts calling for tasks such as uniform and equipment issues (six stops), barber shop, ID photo, several drill periods, and lunch. These tasks are checked off by their firstie instructors as the beasts scurry at double-time from place to place. It looks like the ultimate in confusion and disorder but these appearances are deceptive. It is a highly structured process worked out over a century of trial and error with the purpose of transforming civilians into new cadets in a period of one day. Nothing is left to chance. Every last minute is accounted for.

By afternoon all the new plebes are in uniform and standing straight. They are formed into squads and companies and marched to the wide green parade ground on the Plain where they take the oath of office. It is a moving ceremony they will never forget.

Bugle Notes, the Plebe Bible, leads off with "The Mission of the United States Military Academy: To educate and train the Corps of Cadets so that each graduate shall have the attributes essential to professional growth as an officer of the Regular Army, and to inspire each to a lifetime of service to the Nation." This seems somewhat tautological. What purpose are these fine qualities to serve? Nowhere is it noted that officers will be the guardians of our national defense. General Douglas MacArthur told the cadets in 1962, "Your mission remains fixed, determined, inviolable: it is to win our wars."

Bugle Notes of my day contained no mention of the West Point mission. It was generally understood that the Academy was to turn out successful military leaders who would wield the sword against our country's enemies.

The Area of Central Barracks where I reported has been enlarged. The ancient four-story Tudor-style sandstone barracks have been torn down and replaced with modern granite-faced quarters, and the new digs were set back about fifty yards on the north side. However, one division of the old moated structure was saved as a museum and now sits forlornly in a corner of the Area like a narrow town house. This division of barracks, built in 1851, had housed such historical personages as "Blackjack" Pershing and Douglas MacArthur.

Thomas J. Fleming wrote in his memorable history, *West Point*, that one of the early North-South encounters took place in a ground floor room of this first division. Wade Hampton Gibbs of South Carolina had insulted Emory Upton of New York. Gibbs had said that Upton liked the black girls and for that reason was an abolitionist. Crowds of cadets gathered to watch the bloody fist fight. Cadet guards were incapable of stopping it. Finally Upton stumbled from the room, bleeding and defeated by the larger Gibbs. Thus, as at Bull Run, the first round of the War Between the States went to the South.

Gibbs never graduated. He resigned, was commissioned a lieutenant in the provisional forces of South Carolina and pulled the lanyard of the mortar that sent the first shell screaming on its way to Fort Sumter. Emory Upton, class of 1861, became a brilliant combat leader rising to the rank of brevet major general. After the war he served as Commandant at West Point and wrote the seminal book *The Military Policy of the U.S.*, which became the guide for reorganizing the Army following the Spanish-American War.

And it was to this precise division of barracks that I was assigned a room on the third floor. But I had no time to wonder about its historical significance. The room overlooked the parade ground on the Plain with its vast emerald-green turf rimmed by giant oaks. Nor did I have any time to gaze out the window and appreciate the summer beauty, or do more than hastily shake the strong hand of my roommate, curly-haired John Lawlor from Boston (or Ba-aston as he said it), a good-humored, friendly fellow who was as harassed as I.

As is true today, the Beast Detail (those upperclassmen selected to make soldiers of us) kept us always on the run. We drew everything from mattresses to toothpaste at the Cadet Store, located up three flights of stairs in the massive mess hall. Clothing and uniforms from caps to shoes were to be kept clean and orderly. Most of it had to be folded and stowed exactly so. Even the mattress was folded, with each blanket and sheet precisely folded and placed on top of it. This was supposed to discourage daytime napping, but the Academy has given up on this. Today mattresses too thick to fold are found on each bed. The narrow iron G.I. cot is gone.

Soon we were in uniform and our discarded civilian things were stored in the basement trunk room, not to be seen for eighteen months. I ran to the barbershop to get closely shorn and there I was handed a Western Union telegram:

THINKING OF YOU TODAY ARE PROUD AND HAPPY CONGRATULATIONS
LOVE   DAD AND MOTHER.

The warmth that came through that yellow message penetrated every part of my body. Their love would sustain me through many trying days but right now I was proud and happy too. None of the yearlings' loud commands and the constant drilling of that bewilderingly busy day could dampen my elation for having finally made the grade and been accepted at West Point. I almost had to pinch myself to be assured that it wasn't one of my countless daydreams of being a cadet. I reveled in my good fortune. This enthusiasm would carry me through the whole of that grueling summer.

My original ambition had been to go to Annapolis, but after passing the mental exams I was informed that I was one inch too tall for the United States Naval Academy. (The popularity of basketball has all but eliminated a height limit at any service academy today.) Next year the compassionate Senator Tasker L. Oddie, who had granted me that first appointment, offered me another, this time to West Point, where the height limit was six feet six inches instead of the six feet four inches at Annapolis. It didn't take me long to switch my allegiance from the Navy to the Army. Aviation was my ultimate goal, and the Army would be just as good a route. The daring pioneers of the air with their leather jackets and helmets, goggles and white scarfs, were the glamorous symbols of my growing years and I was determined to pursue their calling.

My father, a land examiner for the Southern Pacific Company, was able to get me a railroad pass to New Orleans and thence by S. P. coastal steamer, the *Momus*, to New York. It was a great adventure. On board I met a charming New York girl, Sue Williams, who made the voyage doubly interesting.

When the boat docked I was met by Paul and Persis Seaborn, complete strangers who were relatives of friends in Reno. This gracious couple drove me to their duplex in New Rochelle, where I spent a few days before it was time to report to the Academy.

Across the street lived Jack Lofland, who was trying for Annapolis. He introduced me to my first real sweetheart, the lovely Ruth Marschalk, with brown eyes so huge and limpid my knees turned to rubber. She invited me on a swimming party of her high school class and I can still see her exquisitely nubile form diving from the deck of a small boat. She entered the water with hardly a splash and I complimented her, but she explained that she had been practicing that dive for months and could do no other. "I'm built for pleasure," she laughed, "not for speed." I fell in love with her almost immediately, and although she demonstrated some affection for me there was no commitment. Nevertheless, some months later I awoke in a sweat after dreaming that someone had taken her away from me.

I had to court Ruth by mail. Plebes weren't permitted to attend the Saturday night dances at Cullum Hall. (Today the plebes use colorful and historic Cullum Hall, overlooking the Hudson, for various social functions and may attend regular dances at Eisenhower Hall.) And I would get no furloughs for a year and a half. It seemed forever. (Today's plebes get Christmas leave and all cadets are granted a month's furlough each summer.)

The Seaborns drove me to West Point on a beautiful summer day. I was fascinated by the heavy green foliage on the rolling hills, the grandeur of Storm King Mountain, the majestic Hudson River glistening in the sun several hundred feet below the level of the West Point Plain. Awed by the castellated Gothic buildings and the ramrod-straight cadets, I thought, yes, this is for me. Next morning I mailed a letter home:

Dear Mother and Dad:
    Today is the Big Day. I'm just waiting for Weber and his friends to get dressed. [I first met congenial Ed Weber* at the Presidio of San Francisco when we were taking our physical exams.] I stayed at the West Point Arms in Highland Falls last night. I listened to challenges and drunken soldiers all night long (yesterday was payday). So I got little rest. [Cadets were not permitted to visit Highland Falls in my day although under certain rules they may do so today. The soldiers returning to the post were those assigned there for housekeeping and troop duties.]
    This school is certainly the nuts. All the buildings are old fuedal [*sic*] castles covered with ivy. The Thayer Hotel is directly inside the gate and about a mile from the Administration building—where we go in an hour.
    I saw West Point first at 1 p.m. yesterday when I arrived with the Seaborns in their Nash. It was a thrill I'll always remember. The first "Kaydet" I saw was in a full white uniform and I wasn't quite sure

---

*Edward E. B. Weber married Helen "Tammy" Bryant just after graduation and they produced the first class godson, Thomas Weber, now a colonel of Engineers. His twin sister, Helen, is married to a rear admiral. Ed fought in the landings at Salerno and Anzio as a battalion commander and was decorated with the Silver Star and Purple Heart. He was killed in action in the battle of Casalpozzo.

whether or not he was a Point man. As we got further in I saw some marching—about a squad. They were dressed in perfect fitting uniforms—white trou, grey coat, white belts and white hats. They marched like clockwork.

Looked up Alden.* He's larger and looks great. They've certainly made a man of him in one year.

All the Kaydets are blunderless. They don't even see you when they pass—even me. [I was used to being stared at and asked "How's the weather up there?" which was supposed to be humorous. It seemed to be a universal question. But no one ever asked me that at West Point, something I appreciated.] They carry themselves perfectly yet are always at ease.

A lot of them were playing golf on the huge parade ground yesterday. They wore white trou that came nearly to their ribs [all trousers had tight high waists tailored for suspenders, without belt loops], and a light white shirt with short sleeves and open collar.

I had a wonderful week with the Seaborns. Very nice people. Saw all of New York City—subways, "L's," 5th Ave., Park Ave., 42nd St., Times Sq., Chrysler Tower, Bank of Manhattan, Woolworth, Wall St., Broadway, Lower Manhattan, Brooklyn and the bridge, Grant's tomb, the Battery, etc. etc. Did it all alone, tho. Twas great fun—I know how to get anywhere in New York now.

Took Sue (the girl I met on the boat) to see "Flying High"—balcony seats at the matinee. Very good. That's all I spent on her though so don't call me a spendthrift.

Took out a girl in New Rochelle who was very sweet. Ruth Marschalk. The most stunning girl I've ever seen. (Spent $2 on her.)

One thing, girls in New York pay for their own transportation and usually meet you at the theater.

Well, the fellows are here now and the Big Moment is getting nearer. Got your two air mail letters. Sorry about the bad news. Hope Dad gets a good break. Sent a lot of gifts home yesterday.

Lots of love,

DALE

*Brilliant Alden K. Sibley was a boyhood friend from Reno who had entered the Academy the year before and upon graduation became a Rhodes Scholar. He saw action in Europe during World War II and held many high-level staff and command assignments during his career, retiring as a major general with the Distinguished Service Medal, the Legion of Merit, the Bronze Star, and three Commendation Ribbons.

Alden K. Sibley as captain of
gym team, 1933.

The Great Depression had finally hit home. Dad lost his job of fourteen years with the Southern Pacific Company. He was a Mining Engineer and had high expectations of finding a position in the mining field but that too was depressed. I became even more frugal from then on.

On that warm July 1 morning, we of the new class of 1934, in motley dress, lugging baggage of every description, were told to assemble at the sallyport of the West Academic Building which led into the Area of Central Barracks. No parents accompanied us and there were no speeches. The sallyport, a wide arched entryway through the building, is unchanged today but the building has been converted and is now called Pershing Barracks.

In the sallyport a group of enlisted men had us sign some forms and stood each of us on scales to be weighed and measured. My heart sank as it always did when I saw that height-measuring rod. Was I going to be eliminated at the very last moment? I settled my spine, swayed my back, and bent my knees slightly inside wide trouser legs. The soldier read "Six feet five and one half." One-half inch under the limit and my bent knees had not been noticed.

Beyond the sallyport was a large paved quadrangle bounded on three sides by the worn stone face, four stories high, of Central Barracks, and on the east side where we stood, by the West Academic Building. In the center of this quadrangle, the Area of Central Barracks, stood a four-faced clock on a fifteen-foot pedestal. This clock was to rule the rhythm of our lives for the next four years.

Directly to our left, at the end of a barracks, rose a stone headquarters building, the domain of the feared and respected Commandant of Cadets, who, we soon learned, was Lieutenant Colonel Robert C. "Nellie" Richardson, Jr.*

Extending out from his office on the second floor was a cantilevered iron balcony called the "poopdeck" where he and the red-sashed Cadet Officer of the Day were standing to observe the initiation ceremonies.

One of the first duties of a plebe prescribed by the Beast Detail was to write home. I found time to start a letter on July 2, eager to share my adventures with Mother, Dad, younger sister Jean, and still younger brother Drew.

Dear Mother and Dad:

We've just had the first "tac" inspection of our room. A tac is an Army officer. He didn't say a word. My roommate and I feel pretty proud. My roomy from Boston is John Lawlor a nice fellow. He and I have folded our hundreds of shirts, sheets, P.J.s, sox, etc. etc. for hours and finally got everything in its regulation place—folded correctly. Every minute till now has been taken up with duties.

[The "Blue Book" listed all rules and regulations for cadets. It prescribed in minute detail just how and where each item of clothing and equipment should be placed. Most of this was stacked in a two-door steel locker. There were no drawers. The degree of uniformity and the stacks of folded clothing on the shelves had to be the quintessence of neatness. If one item in a stack stuck out as much as an eighth of an inch,

---

*Lt. Gen. Richardson commanded the VII Corps after Pearl Harbor and later became the military governor of Hawaii.

an upperclassman would pull out the whole stack and throw it on the floor, thus undoing hours of painstaking work.

[Once we had prepared a stack that would pass inspection, we were loath to use the folded clothes and when our laundry was returned we'd hide the clean clothes behind the perfect stacks or in the laundry bag. As time went on these ridiculous standards were relaxed somewhat, but for a plebe in Beast Barracks nothing but perfection was acceptable.

[Today cadet rooms are provided with chests of drawers and although neatness is still required, the time-consuming, useless folding and stacking of clothing is not.]

Your telegram was given to me in the Kaydet barber shop just as I started through the mill and it was a great help. I like it here—like it a lot and it will take an awful lot to ever get me to leave.

These two days have been nothing but run, brace, salute, run.

Run is right and now it's Thursday the 3rd. When a yearling (they are the one-year men—just a few of the class are detailed as our officers for ten days until the first class returns) comes into the room, we stand at attention (bracing) and face the door unless he says "At Ease" or "Fall Out." That's what happened last night when I was writing you. Most of the poor devils are so homesick they go down a line of plebes so:

"Who are you, Mister?"

"Where'ya from?"

"Well, pull your chin in—shoulders back—reach for the ground!"

"Anyone here from North Dakota?"

And so on until they find some plebe who knows someone they know and then they're tickled silly but still stern.

[Sometimes they would ask, "What's your PCS, Mister?" Translated literally, "What's your previous condition of servitude?" Read, "What did you do before you came here?" My answer was, "Student at the University of Nevada, Sir," but classmate George Dany* who was almost as tall as I and in my squad answered, "National Guard, Sir." "What was your rank?" he was asked. "Major, Sir." So from then on he was known as Major by our class and later by the whole Corps.

---

*Smart, amiable George B. Dany and I became fast friends and roomed together our last two years at the Academy. Major had a roguish buoyant sparkle in his eye and hazed plebes by having them sing to him while he dressed. He won three minor "As" on the rifle team and captained it. During World War II he organized and commanded our first air navigation school. His outstanding postwar career netted him the Distinguished Service Medal and the two stars of a major general.

[Somehow the yearlings got possession of a clipping that had been published in the *Reno Evening Gazette* about my being the tallest cadet. I was forced to memorize this and recite it frequently.]

It's much like "hell week" at the Sigma Nu house only instead of doing it for fun they do it as a duty—and so never let up when they grow tired or bored. As you know hell week didn't bother me much—nor does this, but some fellows take it awfully hard. The only attitude to have is to be conscientious and stoical, also good natured.

I have one complete uniform now and it gives me a thrill every time I think of it. I have an overwhelming desire for you to see me in it.

[We had been issued ready-made light-weight grey trousers and high-necked dress coats for formal drills and inspections. But these "plebe skins" were to be discarded as soon as the tailored uniforms were ready. We were measured on our first day. A tailor asked me, "Do you dress right or left?" I looked at him in puzzlement thinking he was asking about a military formation until he explained, "Do you carry your privates in the left or right leg of your trousers?" I was astonished at the meticulous detail that went into the tailoring of our uniforms.]

On the first day it rained and we were issued doggy looking grey raincoats with a cape. Later in the aft. we put a white glove on our left hand, carried the right glove in that hand, put on raincoats and double-timed to the gymnasium (we d.t. everywhere). Here the band (enlisted men comprise the band—plenty good—play all the time) was playing and we took an impressive oath, with a speech from the "Supe."

[The oath we took is the same as that administered today and it has the ring of Civil War dilemmas of loyalty in it.

["I, Dale Orville Smith, do solemnly swear that I will support the Constitution of the United States, and bear true allegiance to the National Government; that I will maintain and defend the sovereignty of the United States, paramount to any and all allegiances, sovereignty or fealty I may owe to any State or country whatsoever; and that I will at all times obey the legal orders of my superior officers, and the Articles of War (now called the Uniform Code of Military Justice)."

[The United States was taking no chances that cadets would ever again be confused about their ultimate allegiance as they had been when 294 graduates and many cadets (42 resigned or were discharged in 1861 for refusing to take the oath) joined the Confederacy.

[More of West Point's mission is implied in this oath: To prepare cadets who will be loyal and capable to "maintain and defend the sovereignty of the United States" and who will "support the Constitution." The implication here is that it might require fighting to do this as it has so many times in our history.

[The military oath of the Soviet Union is a good deal more straight-forward and less ambiguous: "I . . . solemnly swear to be an honorable, brave, disciplined and vigilant warrior . . . and, to my last breath, de-votedly to serve my people, the Soviet Homeland and the Soviet Gov-ernment . . . to defend my country . . . sparing neither my life nor my blood for the attainment of complete victory over our enemies. . . ."]

Saw Alden Sibley and he was the first one to "recognize" me. That means I don't have to say "Sir" to him when off duty and he doesn't call me "Mr." A yearling across the hall helps us much—McNair [sic] from San Jose. A good egg—all of them are.

The Cadet Mess is a madhouse but the food is good—lots of milk and plenty to eat. We must sit at attention throughout the meal and two yearlings see that we do. If we want something we must say:

"Does anyone care for the milk, Sir?" as loud as we can yell, and if none answer—

"Milk PLEASE" also as loud as we can yell.

[The yearlings found out that John Lawlor had a loud, well-timbred voice (they called it "balls") and had him mimic the adjutant, who called the battalion to attention when he read the orders for the day. John did so well that the whole battalion stopped eating and the mess hall be-came quiet. When they finally realized that a plebe had called atten-tion, they began to clap and many came by to compliment John.]

Hope things work out well for you folks and Dad finds something. Very sorry to hear of the deaths of Peggy and Dan [killed in an auto-mobile accident]. Both were good friends. Haven't time to mourn much tho—or think of anything much.

Lots of love,

DALE

As a holiday the Fourth of July was a farce for us plebes. The yearlings gave us a tour of the post (never called a campus). We marched at atten-tion for miles with eyes straight ahead. From time to time we would be ordered, "Eyes right (or left)" and the yearling leader would call out, "That's the hospital" (or whatever we were passing), and this explana-tion would be immediately followed by the command, "Front!" Then we would have to snap our heads forward and again look straight ahead—

usually at the necks of the plebes in the ranks ahead of us. The drill went something like this: "Eyes right! The Riding Hall. Front!" all in one breath. We didn't see much of the Academy grounds that day and sweat trickled down our backs clear to our tail bones. But the yearlings had a ball and cracked up over their cleverness.

CHAPTER 2 THE DRILL BEGINS

We settled quickly into the concentrated routine of frequent drills and inspections, daily mass calisthenics, briefings and lectures, and the wonderfully relaxing late afternoons on the Plain pursuing some sport. Our schedules were so tight and the inspections so meticulous that we spent what little free time we had polishing brass, shining shoes, folding laundry, cleaning our rifles, our rooms, our uniforms, and our field equipment. Of course the yearlings were constantly tormenting us and often taking up what little free time we had to get ready for inspections.

We were always on the run. Not only because running was required of us whenever we left our rooms, but because we had to sprint in order to be on time at our numerous formations. We were not permitted to talk when outside our rooms except during the afternoon sports period, and hence we had little opportunity to become acquainted with our classmates. Our roommates were our closest friends during this period, and we shared experiences and observations while we diligently cleaned and polished.

As today, the rationale was that soldiers, and particularly officers, must be able to work and think clearly under the greatest pressure. Nothing would be more stressful than combat, and unless a leader has complete control of himself under fire he can hardly be counted on to win.

Hazing was definitely illegal, we were told, because the year before a plebe had died from having been made to "swim to Newburgh" over an alcove railing and Congress had raised hell. The tactical officers were very strict about this, and an upperclassman caught hazing a plebe was immediately dismissed. But the yearlings still found ways to badger us.

Today hazing has fallen into the ash heap. New Cadets are treated to the "positive motivational model" of leadership by example, as opposed to the more negative approach of my day. Progress under this system toward the acceptable standards of the Corps has been remarkable.

I believe the physical training program today is more rigorous and certainly more scientific than in my day. Before and after, diagnostic physical fitness tests reveal how well the program has succeeded. Considerably more emphasis is given to running and jogging. And the "Warrior Obstacle Course" provides an element of danger which sharpens courage and competitiveness. Fifteen stations are designed to develop all aspects of fitness.

I witnessed plebes at Camp Buckner going through a similar obstacle course. One of the most difficult stations was a wall about eight feet high, which the plebes had to surmount. The men would run at it full tilt, place a foot on the wall, and vault over. As a concession to the women a step was attached to the wall. But do you think they'd use it? No. They sprinted at the wall at top speed and tried to vault over like the men. Few made it but they would try, again and again, crashing into the wall with frightening force. That evening I counted several young women proudly hobbling to dinner and I couldn't help but admire their courage.

On Saturday, July 5, 1930, I began another letter home:

Dear Mother and Dad—

My plebe on the "mail drag" just came by and he didn't have a letter for me. I've just received one from you since I've been here—try to write at least once every three days, please.

We haven't a cent in cash but are given a "boodle book" which is three dollars worth of script—good for the "boodlers" or Cadet Restaurant [which served only candy and ice cream. Boodle books, too, have passed into history. Cadets may now have coin of the realm, while the boodlers' fare is greatly enhanced. In fact, a pizza parlor exists in the basement of the old First Division.]

Sunday now. Went to reveille formation in raincoats this morning. We march to chapel in a few minutes.

Later—Didn't go to chapel but to the gym for services. The first classmen came back yesterday from Virginia where they have been on a "deadbeat" (not much work), flying in airplanes and driving tanks. We aren't allowed to watch any of the upperclassmen march but out of the corner of my eye I saw a lot of gold chevrons which could only belong to the first-classmen. The service was short and after returning we plebes were all given a voice test for the choir. The Choirmaster played four rising notes on the piano and told us to repeat them singing "Glor—y— to—God." I sang my sweetest thinking of the weekend leaves the Choir would get. They took my name and my roomy's or "wife" as they call him here because it takes two of us to get dressed—the high collar with 3 hooks and the tight white belts that cause wrinkles in the back of the dress coats and must be smoothed out—we have to help each other.

[The slang term of "wife" for "roommate" might suggest an element of homosexuality, but so far as I know there was none. In my four years at West Point I never heard of an instance of homosexuality in the Corps. This is not to suggest that sex was not a major topic of discussion, but it was all heterosexual and the opposite sex was fair game. Nor was there any homosexual humor. It wasn't funny. It was simply beyond the pale. However, the term "wife" has been dropped from cadet slang and one never hears it now.

[Another slang term which was deemed offensive to the women cadets was "drag," referring to women who were escorted anywhere at the Academy. It, too, has vanished.

[It was widely rumored in my day that saltpeter was added to the milk in order to diminish our concupiscence, but every authority I've questioned about this has denied it. It was even alluded to in the bit of nonsense a plebe "water corporal" (one who served the beverages) had to recite when asked, "How's the cow?" (meaning how much milk is left in the pitcher). "Sir, she walks, she talks, *she's full of chalk*, the lacteal fluid extracted from the female of the bovine species is highly prolific to the nth degree."

[Today cadets are served milk in individual cartons, so the possibility of doctoring the milk is eliminated and so too the rumor. Yet the doggerel answer to "How's the cow?" has survived the years as "plebe knowledge." In any event, if there was any truth to the rumor the results were negative, for cadets were perpetually horny and sought consenting women at every opportunity. But rumors die hard. Today some cadets claim that saltpeter is put in their mashed potatoes.]

When we first arrived with our bags we had our chins pushed in, chests up, and shoulders back—way back. We've stayed that way since—with persuasion. Even at every meal; holidays too. We get in such overly military positions that some of the fellows faint when we have to stand for very long. Sometimes we stand without moving a muscle for as much as a half hour. We stood through all the Fourth exercises at Battle Monument—lasted over an hour.

When a yearling asked me if I liked West Point I said, "Yes, Sir."

"The hell you do, Mr. Dumbjohn, you don't like anything around here, get that! Poo' chin in!"

"Yes, Sir," sais [sic] I, and so I answer "Hell no!" to all such questions and am left alone. But I can't help from liking it. I'm getting the hang of things now. The yearlings on the Beast Detail who are our officers are all fair—stern and exacting but good eggs who would do anything for you if you really needed it. The yearling across the hall from California, McNair,* [sic] is awfully friendly and nearly recognizes me. I go to his room and B.S. with him but always say "Sir" at the end of every sentence, and he, "Mister."

---

*Popular Thomas K. MacNair, class of 1933, was a major on Corregidor when he was taken prisoner by the Japanese. He later died aboard the *Oryoku Maru*, a prison ship enroute to Japan.

My wife, John Lawlor, is a Harvard man. Sings well and we get together a lot on tight harmony. A good speller, is neat and conscientious too. Comes up to all qualifications.

[Mother had always deplored my atrocious spelling. My unique phonetic word construction provided the family with much humor and sometimes howls of laughter. I knew that if I let her know I was living with a good speller one of her major worries would be lessened. Mother had been a secretary to the president of the University of Nevada. To her, not only was cleanliness next to godliness but spelling was as well.

[Although from far different backgrounds, John Lawlor and I hit it off immediately. His father, a fire captain, died when John was twelve and John's mother, Helen, strict but loving (John worshipped her), raised the family under difficult circumstances. Also at home was older brother George and cousin Fred. Helen had taken Fred in when his mother, her sister, died.

[While I was a deist with little formal religion, John was a devout Catholic, and wrote his mother that he had gone to confession and the priest had told him it was okay to eat meat on Fridays if it was on the menu. But the wide gap in our religious outlooks didn't affect our friendship.

[John had attended the famous Boston Latin School and had done so well there that Harvard offered him a scholarship. After a year at Harvard he won an appointment to West Point and eagerly accepted. He was good-natured, congenial, and helpful; I couldn't have chosen a better roommate than John.]

A plebe named Bill Tank* from Syracuse University came up to see me under orders. He's 5 feet 4 inches and just got in. When I asked him what house he was he said Sigma Nu, and I about fell over. The shortest and the tallest men in the Corps are both Sigma Nus.

[This coincidence inspired my dad to compose a verse which came in the mail some weeks later:

---

*Charles Francis "Bill" Tank had graduated from Syracuse and had no trouble wearing stars for scholarship at West Point. These highly prized awards were worn on the collars of our dress coats. Bill graduated number one in our class and returned to West Point to teach before the war sent him to North Africa. Holding several important command and staff positions, he participated in every campaign in the southern theater, including Sicily, Anzio, and the Rhone Valley. Bill was decorated with the Legion of Merit, the Silver Star, two Bronze Stars, and the Purple Heart for a wound. He retired as a brigadier general.

AND BOTH WERE SIGMA NUS

The long and the short of old West Point,
Were ordered up to meet:
The long Dale Smith, Nevada "U"
Six inches and six feet:
Charles Francis Tank from Syracuse,
With five feet four to spare,
They both were plebes who knew their stuff
And that's why they were there.
They passed a grip and gravely bowed,
As Army men must do,
They were the long and short of it,
And both were Sigma Nu!

ALFRED MERRITT SMITH
Sept. 21, 1930

They say I'm the tallest man in the Corps and that it's a great honor but I don't know. I get too much attention from the upperclassmen. A fellow called Bruce Epler* risked a flock of "skins" (demerits) to come over and see me. He's a yearling and was the tallest before me—6 ft. 4 in.—and says he is going to recognize me when I get to camp.

A flock of high ranking "tacs," among them the "Supe" (Superintendent)** walked through our room to inspect it on Saturday Inspection and found nothing wrong. The Supe asked me about my height, weight, etc. Write soon.

Love

DALE

[The Supe and tacs were concerned about my cot being too short. I assured them I was perfectly comfortable, having long since learned to sleep with my feet dangling over the end of normal beds. Not long after that an extra long cot arrived, but the mattress now was too short and

---

*Robin Bruce Epler, a renowned basketball and track star, became one of my best friends. I usually took second to him in the high hurdles. Bruce was commissioned in the Infantry. He wanted the Air Corps but his new bride objected. In those days aircraft accidents were not uncommon. Bruce finally won her over and transferred to the Air Corps. But her fears were realized when Bruce was later killed in an airplane crash.

**Major General William R. "Bill" Smith, class of 1892, was Superintendent of the United States Military Academy. He commanded the Thirty-sixth Division of the American Expeditionary Force in World War I and was admired by all cadets.

"Mr Smith Sees His Grades."

Cartoon from *The Pointer* about Dale Smith's height.

nothing much had changed. I would much rather have been issued shoes that fit. The largest size available pinched my toes. But I was resolved to complain about nothing.]

P.S. French Monument, presented to the Point by the French Military Academy, L'Ecole Polytechnique, is just outside our window on the "Plain" or Parade Ground. When we are through with French everyone throws their French books at it. DOS

This gilded statue has been moved inside the Area to the corner of the retained old first division. No longer do cadets throw their French books at it, but plebes must be able to recite the four things wrong with it: (1) the sword is curved but the scabbard is straight, (2) a button on the jacket is unbuttoned, (3) wind blows the flag in one direction and the coat tails in another, and (4) the cannon balls are larger than the bore of the cannon.

Mother and Dad wrote on the Fourth of July:

Dearest Dale—

We received your card and first letter from New York and sent them on to Thor and Mary. [Thor was my older married brother who lived in Los Angeles.] . . . We are anxious to hear from you after arriving at the

Point. . . . Dad is really very happy and has been since his first rise from the bump. . . .

    Much love dear

        MOTHER

Dear Dale Boy—

    I have been busy with a number of things since I recovered from the shock of being jobless, and all of them offer something different. I have been more content than usual and sincerely believe that the shove was a good thing for me. . . . [Dad never liked his job with the Southern Pacific, which kept him away from home so much, and he despised his boss, who took every opportunity to demean him for being a college graduate when his boss was not.] And not the least of it is that you are at great West Point, with a high heart for old Nevada State. Lots of eyes in this good old Reno town are on you too. I never go down town but someone—often someone I don't know—stops and asks about you, wishes you luck, and congratulates me. And Daley lad, course that don't make me none blue!

    Had a quite a chat with Doc Turner yesterday who stopped to ask of you. Doc said, "His troubles are probably coming. He'll be a thorn to the runts. They all hate a big man. Cave man times hangover."

    Excitement!—we have all just dashed out into the street to see the Southern Cross fly over Reno enroute to S.F. A great ship and pilot— and speed! I'll say.

    Much love, son, from

        DAD

I doubt if I had received those letters by the time I wrote home on Monday the seventh. Unless specially marked "Air Mail" with extra postage, letters came by rail and took four to seven days.

Dear Folks—

    Things are breaking fine for me here, haven't a skin yet. Those we get in July will not count on our record so it doesn't really matter. It's all in getting into the run of things.

    The first classmen have returned and will take us over tomorrow. I guess it will be a little stricter for awhile.

    When you get a chance will you send me my alarm clock—it's good to get up a little before the Hell Cats start and then you have the jump on everyone. I've managed to wake up early so far but I don't know how long it will last.

We started a routine today which will last for 21 days: Study in Sentry and Guard duty for two periods in the morning—infantry drill, lunch, or rather dinner for the big meal is at noon.

It's after supper now: I spoke too soon for I got my first skin at inspection before supper. It took the tac two minutes to find something wrong and at last he decided that my hat was on a little too far back— perhaps a quarter of an inch. Oh, well, I can't hope to be a second Robert E. Lee who went through the Point without a single demerit.

To go on with what I was telling you: After dinner we have about a half hour to ourselves and then we have manual of arms and bayonet. [We had been issued 1903 .30-caliber bolt-action Springfield rifles, which had to be kept incredibly clean. Mine must have been through the Argonne Forest. The wooden stock was so nicked and scratched that no amount of polishing could make it presentable. Seldom did I come to "Inspection Arms" without the tac grabbing my weapon and finding a speck of dust or a trace of Cosmoline in an inaccessible corner.

[I noticed that tacs seldom took the rifles with well-polished stocks and when I had a free moment I found the ordnance warehouse and asked for a replacement. An obliging sergeant helped me select a rifle with a stock I could rework. After hours of scraping, sanding and polishing with linseed oil, the old stock shone with a smooth patina. Never again was my rifle taken at "Inspection Arms."

[We used our rifles yearling summer to qualify on the rifle range. Today cadets are issued heavy M-14 rifles. They have no firing pins and are strictly props. Cadets qualify with more modern weapons. One wonders why the M-14s are needed at all. Marching would be even more precise without these heavy obsolete weapons.]

Next period we have infantry again [the incessant marching seemed to go on forever, and time dragged] and then a long period of athletics followed by an hour to take a shower and "spoon up" for inspection and supper. After supper we usually have a lecture, do a lot of memorizing (songs, cadet prayer, a lot of nonsense you'll find in the Plebe Bible I'm sending you), and be in bed by 9:30. We must "put our trousers to bed," that is, we dampen the creases with a whisk broom dipped in water, place the trousers between the folds of a blanket, and sleep on them so as to press them "spooney." Thus the day.

With each period we have a complete change of uniform and so are hustled all the time. We have our rooms full of uniforms now and yet haven't received half of them. Tomorrow we'll be issued 7 pair of white trousers.

The football is fun—I hope I can make the squad in the fall. It means the training table where you can eat in peace. As it is now meals are torture—we sit so that if a drop of milk or gravey [sic] falls it's on the braid of our dress coat and if we do one little thing wrong we must sit up "bracing" and not eat for the rest of the meal. We must be very alert at all times too. Sometimes the Table Commandant will knock his glass against the table and if we don't raise our hands to say "glass please" immediately he will throw it at us.

Lots of love,
DALE

A few days later a thick envelope arrived with letters from both Dad and Mother written on July 7. Dad wrote:

Dear Dale—

Your letter of July 3 came this noon—so quickly—and we are so happy you are "in." Your letter has been read two or three times by all of us already, even Drew tried to read it, and listens avidly. [My nine-year-old brother Drew followed me to West Point and graduated with wings during World War II.] Mother read it twice aloud. We also would be thrilled to greet you in that fine honorable uniform, and I know how you must feel. Glad you got our wire. We knew it was to be a great day, and in the evening, thinking and talking of you, wanted to send a word of love and cheer. We know you will not be homesick for you have knocked about quite a bit for so young a chap and that will be a great help to you. We will never let our boy get out of touch with home anyway.

Best of all I like your expression as to how much you like it there and that it would take a lot to get you to leave. West Point would have been my goal if I had had a chance; the world's greatest school, but only a few are—or can be—chosen.

.   .   .   .

Nothing new has broken in the business situation for me, but I keep looking into things. . . .

Much love from
DAD

Mother wrote in much the same vein:

Dearest Dale—

We were so thrilled to get your letters today telling of your first couple of days inside the gates. Glad you like it so well and that the treatment doesn't bother you. I didn't think it would. You are naturally not touchy and would accept it in the same spirit in which it is given.

Watch your spelling, dear. "Says" not sais. I tremble when I think of your writing to people and making mistakes. . . . [Mother always feared that spelling would be my downfall. But worst of all was the *disgrace.*]

·   ·   ·   ·   ·   ·   ·   ·   ·   ·   ·   ·

It's amusing to hear Drew sometimes playing soldier and going on maneuvers, and saying he knows "because my brother is at West Point and he told me." One day they were telephoning to General Pershing "about my brother" . . .

Much love—

MOTHER

My sister, Jean, five years younger than I, was the addressee on my next letter. I used the expensive West Point stationery with a letterhead to impress her.

Dear Jean—

I hear you are a hard working girl these days. Well at least you know that you haven't anything on your brother for he's working harder than he ever did digging telephone pole holes. [A job I had for two summers.] We have each day mapped out for us—even to the minutes, and we are running all the time. It's only on Saturday afternoons and Sundays that we have a breathing spell.

It cost 80 cents a day to eat here. All our food is arranged scientifically and we eat royally with milk, fruit, vegetables and meat. But it's an effort to sit erect tho and to keep our eyes on our plates.

In about a month we'll take a week long hike and Beast Barracks will then be over. It won't be till next June, tho, before we can call the upperclassmen by their first names. Of course a few will "recognize" us but even then it's awfully formal.

Every Saturday morning some officer gives us a lecture in a room the size of a stadium. Whenever the officer enters or leaves the room the whole class rises.

For inspection this morning we wore white cross belts with sparkling Breast Plates (not a flaw in them—takes hours to polish our brass to a mirror shine). We also wore white waist belts with another shining brass plate for a buckle, white gloves and dress grey uniforms. It was a beautiful picture—I could see three of the companys [sic] without moving my head. We stood motionless except for "Inspection Arms," for 55 minutes. I could hardly move when we were dismissed.

I don't get a chance to see my friend Ed Weber much. He's in a different company. I'm in first company and in this company the plebes are all tall. All good eggs, too.

Hope things are getting better at home. I worry about Dad and hope he finds a job soon. You are good to help out by working at Conant's grocery.

Lots of love,

DALE

My older brother, Thor, wrote in answer to a letter that has since been lost. It must have been written aboard the *Momus* enroute to New York.

Los Angeles Examiner
Saturday, July 5th

Dear Kaydet—

Christ but I don't know how to talk to you—being so damn far away. Perhaps I should keep my face out of it and merely say "Congrats," but there's something phony someplace, and you know what I mean. I've been thinking it over ever since Mother forwarded the moonstruck letter which contained the startling info, and I have hesitated writing until now.

To begin with—if you *do* love her, if you are nerts about her, very serious about it all, then chuck this letter out the window, and pay little attention to my ravings. Otherwise, lend a brotherly ear: My idea is that one of two things happened. 1. That you had little respect for the real meaning of hanging a pin [it was my Sigma Nu pin and I knew I could never wear it at West Point], wanted to do something romantic, got moonstruck (as thousands do aboard ship), and decided that hanging the pin would be a delightful gesture toward the Goddess Romance, etc. [More to the mark.]

Or 2. That you *both* were under the romantic spell, that you got in a bit of ultra-necking, that you did things, that she said she wasn't that

kind of a girl (afterwards), and that you, with all honor, proceeded to prove that you were semi-serious by donating the pin as an emblem of good faith. [No comment.]
    Lots of love from both of us,
        THOR

I answered Thor's and Mary's letters (hers is not in the file) on July 14, using the impressive United States Military Academy stationery.

Dear Thor and Mary—
    I received both of your long overdue letters and enjoyed them much. The more you can write the more you will raise the morale of the United States Army.
    They call this place Spartan but it must have taken at least 25 more centuries to invent the means of torture they have here. I don't think a good Spartan lad could have stood it. [My letters home were somewhat tempered so as not to worry the folks, who were having enough trouble with the Depression and Dad's being out of work. This letter to Thor and Mary may have reflected my true feelings.]
    You folks seem to worry more about The Gal than I do. She is a blond, went to some college I never heard of, works in New York in an experimental lab as a private secretary, is built well, not fat or slim you silly Mary, and I'm not going to marry her. Besides, a Kaydet is not allowed to be married.
    An hour later—just 3 minutes till the next formation: The truth is tho, that I'm almost in love with another. Ruth Marschalk in New Rochelle—the most stunning and beautiful bundle of niceness I've ever *seen*. And sweet—Boy but I could stand seeing her again. . . .
    Still later—about a half hour before dinner formation and inspection: I'm all "spooned up" now, with shoes and visor well shined, uniform brushed off, clean linen in my dress coat, finger nails clean and close shaven.
    We have an inspection every night before dinner and I have to shave every day. Tried not to once and got called on it—guess I'm a man at last.
    [John Lawlor wrote his mother that an upperclassman had taken it upon himself to see that John didn't bite his fingernails, and John was impressed by the personal interest taken in him by upperclassmen. He

noted that he never was really cleanly shaven until he came to West Point. The same went for me.]

Right now the Corps is "peerading" just outside my window and I can hear the martial music. But custom says no plebe can watch a peerade. The honor system is iron-clad here, and if they ask you, you must say yes if guilty. I saw one peerade and had to "ride to Albany" at "infinity." This is a little game where you get down with bended knees (sitting on your heels) and bounce up and down at varied command rates of speed with arms extended as if riding a horse. When I could do it no longer they said I was at Albany. "Thank God," I thot, "this is over with." But as soon as I got my wind they said I couldn't stay in Albany and must of necessity ride back to West Point. So down I went again and I couldn't stand up when I finally got back to West Point. Now I don't think a peerade is a bit interesting.

[This kind of hazing was definitely illegal, and dangerous for an upperclassman caught doing it. Only once was I hazed this way, and I never heard of my classmates being so punished.]

The common punishment tho is: "Pull your chin in, more yet! Shoulders back, Mr. Dumbjohn—chest up, Mr. Dumbwillie, it's draggin' on the ground. You have a horrible sway in your back. Get it out—small of your back to the rear, Mr. Dumbcrot, etc. etc." [Today Dumbjohn, Ducrot, etc., are never heard. When an upperclassman wishes to correct a plebe he will use his last name, such as, "Stand at attention, Smith!"]

We spend an hour every day on Physical Drill (mass calisthenics on the Plain), and another hour on Athletics (we get fundamentals on almost every sport). We double time (d.t.) everywhere outside our room and drill the rest of the time in military formations. So you see exercise is much. I've been tired every nite for 2 weeks and I'm sorry for a lot of the others. Last week we had football for Athletics, this week it's baseball, then a week each of soccer, lacrosse, track, and basketball.

[The most boring part of the day was the infantry drill. Formations were complicated and we weren't permitted to talk. Today the drill is much simplified and noisy. Cadets yell at each command and sing rhythmic chants when marching or running. One such:

Around her neck she wore a yellow ribbon
She wore it in the springtime and in the month of May
And if you ask her why the heck she wore it

She wore it for the Kaydet who was far far away.
Far away!
Far away!
She wore it for her Kaydet who was far far away.

Around the block she pushed the baby carriage
She pushed it in the springtime and in the month of May
And if you ask her why the heck she pushed it
She pushed it for the Kaydet who was far far away.
Far away!
Far away!
She pushed it for the Kaydet who was far far away.

Behind the door her daddy kept a shotgun
He kept it in the springtime and in the month of May
And if you ask him why the heck he kept it
He kept it for the Kaydet who was far far away
Far away!
Far away!
He kept it for the Kaydet who was far far away.

[Another one:

The prettiest girl I ever saw
Was sipping bourbon through a straw

I walked right up and sat right down
Her long blond hair lay all around

I put my hand upon her toe
She said "Cadet you're way too low."

I put my hand upon her knee
She said, "Cadet you're teasing me."

I put my hand upon her thigh
She said, "Cadet you're way too high."

I took her to a motel room
The bed did squeak the whole night through.

The wedding was a formal one
Her daddy brought his white shotgun.

And now I have a mother-in-law
And 14 kids that call me pa.

The moral of this story is clear
Instead of bourbon stick to beer.

[One exercise on the Plain in my day was a lesson in sighting a rifle. This allowed us to take the prone position in the shade of an oak on the cool soft turf. A firstclassman was assigned four cadets and he would go from one to another, correcting positions and sighting procedures. The exercise was wasted on me because I had been taught to shoot by my father, but some plebes had never held a gun.

[While I waited for the firstclassman to come to me I fell asleep. The next thing I knew I was being shaken awake by the firstclassman. To my surprise he wasn't angry. "Are you sleepy, Mister?" he kindly asked. "Yes, Sir," I responded to the obvious. "Well," said the firstclassman, "get used to it. You'll be sleepy for four years here." And that was all.]

No upperclassman can touch you unless you give him your permission. It's a regulation to stop hazing. Court Martial is given for hazing and for violations of Honor and the "All Right." It is swift and sure. It doesn't go just for the Academy either, but follows the violator to his grave. He is "Silenced" by all army men. That is, no West Pointer will ever speak to him. We just received a lecture on this. [At this point in my Academy career my concept of the cadet honor system was considerably flawed. "Silencing" was an ancient punishment rarely practiced in the twentieth century, and it has since been eliminated from the Cadet Honor Code.

[The heart of the code was then as now, "A cadet will not lie, cheat, or steal or tolerate those who do." The "All Right" given by one cadet to another in authority, such as a sentry or a cadet Officer of the Day, meant a number of things, such as: "I'm on an authorized visit and will not take advantage of it to go off limits or violate regulations." A cadet subdivision inspector asked "All Rights" from each room during study time, and a response of "All Right" from the room simply meant that all occupants were present or absent on an authorized visit. When a cadet officer of the guard saw a light in a window after taps he would call, "All Right for the lights in room number—?" A response of "All Right" from the room meant that its occupants had authority for late lights because one of the cadets there was deficient in academics. An "All Right" in lay terms might be something like this: "I give you my word of honor that I have permission to do what I'm doing or intending to do."

[The Commandant of Cadets was and is responsible to the Superintendent for the military training of cadets. His staff are tactical officers, or "tacs." One tac is assigned to each company and is the true commander of the company. He supervises the cadet company commander and the cadet staff as much as necessary in the administration and training of the company.

[Since the Cadet Honor Code and system is a cadet tradition, no tac will ask an "All Right" of a cadet nor will he ask a cadet if he has transgressed a regulation. The tac has to catch him in the act. There was and is a certain adversary relationship between cadets and tacs, and when not constrained by the Cadet Honor Code, cadets forever attempt to outwit the tacs, who are the guardians of regulations.

[However, a violation of an "All Right" given by one cadet to another is considered a breach of honor, just as is *any* instance of lying, cheating, or stealing or the failure to report anyone who does so. Cadets who have not given an "All Right" are not honor bound to abide by regulations, and may take their chances at not getting caught in a peccadillo by a tac.]

My hardest job here is to keep from smiling or laughing. We get our chins pulled in if we do. There are a lot of good wise-cracks or "grinds" when the fellows are free, but the strictest attention is paid to the instructors at drill formations.

Yours,
DALE

Mother wrote on Wednesday morning, July 9:

Dearest Dale,

The gifts you sent us came yesterday and also Weekend Pointers for Jean and me. [This was a pamphlet with directions for visitors to the Point.] We are very pleased with them. Dad and I have read every word of the Weekend Pointers and found it very interesting. Wish you were near enough so that we might visit you—and I think we would know how to find you. The little pins are nifty. We shall enjoy wearing them on our coats. Tell us what to call them—West Point Arms? or what? Drew is thrilled with his cannon. It's cute as can be. Hope he can keep it without wrecking it. We are so happy that you are happy.

I was out yesterday with Mrs. Lockman. We called to see Mrs. Johnston—she is a brick—just as composed and stoical, but shows in her face how she has suffered. Peggy's picture was on the table—a beautiful picture. How sad it is.

Love—

MOTHER

All through junior high and high school I had been secretly in love with Peggy Johnston but had been afraid to ask her for a date. She was very popular and always seemed to be "going steady" with the most desirable boys—usually in the class ahead of ours. Moreover I was tall and awkward with little self-confidence. I dreamed of going to Annapolis, coming home a hero, and asking her for a date. Dreaming of her was my most romantic pastime and the song "I'll See You In My Dreams" would fill me with waves of tender emotions. Now she was dead and so was the dream. What little time I had left for dreaming (a minute or two before falling asleep at night) was now devoted to Ruth Marschalk.

On Wednesday, July 16, I penned another letter home.

Dear Folks—

This is the hardest period at West Point—the real *grind*. We are forced to be busy every minute—to be at formations 5 minutes ahead of time and to run always. Many of the men (it's always "men" or "cadets" here we are told, never "fellows" or "boys") are moaning and a few are quitting. Others will quit soon and I can tell just about who they will be. I'm ashamed to say that I like it, and haven't been so happy in a long time. I've found the real secret of happiness and that is to work like Hell, do everything just a bit better than the other fellow, and yet help him to do better too.

I believe I'm the fastest dresser in the plebe class. I can give John Lawlor a head start of two flights of stairs from the 3rd floor where we live and then beat him to formation in athletic uniform which we put on in the basement or "sinks." [I must have acquired this minor skill through a lifetime of daydreaming, which when I was "awakened" left me in a panic to get where I was supposed to be on time.]

Just got your letter of the 11th, Dad, and Jean's nice one. Jean, that camp stuff is *great*—it will be something like Beast Barracks and the secret is in the above. Be clean and work fast and accurately. It's fine that you made your own money to go—I'm proud of you—very. You'll get lots of good sun and exercise which will be the best thing in the world for you.

Later: I have to write my letters by installments, two minutes here and three minutes there. Right now it's two minutes.

(Dinner time) I'm quite sure of making the Choir. About 40 of the class were picked and I was among them. I'm a first tenor and they need them. We're looking forward to 2 weekends in New York with a lot of freedom. I'm going to sing loud and sweetly and be sure to make it. We practiced last Sunday in the Chapel for an hour after dinner. The organ there is one of the best in the world, and the Choirmaster can certainly play it. Shakes the whole building. You should hear him play "Alma Mater." We will practice every Sunday on fundamentals and then he will choose the men he needs in the fall.

[John Lawlor with his deep, rich voice made the Catholic Choir. We called the Catholics "fish eaters" and they went to a short mass before breakfast with the rest of Sunday free. Protestants spent most of the morning after breakfast marching to and from the chapel on the hill and attending services. I almost converted to Catholicism because of their shorter service and better schedule. Today attendance at chapel is entirely voluntary and a new Jewish chapel has been added.]

We march in ranks everywhere, even to the boodlers and we can go there just once a week on Saturday afternoons. I haven't been there today because I must get my last inoculations at the hospital.

[That evening I had a reaction to the shot. At inspection before supper my ears began to ring and spots darkened my vision. Just before passing out I relaxed from the rigid position of attention. The watchful tac recognized the symptoms and ordered me to sit on the steps of the stoop of the barracks until we marched off. It wasn't uncommon for cadets to pass out in formations when the weather was hot.]

We don't march back from meals as do the upperclassmen who are in camp about a mile away. We just run to our rooms. Ed Weber and I run together usually and get in a few muffled words when no upperclassman is looking. That's about the most I see of him.

I'm glad things are working out well at home and the morale is high. [This was a false impression. Dad was still out of work and beginning to feel the financial pinch.] I'm very happy for Jean and wish Drew could do something of the kind.

Love

DALE

p.s. If you get the chance I'd appreciate some boodle. This place is like a convent. DOS

CHAPTER 3 GAINING POLISH

For five weeks we were "New Cadets" and not considered fit to join the upper classes at parades. We were raw material, denied association with the elite. We were even isolated socially so that our boorishness would not reflect on the impeccable reputation of the Corps.

We had learned to perform the intricate maneuvers of close order drill with utmost precision, to keep an erect soldierly bearing, to be skilled in the manual of arms, to be dressed in sartorial perfection, and to behave with good manners. We had learned about military rank and where we stood with respect to it—at the bottom. We had come to accept and instantly obey orders and observe a sea of regulations, along with an initial understanding of the inflexible West Point Honor Code. Our physical fitness had markedly improved along with our self-confidence. We were proud of our accomplishments and more than ever proud of being a part of the Corps of Cadets.

The complicated drill of my day was designed for use in combat with single-shot arms. Today's simplified close-order drill is far better for moving troops from one place to another and is more attuned to modern combat. The manual of arms is simplified too. In my day we had to handle the old Springfields with great care, never letting them strike the ground with force. Coming down to "order arms," we caught the rifles an inch before they hit the ground and then lowered them gently. Today the crash of the steel-plated butts smashing against the cement causes me to wince. But I suppose it doesn't matter with obsolete weapons.

Although much of the ridicule and abuse suffered by my class in Beast Barracks has been eliminated, plebes today are still as taut as scared cats and must perform an incredible number of detailed duties in minimal time. Now as then the consequences of not coming up to the standards of near perfection are demerits, which, after July, remain on one's record and threaten punishment tours on the Area.

For us the end of the "New Cadet" purgatory was to occur on August 4, when we were to "join the Corps" in a formal dress parade of ancient tradition. We looked forward to this military acceptance with considerable anticipation.

I began to realize from Dad's letters that my sticking it out meant as much to him as it did to me. It would crush him if I failed, and this was no time to add to his burdens. Having lost his job in the prime of life, he needed something to bolster his self-esteem. This disposition is revealed in his letter of July 10.

Dear Dale—

Your last two letters, one just before the 4th and the other dated July 5th, have made me feel so good that I want to go out and do somersaults on the lawn, accompanied by loud whoops, and I'm deterred only by the usual and inevitable deterrent "What would the neighbors think?" I keep thinking "Dale is going to make good at West Point—the world's greatest."

Your letters are read over and over. It must be wonderful there. . . .

I have looked around for the letter that came today but find it not; no doubt Mother has carried it away on a visiting tour to read excerpts therefrom to her friends. I recall what you said about the two girls, and the last one listens like she is a dear. Well, none of us can live without the women long, and you will meet many fine ones there before the long stretch is over—for where the nation's finest youths are digging, the finest girls will come to cheer them on—and some not so fine, perhaps, but with money, to try to take a little reflected glory by being seen with a "West Pointer."

.   .   .   .

I'm still busy and hope to land something in time, or embark in some sort of enterprise that will bring us in enough money to live on.

Much love from

    DAD

I wrote home on July 19.

Dear Mother and Dad—

I certainly appreciate those often letters you send me. They help a lot. Mother, if you can't stand my awful spelling send me a small dictionary. If you can wait till the 1st of Sept. I'll be issued one.

There has been an order issued by the high command that takes effect today. Not a bit bad either, I would say, for it is to stop all double timing. We must walk now (with a brace, of course) at 128 steps a minute and turn all corners as in marching. [With the popularity of jogging, double timing is now considered de rigueur. In my day some considered it rather cruel punishment. Today there is no reveille formation, even though the Hell Cats still encourage early rising, and cadets are released from quarters at 5:30 a.m. so that they can take early morning runs. This is voluntary, but most seem to take advantage of the opportunity, and dawn finds the post filled with running cadets of both sexes.]

Just finished the Saturday Inspection and got by pretty well. Each Saturday we go to reveille as usual forming in ranks in the Area and then, after breakfast, go to two lectures. The Commandant of Cadets, Colonel "Nellie" Richardson, told us the history of West Point this morning. He claims West Point is the most historical as well as the most beautiful place in all the United States. [His remark, "You live in palaces, you eat in palaces, you sleep in palaces," was the source of much wry humor when things got bad.] He also said that the school is the best of its kind in the world and produces superior men. Our education here costs the government 25,000 for each cadet. In that case I'm making 6,500 a year and spending all of it. [Today a West Point education costs well over $200,000. Quite a scholarship! And one that assures a job at graduation.]

As for West Point being the most beautiful place in America: It's about the most beautiful spot I've seen in the East, but I don't suppose the Commandant has ever been to Lake Tahoe. However, the country is entirely different here. The trees are low and spreading. They completely cover the hills wherever you look. There are some striking views of the Hudson—especially from Trophy Point. Trophy Point is just a few yards from Battle Monument where they have many of the Sunday services (at which we stand without moving until I can think of nothing but the pain in my shoulders and the numbness of my arms).

The second talk was on the articles of war. They certainly are impressive. I found out that if I should hit an upperclassman that it would be perfectly leagle [*sic*] to shoot me. They certainly don't putter around with things here in the army. [I must have been dozing during part of that lecture and no doubt my spelling of legal provided much hilarity at home—except for Mother, who would worry about my being dismissed for it.]

At 11 a.m. the whole class formed in the Area for the weekly inspection. We wore dress grey, cross belts, waist belts with dress bayonet and a cartridge box at the back of the cross belts which could hold about ten modern shells. We also carried dustless rifles, believe me. My brass was shined so that it nearly put out the tac's eyes and I had my rifle perfect but for the bore. Due to being room orderly I just didn't have time to work on it. Got skinned.

[John and I took turns weekly at this room orderly chore. Duties were to sweep and dust the room and empty the waste paper basket. The name card of the room orderly was posted in a holder on the post between the two sleeping alcoves and he was the one who got skinned if the room didn't come up to standard. The story was frequently repeated that a tac whom we called Fanny Macon, while making his customary morning inspection, had entered a room to find two cadets he didn't know standing at attention. Noticing a dirty name card, JONES, D. C., posted in its holder, he voiced a classic boner. Instead of saying, "Which one of you is Mr. Jones?" he asked, "Whose dirty name card is that?"]

Directly after the formation (which lasted 40 minutes in the hot sun at attention) we had a room inspection. The tac couldn't find anything wrong.

My demerits are down fairly low; low enough so that I'm not one of the Area Birds this afternoon, poor devils. [When our demerits passed a certain limit we were required to march at attention back and forth in the Area with a rifle—an hour for each excessive demerit. It was excruciatingly boring. We couldn't talk to each other, blisters formed on our feet, and our rifles became monstrous burdens that cut into our shoulders. I walked my first punishment tours after we moved to camp and resolved not to walk another, but it was a resolution I couldn't keep.]

A fellow plebe on the first floor, Al Wilson, got a box of boodle from home and invited John and me down to help devour it at 5 p.m. That's the kind of a man I like. [A hint?]

[Al Wilson,* whom we called "Sad Eyes, " and his roommate, Allie Povall, occasionally had a gathering of plebes in their room. Al and Allie

---

*Al Wilson flew missions over Tokyo in B-29s, was Communications Officer of the Twentieth Air Force at war's end, and rose to the rank of major general before retirement. He had been awarded two Legion of Merits. Allie Povall was found deficient in academics in his plebe year and left the Academy.

provided tins of fifty cigarets and we contributed our boodle when we had any. These were the most pleasant and relaxing periods of Beast Barracks as we exchanged stories of our ordeals and talked of home.

[In Beast Barracks I took up smoking seriously. It seemed about the only way to gain a moment of peace and solace. My father had strongly objected to smoking. Dad had promised me his Colt automatic pistol if I wouldn't smoke before my sixteenth birthday. I accomplished this easily but afterwards began to smoke occasionally. At West Point it became a habit that I didn't break until I was forty-nine years old.]

Went to a show (marched) last Saturday nite. It was in the gym and they have a vitaphone. In one of the features they showed West Point and called it "the peaceful training ground of peaceful Cadets." With all the military control they couldn't stop the howls of laughter from us fourthclassmen.

We get to see another show tonite. They cost 35 cents. Believe it or not, but even with the 300 dollar deposit every plebe is now in debt [from buying uniforms]. We must be out of debt to get our leaves—but as you know my first will be 18 months ahead.

I signed my transportation voucher [for reimbursement of travel expenses from Reno to West Point. I needed this cash to go toward the required $300 initial deposit.] Now I think this might have been a breach of honor which could get me kicked out of here within twenty-four hours. For heavens sake, don't tell a soul that I came here on a pass. Never again will I take such a risk, there is too much at stake.

[This worried me deeply, and I was about to turn myself in until a firstclassman on the Honor Committee assured me that no breach of honor was involved. Under the more rigid honor code of today, I wonder if I would have been expelled?]

My love to Jean and Drew and to you,

DALE

Passes for his family on the Southern Pacific lines were an emolument my father had earned by working for the railroad. In that sense passes weren't exactly free but a form of his pay. My asking for government travel reimbursement to apply toward the $300 that all parents of new cadets were asked to deposit could be legitimately construed as a gift from my father.

No doubt some new cadets who were driven to West Point in the family cars had also requested mileage reimbursement, as was then authorized, and this was considered entirely proper. But a more literal interpretation might conclude that to be a breach of honor, because no money changed hands in the travel. Upon such fine points hang the reputations and careers of some cadets.

My impression that the honor system today is more strict than in my day is purely subjective. As the result of the cheating incident reported by the instructors of Electrical Engineering 305 in 1976, over 200 secondclassmen were charged with honor violations and 152 either resigned or were discharged. A drastic revision of the honor system resulted, and far more emphasis is given to the subject now than in 1930. Understandably, cadets are much more concerned today about the subject of honor and probably more literal in their interpretations of the code.

The Department of Electrical Engineering had given all 823 secondclassmen identical graded homework assignments at different times, and the department's analyses of the papers resulted in the allegations that about one-fourth of the class had cheated. This opened Pandora's Box and a national "scandal" resulted. The very capable and highly qualified Superintendent, Lt. Gen. Sidney B. Berry,* was caught in the middle, as the Cadet Honor Committee was incapable of handling such a large number of accused. He was thus forced to step in and revise the honor system. Out of this tragedy that nearly destroyed the Corps came two good things. The Superintendent may now overturn the findings of the Cadet Honor Committee or even use "discretion" by invoking a lesser punishment than dismissal. In my day a rare finding of guilty by the Honor Committee resulted in automatic dismissal.

The other much-needed reform was the discontinuance of assigning graded homework, which trivialized the honor system by using it as a means of facilitating academic administration. Little was said in all this about the errors of the Department of Electrical Engineering and its sophomoric actions of accusing hundreds of cadets. The department could have declared the examination compromised and given another under different conditions. A noble tradition in the Corps is for the smart cadets to help the dull ones. With homework floating around the

*Sidney B. Berry, class of 1948, saw combat in the Korean War and was awarded two Silver Stars, a Bronze Star, and a Purple Heart. He also served in Vietnam, winning two more Silver Stars, a Distinguished Flying Cross, eighteen Air Medals, and another Purple Heart. Two Distinguished Service Medals and three Legion of Merits also graced his chest when he retired in 1980.

barracks, it might have been difficult for cadet coaches to determine which answers were or were not part of a graded assignment.

On Monday, July 14, Dad wrote from Reno:

Dear Dale—

.   .   .   .

... as to athletics, you are still pretty young and have grown very fast; in another year, or even 2 years, you will be much better than you are now.

I begin to realize, in a way, why so many strong men weep on leaving West Point. Behind all the grim discipline lies a loyal fellowship that will stand by while life lasts, even unto death. [He hit the mark there.] No other institution of learning has anything like it excepting Annapolis, and the Naval Academy has no such ancient creed; it is younger. [Naval Academy graduates have similar loyalties but Dad was slightly biased.]

You would be amazed if you knew how much you are in my thoughts. West Point was to me an utterly unattainable dream, and it was the acme of all things desirable. Vicariously in you I try to live the life there and be a West Pointer. Yesterday Mother said "I feel so sorry for Dale, so sorry. So much terrible discipline seems unnecessary." Hard boiled Dad replied "And you also feel so sorry for the other 300 poor plebes, too, don't you Ma?" But in her heart I don't think she is feeling too sorry for any plebe but her Daley-boy. Mother love is a wonderful thing and passes understanding.

I can well understand how the ultra military decorum at meals must irk one who is accustomed to the free and easy manners of the West. But it will very soon be easy for one as clever and adaptable as yourself, and ere long you will even cease to think of it. Habits become fixed. I often think of the great strain and difficulty I had in learning to drive an auto when over 30 years of age, yet now it is all so automatic that I drive with hardly a thought of it.

Much love from all of us,
    DAD

Enclosed was a letter from my nine-year-old brother:

Dear Brother:

I am writing to thank you for the cannon you sent me. I am working at conants market and get one dollar and fifty cents a week. When I work about a month i wil buy you something.

Just writing a note.

Much love, DREW

My next letter was dated 21 July 1930:

Dear Mother and Dad—

I received your letters and the clock and pen yesterday. The pen is a beauty and I'll always keep it. At least the 4 years that I'm *sure* I'll be here, for a cadet never loses anything—it is *always* returned.

I laugh long and loudly when I hear you say "I hope you can stick it out." I never give it a thought. [This was a slight exaggeration but I was in an up mood.] It's really easy here and I'm making a success of it too. For instance:

I've had my name taken for the plebe football squad. I've practically made the Choir. . . . I went swimming one Saturday and the Coach has now picked me along with about 6 other fellows from our company as prospects for the swimming squad. By special act of Congress [he said] we (just we who have been chosen) are allowed to swim every nite from 5 to 6 and go to the swimming pool (in the gym) in any uniform—it is "off limits" to boot [to the rest of the class.]

I'm riding high and this is supposed to be the worst! All the worries I have are back in Reno, Nevada, at 229 Maple St. I only hope you can get an equal share of the breaks I'm getting.

Have you read of any heat waves striking New York with people dying etc.? I haven't but I imagine that such is the case for here it was 112 degrees in the Area today! 90 degrees in my room. Imagine that in New York where they die at 85 degrees. It is 90 right now as I glance at the thermo and it's 8 p.m. Funny though, I don't mind. My only objection is that we must change clothes so often and we use up so many collars and cuffs. [Heavily starched white collars and cuffs pinned in our dress grey jackets quickly wilted with sweat.]

I thought that if there was an earthquake and the middle of the Area sank underground that we would still go to formations like clockwork, regardless. I formed my opinions due to the way we don the long raincoats, put the rain covers over our caps, wear rubbers and drill in the rain. But today the 4th class was decimated by men getting sick from the heat. The drills were lousy and they finally cut each period in half. I was surprised. They were good enough to let us drill in shirts, too, when dress grey and cross belts were prescribed. The upperclassmen drilled in all white—very striking.

They have full white uniforms and rarely wear them to formations. They are called Hop Uniforms, I believe, and they wear them off duty. [The two firstclassmen across the hall looked like paladins in their all-whites. One, Charles H. Bonesteel III (a third-generation cadet), was called Tic* and I admired the white meerschaum pipe that matched his uniform. Soft-voiced, brilliant, with an arm full of chevrons, he was obviously on his way up.

[Occasionally Mr. Bonesteel would saunter into our room, order us to "fall out," and shoot the breeze. I imagine this would be frowned on today under the more structured Fourth Class System. "Fraternization" is prohibited. Mr. Bonesteel had a wealth of information about cadet life and the Army and we enjoyed his visits.]

We started Lacrosse today. Of all the queer games, that's it, yet it's a major sport. Directly after that I take my daily swim.

Only a week more of this routine then we start walking guard tours at camp (still living in barracks, tho). In the afternoons we will have dancing class and do a lot of other things that are "deadbeat." Just before the Cows come home (2nd class) we take a week hike and that ends Beast Barracks.

Those pins I sent you should be worn as fraternity pins—over the heart. They are miniature shoulder ornaments that every soldier, officer and cadet wear. The helmet and sword are part of the crest. Dad should wear his on his watch chain. [And he did for the rest of his life. The small Grecian helmet with the gold watch I so admired as a child hangs in my office today.]

My love,
DALE

Next week came a most welcome letter from Ruth Marschalk, but it contained disturbing news and was oddly cool.

Hello Dale [she couldn't even write the customary "dear"]
We went through dear old West Point twice today going and coming

---

*"Tic" Bonesteel graduated seventh in his class and won a Rhodes Scholarship. His career took him to the highest military levels and he retired with two Distinguished Service Medals, three Legion of Merits, and four stars on his shoulders.

from Newburgh and Pine Bush. Mother said we couldn't go anywhere near the buildings unless with a special permit, which we didn't have. . . .

Be a good cadet D,
RUTH

To think that Ruth had been right there on the post and hadn't looked me up! I couldn't understand it. Then I began to suspect that perhaps Mrs. Marschalk didn't like me as much as she had pretended to when I had visited in New Rochelle. I then recalled some disparaging remarks she had made about the military profession.

I wrote home again on July 26, a Saturday.

Dear Folks—

Got a note from Senator Oddie a while ago to meet a fellow, Tom Foote,* whose Dad is a Capt. in the Navy and a friend of the Senator. Tom is in our class. I know him a—good egg.

We've been busy as sin for two days and a half—not a second to ourselves. They're rounding us off now and we'll go into the Corps next week.

We have a very long hour of bayonet drill but it's interesting. We carry rifles at all drill formations now and walk post (practice) for Guard Duty.

Lacrosse is over. Soccer Monday. The Lacrosse coach wants me to come out in the spring. Said I handled the stick well. He played catch with me for some time one aft. On the last day he picked a team of 12 men out of our company and had us play the varsity. We did well, too, considering.

[John Lawlor vividly described these athletic periods in a letter home: " . . . you shouldn't miss seeing the Plain on a weekday afternoon. It fairly breathes with activity. There are six companies of plebes and each company practices a different sport each week on the Plain (all at one time). The Plain is a great level expanse of green surrounded on all sides by mighty hills, here and there speckled by the grey of the academy buildings—a great plateau alive with us plebes playing baseball,

---

*Thomas C. Foote and I became good friends. He fought valiantly in Europe during World War II as a colonel in the Seventy-ninth Division and was decorated with the Silver Star, the Bronze Star, and the Purple Heart. Years later he was decorated with the Legion of Merit for his service as Chief of Staff of the Berlin Command.

football, lacrosse, soccer, basketball and track. Then suddenly a bugle call and the Plain is cleared. In a few minutes the Corps is having its daily dress parade." But not with us plebes. Not yet, but soon.]

This morning we had a field equipment inspection out on the Plain. Marched out with everything on our backs as we will on the Plebe Hike—took interval to the right and pitched our pup tents. They had to be directly in line four ways, and everything in its proper place. Some plebe had packed an alarm clock which began to ring inside his pack. The firstclassmen didn't know what to do about it and we could hardly suppress our laughter. After this we marched back, put our field equipment in its place in our rooms and had the S.I. (Saturday Inspection) at 11 o'clock in the Area. [Today it is called "SAMI."]

We wore white trou for the first time, cross belts, waist belts with bayonet, and rifle. At inspection we stood at attention for 50 minutes in the Area and then went to our rooms and had the room inspection. It's the same every Saturday.

Love,

DALE

A letter from Thor which had been lost finally arrived and I answered it on Sunday the seventeenth.

Dear Thor—

Got your long letter today with all the clippings—I take back all the bad names in Cadet slang I called you.

I like the ads you wrote and got a cheer out of the advice as to a text book. I'm only free to read on Sundays, and so newspapers are out for awhile. When academics start you can send me the Examiner daily.

We went to Chapel services at Battle Monument this morning in white trou. The plebes look pretty good. The upperclassmen who wear gold cheverons and carry sabers have about the best uniform that can be designed. I'm always taking fleeting glances at them out of the corners of my eyes. They wear a red sash, white cap, full dress coat and white trou to Chapel. Nearly all of them are well built and have a perfect set-up.

They're not sure yet whether to "Silence" Cagle or not. [Red Cagle was an Army football star who had been dismissed for being married. There was some question whether he had denied being married, which I believe was resolved in his favor. He was never "silenced."]

Do West Point plebes nowadays still take fleeting glances at upperclassmen from the corners of their eyes?

The "All Right" is a very sound thing here. For a cadet crossing a sentinel's post it means that he has been to an authorized place on an authorized mission and that during that time he has had nothing to do with: 1. Hazing, 2. Liquor, 3. Narcotics, and 4. Gambling. We plebes are considered too inexperienced to handle the All Right yet and won't be asked an All Right for a month.

This is a funny place. No money and nothing the same as things were a month ago. Everything different. We live so much the same that if you feel bad at a certain drill, the whole company makes the same mistakes. If one person goes to the hospital, usually the class is decimated. On the hot days when we stand at attention during inspection before supper, if one plebe passes out twenty will.

All the upperclassmen talk the same way and in the same tone. If it wasn't for their faces you couldn't tell one from another. The meals are different for 7 days and then the menus start over again with some minor variations.

The plebes have worked into wonderful shape in such a short time—

they ought to. We drill better now than the Midshipmen. Some things that make the Corps outstanding in parades are the little differences in doing movements. At parade rest we don't bend our knees, when marching we kick out our heels in a modified Goose Step, we swing our arms without bending the elbows and every movement is executed exactly and smartly.

Write soon and lots.

Yours,

DALE

Had it not been for the supreme pride diffusing me at being a West Pointer I'm sure I would have rebelled at this ultimate in regimentation. No young person should strive for West Point unless he or she is deeply dedicated and determined to complete the course.

A cheerful letter was written by Dad on Monday, July 21.

Dear old Dale—

11 a.m. Yours of the 16th just recd. and read by Jean and me; a splendid letter and we both gave whoops of joy, as will mother also when she reads it. You have got the "guts" all right, to like it, and be in the van and lead during the terrible period in which the weaklings and unqualified are weeded out of the world's most exacting school. It's fine that you are going to make the choir, and your roomy also, you will enjoy both the music and the trips. I have read about that organ. It's one of the world's best.

[As a matter of fact the organ is still renowned as the largest church organ in the world. It was designed by Mr. F. C. Mayer, who was the organist and choirmaster when I was there.]

5 p.m. . . . Jean has been busy making you some kind of "boodle" all aft. . . . Mother thrilled with happiness to read what you said about the joy of hard work and a helping hand. Verily, it is the truth, out of my experience. One is never so happy as when working like sin and getting away with the job.

I don't suppose you like baseball very much never having had any of it, but it betokens the efficiency of West Point to round out a complete development. At boxing and football you will be better and also at fencing and tennis. You ought to be good at fencing with your great speed, height and reach. . . .

How I wish I could see you! I dream of West Point. Once we were there together, you and I. I was pretty old, but dreams have a way of overcoming obstacles by the simple process of omitting them.

I am sure that in your hard earned minutes of rest and relaxation, when you look out over the plain, a feeling of victorious pride must fill you. West Point! The Corps! God bless and help them, for of a truth, so much of our Country's welfare will depend on them in the bright future as it has in the honorable past.

Your loving
DAD

And following on the heels of that poetic letter came another which reflected the hardships of the Great Depression in Reno. It was dated Wednesday, July 23.

Dear Dale—
Mother is beside me making up the daily budget sheet. She has worked 3 days at Conants now, two days on the cash register and today both cash register and selling on the floor. She says she loves it. Jean and I do all the housework. . . .

Much love from us all
DAD

My next letter home was written in the style we had been instructed to use in responding to an official report concerning some dereliction of duty. After submitting this "military" letter we would usually be awarded a certain number of demerits, or "skins," depending on the seriousness of the offense. Rarely did our letters excuse us of the offense, because we were warned not to quibble or make excuses unless they were most pertinent. Paragraph one of the letter (sometimes called a "B-ache") was almost always "The report is correct." And paragraph two was "There is no excuse."

One B-ache which will go down in history was submitted by a cadet who had been skinned for kicking a horse. He responded in paragraph 1, "The report is correct." And in paragraph 2, "The horse kicked me first."

West Point, N.Y.
29 July, 1930
SUBJECT: Explanation of a few days at Usma College.
TO: The Commandant of 229 Maple St.

1. Dear Folks: West Point takes up too much of my time to answer all the long letters you send me. Some days we don't have time to drink a glass of water.

2. They are certainly marching our legs off now. We soon get formally presented to the Corps and will parade with them from then on. We now go to each meal formation in 50–50 (white trou and dress grey coat), and they march us once around the Area in column of platoons so that we will be able to keep straitly [sic] dressed.

3. My table commandant is changing soon and we have it harder just now. I still get plenty to eat tho. [I didn't want the folks to worry.] We move a chair every day around the table so that there is a different "Water Corporal" daily. [The water corporal sat at the foot of the table serving water and milk from two big pitchers. He seldom got enough to eat. I was on a starvation diet every meal at this table for having acted smart, or "B.J."

[At each meal this particular table com, an overly strict firstclassman whom I'll call Mr. Anthony, required each cadet to ask him a question. No doubt he was attempting to help us learn, but we all had to stop eating during this question-and-answer period and endure his verbal flatulence, which took up much of the short thirty minutes we were allowed at the table. One day when I was wolfishly hungry, anger rose in my throat and I asked, "Sir, what do you do for a pain in the neck?" An ominous silence fell on our table as everyone waited for the ax to fall. In exasperation Mr. Anthony commanded, "Sit up, Mr. Smith. You're through eating." Nor did I get much to eat for several days thereafter, which was just punishment for my inexcusable behavior.

[Mr. Anthony was also fond of throwing his water glass to the water corporal at the end of the table. The custom was rather widespread for an upperclassman to knock his empty glass on the table, the signal for the water corporal to put up his hands and yell, "Glass, PLEASE!" Classmate Johnny Diefendorf* tells how he caught a glass that first had shattered a bowl in front of him. Except for the thrower the upperclass-

---

*John E. Diefendorf, Jr., was known at West Point as a skillful mimic, a 100th night thespian, and a reputable poet. A career in Ordnance carried him to West Point as an instructor in Ordnance and Mathematics, to Iran with the Military Mission, to Korea during hostilities, and to Germany as Commandant to the U.S. Army Engineer-Ordnance School. He was awarded two Commendation Medals and a Commendation Ribbon.

men at the table applauded his skillful catch, worthy of a Yankee first-baseman, and the thrower signed the chit for damages.

[Fortunately the table coms changed every week or so and I was not long in purgatory. My relief is expressed in the letter:]

This particular Table Com is leaving Saturday so the world is round after all.

We are having Track for athletics now. I certainly enjoy it and intend to break their high jump record of 6 feet before I'm thru here. [I never did.]

Tomorrow we will practice parades and wear all the uniforms we own I suppose.

Lots of love,

DALE

The practice of having plebes "sit up" and not eat has been discouraged by the authorities so that now plebes always get enough to eat. Nevertheless there is still plenty of horseplay at table and, of course, much guidance in good table manners. I was told that at one football rally cadets stacked tables one on top of another until they almost reached the high vaulted ceiling. There a brave cadet stood and led a yell.

Then as now plebes had to memorize certain "plebe knowledge" and recite it when called for. An upperclassman might ask, "Who does a plebe rank, Mister?" The answer: "Sir, a plebe ranks the Superintendent's dog, the Commandant's cat, the waiters in the mess hall, the Hell Cats, and all the Admirals in the damned Navy." The modern version has added "the Generals of the Air Force."

Another question: "How are they all, Mister?"

"They're all fickle but one, Sir."

"Who's that, Mister?"

"The woman on top of Battle Monument, Sir."

Depending on the circumstances the answer might have been, "Your O.A.O., Sir." The O.A.O. was the upperclassman's One And Only girl-friend. Sometimes they'd demand more details about the woman on top of Battle Monument. The model was the famed beauty Evelyn Nesbitt, whose husband, Harry Thaw, shot and killed the architect Stanford White. Perhaps even she wasn't constant.

As in any social situation, animosities sometimes developed between upperclassmen and plebes. A plebe who seemed to be taking the system too lightly would be labeled "blasé" or "indifferent" and be singled out for special attention. On the other hand, a plebe taking the system too seriously would be let up on. Almost never were there instances of sadism. Often when a particular plebe received special attention he deserved it, as when I popped off with a flippant remark at dinner.

Another time I imagined that a secondclassman, a Mr. Bigelow, was crawling me too frequently and unfairly. In a fit of anger I "called him out"—challenged him to a fight in the gym with boxing gloves. Ordered to "drive around" to his room he explained very carefully that there was nothing personal involved in his instructions. He wasn't chicken; he was sincere and hadn't realized he was being overly strict. By then my anger had drained away and I felt guilty for having taken such a drastic step. Nothing more was said about a fight, but from then on Mr. Bigelow* seemed no more severe than other upperclassmen.

Plebes not only had to stand, march, and speak according to Corps

*Horace Bigelow became Chief of Army Ordnance, was awarded two Distinguished Service Medals, and retired as a major general.

standards, they were expected to have the proper attitudes. A "B.J." plebe (I never knew what the initials stood for until reading the modern Plebe Bible; "Bold before June" was the explanation there) was a smart ass, as I had been at Mr. Anthony's table. A "gross" plebe was mentally or emotionally incapable of coming up to standard. I soon learned to be adequately serious even though much of the fourth class training struck me as humorous.

A plebe was not required to perform personal duties for an upper-classman, such as shine his shoes, run errands, or sweep out his room. Any dog robber or batman duties were frowned upon. In spite of all the military hazing, a plebe was permitted to retain his dignity. Some few upperclassmen in my day came close to violating this unwritten rule by having plebes run errands to the boodlers. Mr. Anthony was one of these. One Saturday afternoon he awakened me from a nap to send me on such a mission. I thanked him for awakening me, told him I was late for football practice, and ran out the door. He never again asked me to run an errand.

Something that disturbs me today is the codification of "the Fourth Class System" in an official circular. This lists much nonsense a plebe must memorize and when it should be recited. Certainly a plebe should learn the details of military life, but to prescribe that he recite the menus for breakfast, lunch, and dinner; the generals who commanded the major battles of the Civil War; the names of the Army mules; the number of days to the next football game, Navy game, Christmas leave, 500th night (whatever that is), 100th night (before graduation); the senseless "Definition of Leather," etc., strikes me then as now as time-consuming and ludicrous. For the Tactical Department to put this in a circular seems to lower the dignity of the officer corps and deny upper-classmen the initiative they need to make cadets out of plebes.

Something else this circular prescribes is a bundle of paperwork to report plebe infractions and the disciplinary actions to be taken. Studies show that the most effective punishment is that which can be given immediately after an infraction. For violation of fourth class customs (not USMA regulations) a rebuke, or repetition of some military maneuver, should be all that is necessary.

CHAPTER 4 WE JOIN THE CORPS

Mother's letter of July 24 indicated that their Depression trials were appearing more often. It worried me deeply when I had a chance to think about it.

Dearest Dale—

We had a feast today. Two letters from you. One coming by air mail, and catching up with an earlier one. Your letters are such a pleasure to us—we read them over and over and enjoy everything you tell us. The one from Thor was a peach—telling about going to Albany. [I hadn't wanted that story to get home, but neglected to tell Thor not to forward the letter.] Is that the worst torture you have received?

. . . .

We are getting along fine. Dad and Jean are finding plenty to do to run the house and be my taxi. I have worked for 4 days and am on my feet all that time—got pretty tired the first two days, not so tired last night and tonight. . . .

Must quit now and rest—we all send you all our love—
MOTHER

On Saturday afternoon, August 2, I wrote:

Dear Mother and Dad—

At least I have time to breathe and so I'll give you a long letter. With Jean's delicious box of boodle in front of me supported by a box of John's, I'm in perfect bliss. It's surprising how much I enjoy little things.

I've received lots of your letters and Jean's nice long one. I'm glad she had such a wonderful week at camp. I'm afraid you two are working too hard—for heaven's sake don't let anything interfere with your health. Here it's "Duty, Honor, Country" and an unwritten, "Health and Cleanliness."

I'm thru dragging mail. It was like Xmas today—boxes of boodle for nearly everyone. We can only eat it during the weekend, and John's and mine were kept till then.

Monday we join the Corps. We've been having practice parades for the past week and are now almost molded into West Pointers. Much ceremony at the Parade on Monday will make us "Cadets" instead of "New Cadets."

Tuesday we start the Plebe Deadbeat which consists of a half hour of infantry in the morning with the whole Corps, dancing, swimming, lectures, classes in social and military customs, and Parades at 5:30 every evening.

At our practice Parades we had an audience as large as the Corps usually has. With the wonderful Usma College band trouping the line, it was a thrill. We certainly kicked our heels out and from the corner of my eye I could see that our Platoon front, as we passed in review, was just as strait [sic] as a die. Of course, our guides and officers are first classmen.

While the band troups the line we stand at parade rest. We must "freeze" and not move a finger. This goes for all other movements while on the parade ground. Major General Smith (the Supe) says that ours is the best class since 1838. [A real leader, he.]

The band is supported by the Hell Cats—twenty bugles and drums [played by enlisted men. The cadets had no band of their own.] Every evening the band gives a concert that we can hear—we hear the Hell Cats in the morning!

The bells in the Chapel play every Sunday morning as we march to battle monument. They can be heard for miles.

We've been having extended order drill for two weeks. It's the same as drill under fire. I'm a scout (no. 1 in front rank) and I run out till I'm fired upon and then drop. The line of fire is brought up by infiltration to this line of scouts. It's interesting but plenty of exercise.

John and I worked every spare minute yesterday on our equipment and got up at 4 a.m. this morning. Even at that we didn't quite finish and I'm afraid I got a skin or two on room inspection. The skins count from now on.

We've been taking intelegence [*sic*] tests for two days. They last 3 hours each. It's an awful mental strain. [No doubt Mother imagined my failure because I couldn't spell intelligence, but these were only diagnostic IQ tests, fortunately with no spelling.]

We took some track tests and I got a score of 98. I could have done better but the time was cut short and I didn't get a chance to show them how high I could jump. John got a score of 96. The only one higher than that in our company was Glen Thompson with 104. I surprised myself by broadjumping 19 feet and running the hundred (tennis shoes and turf track) in 11⅗ sec.

Have to go take a shower now and then catch up on some sleep. I hope everything is going well at home.

Lots of love,

DALE

A rather sad letter came from Mother written on July 29.

Dearest Dale—

I have not been able to write to you for some time because when I would get home from work in the evenings I would be too tired to do much of anything. Dad has written to you often and I really did not have much news for you.

. . . Tonight after supper I finished up the ironing and then some mending. Jean and Dad have been getting along fine, Jean preparing most of the meals and Dad coming for me after work.

.   .   .   .

Dad has the double garage a going—framework all up—using up all the old scraps in the barn and buying as little new as he can. [Dad was converting our old woodshed into a double garage in hopes of renting it.] He felt very tired today—quite early and has gone to bed. . . .

Much love dear—from us all,

MOTHER

On Monday, August 4, I managed to get a letter off to the folks just before the ceremonial parade.

Dear Folks—

I'm just waiting to be called to drill. No special program today for we are to be presented to the Corps this afternoon. I've everything spoony and so I'll write this note.

Alden Sibley sat at our table for one day as a Corporal of the Guard. I sat right next to him and didn't know who it was until he asked me if I had forgotten him. "Funny place, Mister," he said. [We plebes had to sit erect, heads up and chins in, but with eyes always on our plates. It was no wonder I didn't realize that Alden was sitting next to me. Today plebes may look around the table, but still must sit straight with backs not touching their chairs.]

Our class starts Guard duty at Camp Clinton tomorrow. [Camp Clinton was across the Plain on the bank above the river, where the upper classes lived under canvas in the summer. Camp Clinton, too, has vanished into history.]

We have a good table com now. I'm getting sleek and fat. This fellow makes us do saber manuals with our knives and have bayonet duels with our forks at his command, but we don't mind that. He has a sense of humor. Yes, the world is round again.

A week ago Sunday Ed Weber and I went up to Fort Put[nam]. It is a very interesting and historical spot with a beautiful view of the post. This Sunday I took a short walk and saw hundreds of good looking girls which we are not supposed even to look at. There are hundreds of visitors—mothers of plebes, etc. I would have liked to have seen you here—

Love

DALE

                                      Aug. 5th

Dear Folks—

What a deadbeat! We're leading a life of luxury now. We'll be softies after a month of this. We are Kaydets now—not New Cadets. We don't have to salute anyone but officers and we drill just ½ hour a day. It seems like ten minutes after the hours we've been used to. There was no Pee-rade today because of the heat and we had two hours free. We didn't know what to do with ourselves.

The morning is taken up with drill first; swimming which is a pleasure; dancing, where it's such an effort to look serious and keep a strait [sic] face while gazing into the fluttering eyes of the "ladies" (our classmates). [Today there are no obligatory dancing classes for plebes. An optional class is provided for upperclassmen, and of course there are ample numbers of female partners.] Then there's a vacant period in which we usually get a new piece of uniform. I tried on my F.D. (full dress) coat today with its 26 brass buttons at 40 cents apiece. It had to be altered a trifle. We *have* to stay braced in those things; they are very heavy and fit so perfectly. [It was a pleasure to have clothes that *fit*. Before West Point my long thin frame was draped something like Ichabod Crane's.

[John referred to dancing class as "tripping the Terpsichorean measure." He must have learned that in Boston Latin School. I had to look it up. My partner in these exercises was George Dany, another tall plebe. We clowned around so much our little effeminate dancing master, Monsieur Vizay, would never qualify us. We were called "elephants" and had to attend extra instruction. I don't think we ever qualified. George Dany claims we had to attend dancing class firstclass year, but I have no recollection of that.

["All American Free Style" dancing is the vogue at cadet hops today. I recall when we had to gather around Bill Craig and his "drag" to shield them from the eyes of the tacs as they danced the forbidden shag.]

This afternoon we had a lecture on etiquette followed by an hour of soccer—then the deadbeat which I have mentioned. [I recall a lecture by Major Hubert R. Harmon,* one of the few Army Air Corps officers in the tactical department. His subject had to do with the marks of a gentleman. One of these was that a gentleman is *clean*. Clean in every detail from hair to toes. It made quite an impression on me.

[There were several lectures on personal hygiene. How to cut toenails, for example, and care for blisters and corns (not uncommon ailments with all the marching), and, of course, the age-old scourge of armies, how to avoid venereal diseases.]

Tonite we are ordered to go to a movie. Imagine that! Isn't it awful the things they require us to do? The show is "Dress Parade," a picture about W.P. There will be another, "West Point," on Thursday. [I'm still hoping to see those excellent shows sometime on late night TV.]

.   .   .   .

The presentation of us to the Corps was a riot. We tied everything up. They put us in a new position and with the help of the yearlings yelling

---

*Hubert R. "Doodles" Harmon, class of 1915, commanded the Thirteenth Air Force in the Pacific during World War II and became the first Superintendent of the Air Force Academy at Colorado Springs, Colorado, in 1954. He retired as a lieutenant general with two Distinguished Service Medals, a Distinguished Flying Cross, and a Legion of Merit.

at us (me especially—I'm too tall) our lines were very wavey [*sic*]. Will tell you more later.

Lots of love,

DALE

For me the oppressive routine was lifted for a short period. I was attending a class in Customs of the Service held in the gym. We were told that we should never touch a woman or hold hands in public and that when we were allowed to attend hops we should wear white gloves.

About that time in the lecture I developed a nosebleed that wouldn't stop and was excused to go to the hospital.

I wrote about my hospital holiday to the folks on Saturday, August 9.

Dear Mother and Dad—

I'm certainly enjoying a delicious deadbeat right now. I'm in the hospital with a cold—will be out tomorrow morning. I came here on sick call yesterday morning and they sent me home with a box of pills. While we were having our class in Customs of the Service I got a nosebleed and the Lieut. in charge sent me here.

I believe the rest is doing me good—no jumping to bells and bugles and no worries. I slept a lot yesterday in their soft bed. I thot they were starving me with a bole [*sic*] of soup for dinner and a glass of milk for breakfast but this noon they fed me royally and with a radio over my head I'm in perfect luxury and comfort. We have just been told that ice cream will be served this aft.—not bad! We can wander around most anywhere in our bathrobes and B.S. on a spacious porch. Up to now I had disliked hospitals but I find this a wonderful place—nice nurses too, the first females I've talked to in weeks.

Sorry to hear of your sickness, Mother. I was afraid of that—for gosh sakes don't work so hard. Sometimes I feel that I ought to be home turning out some gold. . . .

Lots of love,

DALE

Four days later, on August 11, I penned another letter.

Dear Mother and Dad:

I was in the hospital 2 days and plenty tired of the idle life. Unless I keep moving I always feel groggy—of course resting is alright [*sic*] until I'm rested.

I go on Guard Saturday after parade. We will have very formal Guard Mount and then I will walk post no. 7 for 2 hours on and 4 off, Saturday nite and Sunday, till the Sunday aft. Guard Mount. This takes place every evening directly after parade. The band plays for about a half hour and there are a lot of "present arms" and "eyes right." At Buckingham castle in England the guards are given 4 days to prepare for 24 hours of duty, and here which is the most spectacular Guard in this country, we get just as spoony in an hour. It will be interesting being my first time on, but I'll have to be on my toes continually for it's an easy soiree [unpleasant duty] to get gigged on [put on report or skinned].

I haven't told you much about The Parade yet. When we were presented we marched out in front of the Corps and did "Present arms," they also did this. Then each plebe company marched thru the intervals of the upperclass companies and formed behind them. After the band trouped the line we "passed in review," which consists of a flock of platoon fronts passing the reviewing stands and giving "eyes right" as they pass. I suppose the visitors think everything is stiff and quiet out there on the Plain, but it is as noisey [sic] as a pink tea. Especially on that first day, the Yearlings made a lot of noise telling us to pull in our chins and pop up our chests.

Now we have new positions in the rear rank with upperclassmen in the front ranks. Sometimes a bug gets on the neck of the man in our front rank file and he orders us to blow it off. Of course at that distance it's impossible but we have to make a lot of noise blowing to convince him that we are trying to blow it off. Sometimes we are ordered to count the drum beats in the Star Spangled Banner, and it is 34. [All kinds of diversions were used by cadets to keep their minds off the trial of having to stand rigidly for what seemed like hours.]

When the cannon fires we do "present arms," the flag is lowered and they strike up the Star Spangled Banner. No matter how tired and hot I am a queer shiver runs up my spine. Sometimes there are thousands of people watching us and they all rise and uncover. There is usually a troup of scouts or some other order—today it was Girl Scouts, and they always salute.

My company, A Co., has gotten first line for 3 consecutive [sic] Peerades. ["First line" meant the straightest company front on passing in review.] The Adjutant announces at dinner: "Best appearance at Parade tonite, A company." And then, "First and 3rd classmen—RISE." Soon afterwards comes, "First and second companys—RISE." That's us plebes who marched with A Co.

[I used this effective method of recognition to improve the formation flying of my B-17 group during the Second World War. On return from a mission against Nazi Germany each squadron would fly over the field, and the best formation would be announced at dinner. It worked. We soon were flying one of the tightest and formidable-looking formations in combat, and the enemy avoided us for easier game.]

I was late to the 5 minutes bell at lunch—not a skinable offense but a violation of 4th class custom. I spent too much time spooning up. So tonite the dozen or so who were late ran a "Late formation." We were formed in the basement and told to report in "Athletic B uniforms." [We had to run up to our rooms, change, and return.] The first down would be excused from the formation. I won easily and the others are still running up and down in everything from Cross Belts to bathing suits. They just asked: "Who's the fastest man in A Co.?" and someone answered (not me) "Mr. Smith." "Who's the second fastest man?" "Mr. Womack."*

Love
DALE

Soon a letter arrived from Mother, dated Thursday, August 7, with exciting news about Dad. He had landed a temporary job!

Dearest Dale,—

Your wonderful letter came this noon—so much fine news in it— about your good record and all the interesting things you are doing. We do enjoy them so much and are always so happy and buoyed up after hearing from you. Dad is so proud of you—and of course Mother is. What pleases me so much is that you are happy and are kept so busy that you do not have time to think and become dissatisfied and want to try something else. Everything is fine here and we are convinced the world is round too!

---

*Classmate Carl Womack was almost twenty-two, so of course we called him "Pop." A good-humored, relaxed Texan, he seemed to have been born in the saddle and played polo four years at West Point. The Cavalry was his love but he lived in the wrong era, as horses were on the way out. He served honorably in World War II and retired as a lieutenant colonel.

A nice break for us is that Dad has a small job—just a few days perhaps but at a nice fee—and it shows that his friends have not forgotten
him. He leaves for Sacto tonite. . . .
We all send you much love and good luck,
MOTHER

I responded to that wonderful news on Wednesday, August 13.

Dear Mother and Dad—
Great to hear that Dad landed a job. I knew he would. Hope it lasts
a long time.
Enclosed is a picture of Sue and me on the Momus. What a carefree
life that was! I'm sending a bundle of old "love" letters for you to file
away among my souvenirs. Read all you care to—they really aren't good
love letters anyway, much to my sorrow.
Humber,* the Army football captain, made a special trip across the
Area to crawl me, and then he said to be sure and "drive over" as soon
as academics start. This means that he intends to recognize me.
Several others have told me the same thing. Some, as in Humber's
case, because we are both Sigma Nus, others because I'm taller than
them, and others because they know someone I do. [Today recognition
is forbidden during Beast Barracks and at all other times "unless there
exists a prior friendship." This seems unnecessarily restrictive, but perhaps has something to do with discouraging fraternization between upperclass males and female plebes.]
Shepardson** crawled me today and said to "drive over when academics start."
I'm riding well with only six gigs [demerits] so far this month. We are
"found" [dismissed] for more than 150 to December. I go on guard duty
Friday instead of Saturday—post no. 4 on Fort Clinton parapet (you've
heard of it—how the upperclassmen toss plebe sentinels over the par-

*Charles I. Humber, Jr., from Georgia, commanded an infantry battalion on Bataan in
the Philippines; he survived the Death March but succumbed to cruel living conditions
on a Japanese prisoner-of-war ship. He was a lieutenant colonel and was awarded the Legion of Merit.

**Frank H. Shepardson was a yearling from Reno. He served with the Twelfth Army
Group in Europe during World War II and was commended twice for bravery. He retired
as a colonel and lives now in Tucson.

apet. When they feel the urge I'll brandish my shiny bayonet freely and nothing out of the way will happen to me).

Love

DALE

I wrote my next letter from Rocky Swamp Camp while on the Plebe Hike on August 19, a Tuesday.

Dear Mother, Dad, Mary & Thor—

Got a letter out here from each of you and it was a great treat. I'm writing this on a mess kit with my head sticking out of a pup tent, so you can expect anything.

I had a very strenuous week, last. John Lawlor, my "wife," broke into the hospital with tonsilitis which made much extra work around the room—they took away our vacation period—I went on Guard Friday and had a million things to do on Sunday besides having visitors and a two hour guard tour of the truck train (about 15 of them) for the hike. Monday we started—just as if we were going to a field inspection. A "Squads Right" and we were off without a seconds [*sic*] delay. Officers and Bat. cadet officers rode horses and as we marched out of the sallyport the band started playing in front of us and escorted us to the gate (about a mile). People of the post lined the way to watch us—we were thrilled because everyone clapped and seemed to take so much interest in us and because it was the real end of Beast Barracks.

I got Mother's special on Sunday and read it in my song book during choir practice.

My visitors were Ruth Marschalk and some of her friends who arrived in the morning. It was a great treat to see Ruth again.

[Ruth hadn't let me know she was coming, so the awkward half-hour visit caught me by surprise and during a morning when I was overwhelmed with duties. Moreover, a boy drove her up with another couple in the back seat. It wasn't exactly a situation to enhance my romance. Nevertheless, I was once more stricken by Ruth's exquisite beauty and the pangs of young love again rushed through my body. My dreams of her became more intense and I was more than ever determined to woo her in whatever ways I could under the confining restrictions placed on me by the Academy.]

Once I felt pretty confident about how to act—the glad hand rough method of the west. But now I must do everything differently. Introductions: Heals [*sic*] must be together. "How do you do, So-and-so" said to both male and female, handshaking in the prescribed manner but not for the ladies, a regulation bow for them. Even conversation is according to regulations. It seems awkward.

Guard duty at Camp Clinton on Post No. 4 was something of a grind. We had just 2 hours of troubled sleep in full equipment, for the O.C. [Officer in Charge] turned us out for inspection.

We went 15 miles this morning at 128 steps a minute! Then—like nuts—we swam a mile across a lake only to find that the colored swimming suits contained Girl Scouts. Too dark to write more.

Love

DALE

A letter from Dad written on the seventeenth and received after the hike made no mention of his job. I guessed it hadn't lasted very long, whatever it was.

Dear Dale boy—

Yours of the 11th and 13th at hand, and read over several times as usual.

It was fine of Humber to come to see you, and you may do something in football now as you have your growth and have matured. Incidently you mentioned that Humber and also Shepardson crossed the Area to "crawl" you. The Bugle Notes defines crawl as to correct or rebuke a plebe. I take it from your text that it has another meaning aside from that, hasn't it? [Upperclassmen needed no reason to crawl a plebe. It was done just because he was a plebe.] To "drive over" evidently means they will recognize you when you come. West Point slang is all its own, exclusive, and over a century old, for the most part.

I hope you didn't get tossed over Fort Clinton parapet while on guard duty, and am sure whoever tried it would have his hands full. [No one tried, although there was some horseplay by upperclassmen. Several came near my post and I challenged them with "Halt! Who is there?" One responded, "Cleopatra in tin drawers." Another called, "Advance, Cleopatra, and bring a can opener," and they all laughed. None tried to cross my post and they soon disappeared in the darkness.]

I know that already the great old Academy with its grim and inexorable rules and standards is taking hold of your heart. It could not be otherwise. The world's finest young men are there, and the best instructors. They all know the school is the world's hardest and best, and therefore unyieldingly exact the best from every cadet.

The spirit of West Point—what makes her graduates truly great—is admirably set forth to the Plebes on pps. 128–130 in Bugle Notes. I cannot read those three pages, so simply yet beautifully written, without being deeply moved. "Play the game, look around and see what it is all about, look back over 128 years and see the great multitude who have so gallantly raised the prestige of West Point to what it is today."

Yesterday was our silver wedding anniversary—25 years. Jean ran a splinter in her knee at the store yesterday and came home bandaged and in tears one hour before quitting time, but she had her $2.00. . . . Drewdy racing all over on his bicycle, not too willing to do chores, little dickens . . . Mother out in the kitchen cooking up the usual good dinner. . . . last night Conants called us up to go to a show with them as an anniversary treat. We got ready and were waiting when the gang trouped in—Drewdy outside weeping because after getting all ready we were not going to a show after all—good old Frank Conant and Currie Jamison rounded up all the kids and drove them down to the Majestic, so they *did* see a show—the great quantity of ice cream and cake they put away on their return. . . .

Wish our two fine boys were here.

Much love from

DAD

After the Plebe Hike I submitted my impressions to *The Pointer*, the cadet magazine, and the story was printed soon afterward. Cadet Eric Williams, class of 1983, was kind enough to find this article in the West Point Library and send me a copy. Here are some excerpts from "Poison Ivy and Highways":

> After giving the world the impression for forty-eight days that we were all extremely proud of ourselves, we were given two dollars and a "Squads Right" . . . just like soldiers going off to war. . . . It wasn't long, though, before we began wishing we were going to war—war would have been a pleasure. . . .
>
> They told us the rests would be given every forty-five minutes, each rest to be of fifteen minutes duration, and for awhile . . . it looked as if we had been told the truth. It seemed that the farther we marched, the fewer were the rests, and we would no sooner get set-

Cadets taking break
during hike. From 1934
Howitzer.

tled than the bugler would blow attention, and off we would go for
another walk.

[Full field equipment in those days weighed about thirty pounds,
and as the day wore on our Springfield rifles turned to lead. A few of
the smaller plebes found the going very rough but there were always
stronger classmates willing to carry two rifles or an extra pack. We
had become a band of brothers.

[We pitched our pup tents the first night by Popolopen Creek,
where now exists a well-equipped field training area called Camp
Buckner.] It was a sorry looking rabble which left Popolopen Creek
for Bocky Swamp. Faces were embellished with scratches caused by
shaving without a mirror and with mosquito bites. Packs were a mess
. . . it was fourteen miles . . . there are 762 ways to carry a rifle with a
sling and . . . there are 762 ways which are uncomfortable.

. . . Alas and alack the swimming suits contained . . . Girl Scouts
averaging fourteen years in age. Picture the effect on our ego when
they demanded, "Are you Boy Scouts?"

[The next halt was] Round Pond, eleven miles away. . . . We went
over the hills without breathing hard, feeling like seasoned troopers.

James Walsh. From 1934 *Howitzer*.

[Classmate Jim "Turkey" Walsh,* a graduate of Boston College, on reading my manuscript scoffed: "Troopers ride horses." I was deeply embarrassed at my ignorance.]

[Big George Dany from California amused us by singing his version of Gilbert and Sullivan tunes as we marched, the lyrics of which seemed highly appropriate to Beast Barracks: "Oh I polished that brass so carefully/ That now I'm the admiral of the queen's navy."]

The Pond promised some excellent swimming, but along in the early afternoon, the sky grew dark, and the tears of the Gods fell thickly upon us. The shelter tents hardly live[d] up to their names. . . . It was great fun to attempt sleeping in the middle of a stream. . . .

*James E. Walsh played football four years and we were rivals plebe year for the class heavyweight boxing championship. Immediately after graduation, Jim, myself, and four others were invited on a midshipman cruise to Europe, where I ran out of money and Jim lent me enough to continue with our adventures. Jim ranked high in our class and joined the Engineers, serving with distinction on a number of boards and missions in both the European Theater and the South Pacific during World War II, and as commander of an Engineer battalion during the Korean War. He was decorated with the Legion of Merit, two Bronze Stars, the Air Medal, and the Commendation Medal.

That night John Lawlor and I (or maybe it was George Dany) abandoned our leaking pup tents and found shelter in a nearby barn where many of our classmates were already buried in the hay. Late that night a tac inspected the barn. "Any cadets in here?" he called. "No, Sir," yelled one wag from the depths of a hay stack, evoking suppressed giggles from the rest of us. The sympathetic tac turned around and left without another word.

In a literal sense this was an honor violation. Sleeping in the barn was not a breach of honor but lying about it was. I wonder if today the cadet who responded would have been charged with violating the Honor Code, and all the rest of us there, too, for having "tolerated" his dishonesty.

Heavy rain had so drenched us and our equipment that the hike was curtailed and the next day we headed back. The band came out to lead us down the last lap through Washington Gate as we stumbled home in our soggy shoes, wincing at the blisters. I counted nineteen on my feet after we had been dismissed.

Beast Barracks had ended and the frightening first academic semester was about to begin. How many of us would survive?

CHAPTER 5 ACADEMICS

Two challenges dominated my life as the academic year began: French and football. Although I stayed on the ragged edge of proficiency in both, I couldn't perform well enough to find a comfortable berth in either. Excelling was simply out of the question. The high hopes I had held during Beast Barracks, when I began to believe I might cut a wide swath at West Point, began to fade. Nevertheless the next six months were full of adventures.

We were issued a stack of books and student materials, together with a slide rule. That, too, has gone the way of the buggy whip. Each survivor of the class of '90 received a Zenith 248 personal computer. But with all the modern thinking, Beast Barracks remains an ordeal. Attrition in that class of 1,329 entering New Cadets came to 114 during the summer training period.

Today's plebes all take the same core courses, which include math, English, chemistry, history, and computer science. French is still required but provided in the yearling year. After plebe year a dual-track curriculum is offered. The yearling may pursue either a math-science-engineering track or a humanities-public affairs track. Core courses are prescribed in each track but a great variety of electives permits a cadet to specialize in a field of his choice. Additional electives are possible for a cadet who has been excused from certain core courses by demonstrating sufficient knowledge of the subjects.

In my day as today the design of a curriculum is an exercise in divination. What knowledge and mental skills will the future army officer need to perform his duties? What will his duties be? What will the world look like ten, twenty, thirty years from now? West Point graduates, besides being military leaders, were renowned for their engineering skills in the nineteenth century and contributed much to bring America into the industrial age. Thus the importance given to engineering studies in my day. But today there are many equally fine engineering schools, and with the burgeoning of knowledge in all fields it is felt that the army officer should be less specialized and able to pursue many fields of study. Among other skills, leadership is an amalgam of behavioral studies, history, political science, geography, management, public affairs, and philosophy, all of which are offered to the cadet who chooses the humanities-public affairs track. The United States Army must be a reservoir of all the knowledge and skills necessary to maintain a military establishment that will win wars. But who really knows what the future may demand?

Our class of '34 all took precisely the same curriculum, with a four-year emphasis on math, English, and technical subjects, leading to a Bachelor of Science degree. Plebe year it was a large dose of math, English, and French along with an hour each morning of gym. Today's plebes, too, have a comprehensive physical education program.

The following letter to my older brother and his wife, Mary, in Los Angeles shows how we ended the summer. It is undated and their letters to me are missing from my files.

Dear Thor and Mary—

I got a letter from each of you while in the field and another from Thor today. You are very good to me.

Today the camp was dismantled and everyone moved into barracks. [We plebes had moved to camp after we joined the Corps.] I have a new room now on the first floor, and another roommate—Mr. George G. Corley from Tenn. My old "wife," John Lawlor from Harvard is also with me—3 in the room, a westerner, a southerner and an easterner.

[We called Corley "Showboat." I've forgotten how he acquired that nickname. Perhaps because he was such a colorful character. Corley was a turnback from the yearling class. I believe he and a plebe named Mulcahy had been cruelly hazed and hospitalized. Mulcahy died and Corley almost. Corley was from a notable family, his cousin being Senator Cordell Hull, who later became secretary of state. Corley was given sick leave and returned to the Point with our class. John wrote that "he knew Red Cagle and has been all over God's world." Showboat claimed to have been valedictorian of his high school class in Murfreesboro but he was woefully unprepared for the stiff academic routine of West Point. I often wondered what they had taught him at Murfreesboro High. John and I spent many an hour tutoring him, but it was a hopeless task.]

This is the first night call to quarters has been enforced—they're getting us ready for academics. John is an assistant subdivision inspector and goes around asking All Rights from the rooms—the times are different each night and so no one knows but him when the All Right will be asked. [This "All Right" meant that everyone was present in his room or else was absent on a legitimate mission such as a visit to the latrines in the basement, or sinks, as we called them.] In addition, starting tomorrow and continuing until June, there will be guards walking in the halls of barracks on weekends who will ask All Rights from anyone crossing their posts. You see we are in a very secure prison and there is no possible way out. [That wasn't exactly so. Some brave souls risked going out after taps when no guard was posted, and at least one classmate, Paul Hanley,* even made it to New York City without being caught or being asked an All Right. But not plebe year. I doubt if anyone took such risks as a plebe, and Paul eventually paid dearly for his many escapades by becoming "King of the Area Birds."]

An interesting thing is the way they start off the academic year here. We were given a printed "poop sheet" containing the assignments for the entire year. The first class will begin on the first day fully prepared to recite—some system.

Yours,

DALE

Two letters from Mother and Dad arrived dated August 27.

Dearest Dale—

Your letters written after the hike just came today. I'll bet the old army cot felt good to you after sleeping on the ground three nights.

---

*Dynamic Paul T. Hanley graduated from Flying School and was assigned to March Field, California, where I had the opportunity to become well acquainted with him. In the early years of the war he was at the Engineering School at Chanute Field, Illinois, and invited me to speak before his students. His knowledge of languages led to his assignment as Chief of the U.S. Air Mission to Santiago, Chile, and later, after duty at several service schools, as Air Attaché to Italy. He continued to study and after retirement garnered a Ph.D. at Stanford University, where he served on the faculty for several years. During his service as a colonel he was awarded a Legion of Merit, an Air Medal, and two Commendation Medals.

Their "week's hike" dwindled down to three days but I guess you were glad it was no more. . . .

Much love dear boy. We are glad you are happy.

MOTHER

Dear Dale—

It is easy to see that the spirit of old West Point has crept into you; that the iron of our great country has entered your soul. The stern old Army mother makes you grind always and weep at times perchance; but she will make you great if you have the hickory in you to survive—and you are proving that you have it. It makes us grind harder, too, and makes us happy. There is no joy in life comparable to the joy of achievement, and no worthwhile achievement without work of the hardest kind. Good breaks do not come to the lazy man as a rule. They pass him by—and even if he does get one once in a while he can't appreciate it.

You certainly had a great march. It was hard on the poor fellows who could not stand it. They sure find out who has the strength and guts, both so essential.

Much love to my dear boy from

DAD

Before receiving the above letters I wrote this one:

United States Military Academy
West Point, New York
Thursday, 28 Aug. 1930

Dear Mother and Dad—

I'm using this good stationary [*sic*] for I have good news. First, I made the Plebe football squad and now will eat at a training table, *AT EASE*. I couldn't hope for anything better and I'm going to surely give 'em hell in football to show my appreciation. It means no more boodle so you needn't send any more—we sign a poop sheet to the effect of no boodle nor smoking, so you see if we break training it is a breach of Honor. By the way, that box of boodle came from New York, and it was delicious—lots of nuts and things. Muchas gracias.

Yesterday the entire 4th class turned out in FD [Full Dress coats with tails and many buttons like brass marbles] for a Howitzer (yearbook) picture. They formed us into two sections that stretched from "hell to breakfast," and the firstclassman in charge came over and instructed me to command one of them. When I got out in front my knees were shaking but I felt like a major general. I yelled my commands out at the top of my lungs and kept the 150 odd men in step. It was a great thrill. The picture was taken on the steps that go down to the depot— you'll see it in June when I send the book—and after it was over I formed the mob out in the street, "drove" them back to the Area and dismissed them.

This morning the gunner at our table [the plebe who sat next to the water corporal and helped with the serving] gave the days as usual— "Sir, today is Thursday, August 28th, 1930. Today the Cows come home, Sir. etc. etc." It will be a big event and 300 more men to pull our chins in.

We (4th class) have been having drills in the Area ½ hour a day for the last 3 days wearing tarbuckets [tall black shakos with plumes and large brass insignia called fried eggs]. They are clumsy and it is difficult to handle a rifle well with them on. The first Full Dress Parade is this afternoon—it will be very pretty for the visitors. The Plain is green again from the many rains and the plebes have worked into the swing of things well enough now so that it is hard to tell one from an upperclassman at a distance.

(Pardon my many scratches—the tac is about to inspect and I keep listening for his footsteps and jump at every noise.) I went over to see Shepardson last nite and both he and his roommate recognized me. We talked about Reno for awhile and then went to a show. It was Helen Kane in "Dangerous Nan McGrew." We plebes can go any Saturday night now, can even go to the boodlers when we care to if there is no conflicting duty.

They have a wonderful academic system here. Never more than 15 men—usually 8 or 10—in a section [class]. Each man must be prepared every day or he is skinned. We go to the blackboard each day and are given problems to work. When the instructor decides we have had time enough we must stop work. Then, using a pointer, each of us must recite how he solved the problem. In this way each is graded every day. The grades of every man are posted each week in the sallyports; monthly his position in the whole class is posted, i.e., 100 would be 100 from the top of his class, 1 would be the highest in the class, etc. A lot of writs [exams] are given. [Since 1978 cadets have been ranked alphabetically within their class. This egalitarian measure has probably omitted a lot of the competition that caused cadets to strive for excellence.]

Sections are marched to and from the classrooms by section marchers. He is the highest ranking man in the section in that subject. After the first month the sections will be rearranged according to the grades made that month—we begin alphabetically. [Today cadets go to classes individually.]

[When the call for class was blown, each section would form in the Area in a double rank, led by the section marcher who would call the roll. Interval was taken by extending the left arm, then we left-faced to a column of twos. The Officer of the Day standing on the poopdeck would command, "March off your sections. March off as a unit." This meant that each man in the section was to step off with his left foot at the same time, something that was rather awkward with the files so close together. Consequently the cadets repeated this command as, "March off as a eunuch."]

I'm glad Dad got such a good job—hope he gets more of them. I would have liked to send something for the wedding annaversary [sic] but there wasn't a Chinaman's chance.

I guess the tac isn't going to inspect. A.M.I. is 8:00 a.m. to 10:30, and it's after 10:30 now. [Today cadet rooms are subject to a cursory inspection between 7:30 a.m. and 9:30 a.m.]

Love

DALE

Academics began on September 2 and I wrote home that day.

Dear Mother, Dad, Jean & Drew:

Well the big day of academics is under way. I went to Math at 7:55 and much to my disgust we had a dry lecture (all sections together) by an officer who looked too much like a college professor to be military. My lesson was prepared cold—I'd been studying for the past week—and it was a disappointment not to get a chance to show my stuff.

We carried our "gym rolls" to math with us and marched directly to the gym afterwards. We dressed in the Gym suit (long grey trou, tight grey sweater, and boxing shoes) and had another lecture. They will teach us fencing, boxing, wrestling, gymnastics and swimming this year.

This morning I have from 10:30 till noon to study and from 1 to 2 to study again. This aft. I have a "Frog" [French] class from 2 to 3 which will alternate daily with English. I've been picked as one of the first 40 men in the C squad (Plebe football team) and won't have to go to Parade on Tuesdays and Thursdays.

[For some reason John Lawlor was cut from the plebe squad. But he showed unusual ingenuity in getting back on. In his words, "While running back from intramural football I saw end coach Eddie Doyle. I broke ranks and asked if I could stay on the C squad without being on the squad list. This must have impressed him for he put me back on the squad and by the end of the season I was first string (along with Kopcsak). On the first day of practice I was on the 13th team."]

By the by, I made the Choir for sure and have two trips to New York cinched. We had services last Sunday for the first time in the Chapel and we sat up in back of the Chaplain. [By finding a seat behind a thick pillar I was hidden from the congregation and able to snooze from time to time.] There are about 120 men in the Choir—the largest of its kind I think.

Last night we had a Labor Day dinner with chicken and icecream, followed by a big football rally in the mess hall. The yelling could have been heard back in Reno if they had left the doors open. All the big shots talked to us and the coaching staff was introduced. Why, the Plebe team here has a football staff larger than the whole athletic staff at Nevada.

I've been recognized by a pile of men for no good reason, and I haven't yet got around to see half of the names I have listed. It doesn't do an awful lot of good unless they are in my own company for I rarely see those in North Barracks or even in Central Barracks where I live.

Try sending me some newspapers. Especially the Sagebrushes and the Desert Wolfs. [Student publications at Nevada. I had been on the staff of the *Desert Wolf* humor magazine.] Now and then a magazine that you have finished would serve as reading matter on Sunday when my friends whose homes are nearby are P.S.ing [escorting] some femmes around the reservation.

Tell me about college starting and what you know of all the gang—tell me about Jean and Drew. If you get a chance send me a pair of plyers [*sic*].

Love,

DALE

Homesickness was a common disease at West Point but the plebes suffered most. I wrote again on Sunday, September 8.

Dear Mother and Dad:

Well a week of academics is past and I'm still alive. The marks are 2.0 as passing and 3.0 as perfect. I made a 2.3 for the week in French and a 2.7 in math. I guess there'll be no stars for me. I'll do well by staying in the upper half of the class. A 2.76 average or better is needed for stars = 92%.

Each day it's necessary to be prepared—they don't let you get by with a thing, and they take up each word in the lesson. It's the most thorough place in the world—so systematic and complete that it strikes me as being hardly human. We are instructed in everything from the method of carrying our books to the manner of holding the blackboard pointer.

There's nothing to do but study in the evenings, and everyone does. Cadet sub-division inspectors may ask for an All Right from the room at any time (4 times between 7:15 and 9:30). This is to make sure that all occupants are present. The tac inspects once and we must be in proper uniform (sport shirt with a tie & grey trou) and the room in order. We must also be studying.

Football is advancing well. There are 67 on the plebe (C) squad—40 who get out of parades. They work us hard and feed us the best food at the training table—steaks, always brown bread toast instead of bread, lots of milk, cream, butter. Usually baked potatoes, a good fruit salid [sic] and grapefruit. We get icecream pretty often also. With this and the hour of gym in the morning I ought to be a moose in a year or so.

Have been kept frightfully busy last week with a mail-dragging job and all. [Plebes delivered the mail to the rooms. Today cadets have mail boxes.] I doubt if I'll be able to write oftener than once a week from now on.

I wish you would send me some pictures of yourself, Mother. I have one of Dad and Thor but none of you. I'd like some snaps of Jean and Drew too. [The only personal decorations permitted in our rooms were photos *inside* our steel lockers.]

Try to send me all the news of the [Sigma Nu] house and school. [I felt cut off and isolated from all that I loved back in Reno.]

Something that impresses me is the way we act at retreat. Friday there was a Parade, with [the excused] football squads practicing on separate fields, also the soccer squad, all on the Plain. The Hell Cats played "To The Colors" and then the gun went off. BOOM. Things were moving on the athletic fields at the time—we were taking a couple of

1. Entering plebe Dale Smith being measured for height. John Lawlor is standing in dark suit at edge of sallyport. Edward Weber is third from right, with straw hat and light suit.
2. The Smith family: left to right, Dale, Mother, Jean, Drew, Mary, Dad, Thor and daughter Diane.

1

2

3. John Lawlor.
4. Ruth Marschalk.
5. Beast Barracks: montage from *Howitzer* for 1934.
6. Commandant inspecting A Company.
7. Plebe football squad, 1930. Dale Smith is third from left, second row.

3

4

5

6

7

8

9

10

11

8. Plebe getting the word, ca. 1976—*U.S. Military Academy*.

9. Plebe Smith getting the word, 1930.

10. Color Guard, from 1934 *Howitzer*.

11. Dining hall, West Point, from 1934 *Howitzer*.

12. Drew M. Smith, 1930 or 1931.
13. 2d Lt. Drew M. Smith, 1943, after graduation from USMA. He was killed in a B-29 crash a year later on Wake Island.
14. Jean and Mother with Viking automobile, 1932.

12

13

14

15. "Recognition."
16. Cast of the Hundredth
Night Show, "The Camp Has
Gone to Hell," 1931.

15

16

17. Albert Wilson and John Lawlor on their way home from football practice.
18. A Company friends in summer camp, 1931: left to right, Pete Kopcsak, John Lawlor, Dale Smith, Al Wilson, Bill Bunker, John Smoller.

17

laps around the goal posts. Everyone stopped dead still at the report of the gun and faced the Colors while the band played one verse of "The Star Spangled Banner" and the Colors were lowered. Those in athletic uniforms do not salute but only remove their headgear, drop them to the ground, and stand at attention.

The tac inspected last night at 2 A.M. but I pretended not to waken. Our room was a mess but the locker doors were closed and the absence cards were marked correctly so I doubt if we got skinned. He was probably looking for someone who was staying out late without authorization.

I'm certainly piping the football trips. They will be big times for us Plebes. [To "pipe" something was to anticipate it, as with a pipe dream. Much time and yearning was taken up by cadets in piping everything from a football trip to graduation. Yearlings would gather in the Area around the clock tower in the spring and wail "Yea furlough!" over and over. We spelled it furlo and it was that heavenly time when, after almost two years, we could go home.]

Glad to hear things are working out so well with Dad.

Lots of love,
DALE

A long typed letter came from Dad written September 18.

Dear Dale:

Your letter of Sunday at hand. It doesn't seem to take long for letters to span the continent in these days of fast transportation. Your grades are certainly splendid for a man at West Point. I am not at all sure that you will not wear the gold stars. However it matters not, if you try—to try is the main thing.

The same is true in football. [Dad was an authority on this subject. He played guard on the Nevada team that beat the University of California in 1899. I had played only sand lot football before attending the Academy and when asked "What position do you play?" I said, "tackle," the first thought to come into my mind. This was an error that probably contributed to my poor performance. With my center of gravity so high I wasn't built for the pushing game on the line and probably would have done better as an end. Dad's letter continued:]

I don't think you will make a great player but you will make a good player. The very tall man is at a disadvantage [he, too, was 6'6" and spoke from experience] but you have great strength and considerable speed to offset it. In any case I hope you will be able to stay in the first 40. I would give a great deal to see some of the big army games this year, but it is not to be.

Regarding the Pyramid project I'm still in line as mill manager, and may get in on the construction—if they ever get money enough to go ahead. It beats hell how business keeps up, only I wish it would bring in a little money my way. Still, by close economy we are healthy and happy and are apparently holding even and are in the best of spirits.

We get a big cheer out of your song for rain, and a bit of worry about the tac finding your room in disorder at 2 A.M. I'll bet it will be in good shape next time, still, I wonder often how you find the time to make all ends meet.

[We called the rain song "The Missouri National" and the lyrics went like this: "Everytime I pray for rain/ The goddam sun comes out again/ The sun shines bright when I get dressed/ But it rains like hell at Peerade rest." If it rained before "Assembly" was blown by the bugler, the parade would be canceled, but once begun, the parade continued regardless of the downpour. So when it looked like it might rain the barracks rang with song and whistles while the cadets dressed for parade. "The Missouri National" was sure to bring the rain and we plebes were required to sing it at the top of our lungs.

[When I visited West Point for my fifty-year class reunion, I happened to be in the Area of Barracks when cadets were forming for a parade. It was threatening rain but I didn't hear anyone singing "The Missouri National." I asked a firstclassman how come? He had never heard of it. They paraded in the rain. Served them right.

[Dad's letter went on to tell about a school teacher who was rooming with them. They did everything to make ends meet, even renting Thor's and my old rooms.]

I have about run out and will now quit spoiling paper. Much love to you Daley, from all of us at home; we are with you in spirit all the time.

As ever,
DAD

I wrote home again on Sunday, the fourteenth of September.

Dear Mother, Dad, Jean and Drew:
As a very dutiful boy should do, I present my weeks report card. Keep in mind that 2.0 is just proficient and 3.0 is perfect and that those

who have 2.76 averages for a year wear gold stars. I won't wear them so don't get your hopes up. This is just to give you an idea of the grading system.

Math. 2.2, 2.3, 2.6, 3.0, 2.8
Eng. 2.6, 2.7, 2.8
French 2.2, 3.0, 2.3

Not bad for a slow head like mine!

[One Saturday when I was studying my grades posted in the sally-port, a group of runt upperclassmen began to crawl me. As I stood there braced and sweating under the storm of commands from the short men, big Jack Price* from A Company came by. Jack looked like he had been molded from the barrel of a cannon and he commanded respect from all.

["Mr. Smith!" he shouted.

["Yes, Sir!" I responded.

["About Face!" and I made a snappy About Face.

["Double time, MARCH!" and I took off like a shot, being thus saved from the runt assault.]

Football is progressing swiftly around here. The practice fields (vicinity of summer camp) are now equipped with six huge towers with floodlights on them for nite practice. There are many machines of torture to be knocked over and pushed around, and there are 3 complete gridirons with 6 goal posts.

I'm not as good as I hoped to be. I find it hard to keep on the first 40. Lots of collegiate material out there and two All Americans: Rebholz and Jablonsky.**

I'd like much to be a great football player but I guess I haven't the right build. It's hard to get down low.

---

*The next year Jack Morgan Price captained a highly successful Army football squad, and he graduated toward the top of the class of 1932. He commanded a heavy bomb group in Italy during World War II and was decorated with the Distinguished Flying Cross and two Air Medals. In the Korean War he commanded a fighter wing and was decorated with the Distinguished Service Medal.

**Rebholz was found deficient in academics and left the Academy after Christmas, while Harvey J. "Jabo" Jablonsky from Missouri became an outstanding scholar, cadet leader, and football captain. He continued to be outstanding after graduation as commander of a parachute regiment during the Second World War and Chief of Infantry later. After a military career replete with honors and accomplishments, including a Distinguished Service Medal, the Legion of Merit, the Bronze Star, and Commendation Ribbon, and the two stars of a major general, he became a successful businessman. No classmate is more highly regarded.

I'm sending the Pointer to you today and a picture of a Saturday inspection during Beast Barracks. You won't be able to see much of me but you can use your imagination.

The Corps goes into grey tomorrow. It will be much easier and cheaper. The white trou are an awful bother. Last Parade in white will be today. It's been raining lately—I hope it rains today. No parade, you see. We went to Chapel in Full Dress grey today and raincoats and caps. The sermon was the best one I have slept thru.

Went to the show last night with Alden and saw "The Social Lion" with Jack Oaky.

I enjoyed Drew's letter very much. If it wasn't for the Choir I'd sure be a Sunday school teacher in order to be around some little kids.

Lots of love,

DALE

A letter came from Dad written in Reno on September 22.

Dear Dale—

Today we received the photo and the Pointer. The picture is fine and we get a good view of your face by means of a magnifying glass. Those boys are sure braced! And the pride of West Point radiates from every one.

Buzz Morrison [a local aviator] advertised he would take up anyone for 1 cent a pound and did a rushing business yesterday. We didn't want Jean & Drew to go up but they staged such a weep that we had to relent, and took them out to the field but it was too late—an awful mob ahead all day, and two planes never stopped except for fuel—just up, a turn about and light, all day long. No doubt they will do it again, and the kids can go up then.

Thor sent back your pictures today and we took a new interest in picking out Weber, Lawlor and your other friends. I never look at any of the pictures of old West Point that the patriotic thrill does not creep over me at the thought of the Nation's cradle of valor and honor.

Much love from all of us and

DAD

Mother's letter came in the same envelope with Dad's.

Dear Dale—and Thor and Mary too— [They got the carbon.]

We were so happy yesterday to get the Pointer—enclosing the picture of the plebes in uniform. Sorry you had to be way off in the middle so that only the top of your cap was very plain, but when we put the magnifying glass on the picture your profile was discernible—and so we know you were there!

Last night the boys at the [Sigma Nu] house entertained the mothers. Bob [Merriman]* makes a fine house manager, also Bill Blakely seems a very good EC [president]. Both seem to be able to unbend and be more hospitable than some of the other boys—just personal qualifications that every boy cannot possess. Of course all the pledges had to come in and meet all the mothers. Some of them were very shy.

Mrs. Wilson called for me and Mrs. Seaborn also phoned and asked if she might come by for me. Each mother was given a corsage. I took over the Pointer and the pictures of the plebes.

All the boys ask for each of you.

Much love—MOTHER—

---

*Robert Merriman commanded the Lincoln Brigade in the Spanish Civil War on the loyalist side and was killed in action. According to several authorities Bob was the model for the character of Robert Jordan in *For Whom The Bell Tolls*, by Ernest Hemingway. Gary Cooper played the part in the movie. Merriman, a tall, handsome former classmate at the University of Nevada with a broad grin, captured the heart of Marian Stone, one of our most attractive freshmen, before any of the rest of us had a chance to date her, and he had become one of my good friends. We marched side by side in ROTC drill and sang the popular song, "Louise," arguing over the correct lyrics.

CHAPTER 6 PLEBE FOOTBALL

We used to refer to the Corps as "the twelve-hundred mule team," and we obviously couldn't field many athletic teams with such a small student body. But today, with the cadet strength numbering well over four thousand, the Corps of Cadets fields a wide variety of competitive teams. At the top of the list are the "Corps Squads," those twenty-three teams that compete at the intercollegiate level in such sports as football, basketball, baseball, and track. Next on the list are the athletic clubs, which may likewise participate at the intercollegiate level. These clubs include such sports as bowling, cycling, judo, riding, and parachuting.

Finally, those cadets who don't find a spot on either a Corps Squad or a club sport are required to participate in intramural athletics, which somewhat parallel the sport seasons of the Corps Squads. Many a cadet has worked his way up from the minor league of an intramural sport to an elite Corps Squad. So the motto "Every cadet an athlete" is more than an idle boast.

In 1930 intercollegiate rules prohibited freshmen from playing, so each university fielded freshman teams which competed with similar teams of other universities. This rule has gone by the boards and today plebes may play on Corps Squads.

Perhaps the most valuable and practical athletic program at West Point is the daily physical education class in the gym required of all fourthclassmen. This includes combative sports (boxing for the men and self-defense for the women), swimming, gymnastics, and a fundamental course in physical fitness. Instruction is also given in those activities which a cadet might engage in after graduation, such as golf, tennis, handball, SCUBA, close-quarters combat, skiing, badminton, water safety, volleyball, and bowling.

Except for instruction in these "carry-over" sports, the program is similar to that given in my day, although we took fencing, as moribund in 1930 as it is today. No doubt the authorities have finally decided that an Army officer will have little need of this skill.

I wrote home on Sunday, September 21.

Dear Mother, Dad, Jean & Drew:

I'd like to write oftener but I can't seem to make it. Football takes up all my spare time. We practice Saturday and Wednesday afternoons while everyone else is deadbeating. Sunday I spend the morning in Chapel—Choir practice and service. In the afternoon it's Parade and in the evening we study.

My skins this month are:

"No belt at p.m.i." (Study hour inspection)	2	gigs
"No draw string in laundry bag" (the laundry sent it back without one).	1	″
"Failure to fill out Vocabulary Builder Notebook as instructed."	2	″
"Numbering problems incorrectly at mathematics."	2	″

Total 7. This is a fair record for 20 days. If a Cadet gets over 14 in one month he walks the Area—1 hour for each gig over 14. Last month I got 20 and have 6 tours awaiting me when football is over. To be "found" [dismissed], you have to get over 30 a month until Xmas.

Lots of men who are found in only one subject can come back the next year if they pass an examination in it. They are called "turnbacks." A yearling across the hall is one—he wears stars on his bathrobe.

My grades weren't so good this week. We had "writs" all week in Math and I fessed [flunked] one (1.6). I was only 8 tenths proficient for the week. Did better in English, 5.8 out of a possible 6 (2.8 in a writ). Went deficient for the week in French, 1.5 and 2.2. No, you won't see any stars on D.O.

Over half the plebe football squad is deficient. There are about 50 deficient in my class of 300.

We scrimaged [sic] yesterday in football and I did pretty well. I believe I have my position cinched now.

Did I tell you that I broke my nose last week? I won't be able to get it fixed till after football. The Dr. said it would make it weak.

Cartoon from *The Pointer*.

[The nose wasn't noticeably crooked, but I had a deviated septum and could breathe only through my right nostril. The medico said that if he operated, the next time I was hit there the nose would be smashed all over my face. So because of athletics I never got it fixed.

[One of my classmates on the plebe team was so ill coordinated that when he tackled me in practice his arm flew up and hit my nose. We didn't have face masks in those days.]

My roommate, Corley, is deficient, and is piling up a lot of skins. He works hard and we help him as much as possible, but he is pretty gross.

John Lawlor* is doing very well. He has better grades than I in Math

*John D. Lawlor commanded an infantry battalion in Europe during World War II and served with the Allied Control Authority in Berlin following the war. There he met and married Mary McLaughin, a former Women's Army Corps lieutenant. They raised six children. John retired as a brigadier general with two Legion of Merits and two Bronze

and French. He's had 4 years of French. He's also on the plebe football squad. [A graduate of the famous and strict Boston Latin School with a year at Harvard, John was far better prepared for plebe year than I. He was also a better athlete, making first string on the plebe team followed by three years of varsity football. He won the coveted Army "A" in football and hockey and wore the chevrons of a cadet lieutenant his first class year.]

Sue hasn't been up to see me yet, but promises to come soon. I'm dying to see her again—3 months without hardly speaking to a girl is pretty hard.

Alden is coming over this afternoon to read my Artemisia [University of Nevada's yearbook for the year 1930.]

Haven't much more to tell. I'm glad things are going well at home.

Lots of love,

DALE

P.S. *PLEASE* send me a photo of Mother—at least some snaps. Also some of Jean and Drew. DOS

A letter arrived from Dad written in Reno, September 25.

Dear Daley Boy—

Your letter of Sunday came today. Don't be distressed about not writing oftener—you have done nobly by us. I know life at West Point is intense, steady and constant, and only men with guts and perseverance can make it. Plenty never survive the short two months of preliminary training, and another lot go under by the end of Plebe year. You have it in you not only to go through, but to make a good record. So dig in old man, only one day at a time, and give it the best you've got.

[Dad's continued encouragement and enthusiasm for my being at West Point strengthened my determination to remain and succeed. Our mutual devotion was never more profound.]

We are sorry you have a broken nose and hope it will not trouble you much. It will be quite wonderful if you make a place on the plebe team, for you haven't the build for a first class player, and what you lack in that respect must be made up in speed and agressiveness.

I'm sorry you are having a battle with French. You will just have to

___

Star Medals. Now living in Winnetka, Illinois, he says, "I love Mary, my kids, my country and coffee."

dig in like hell when you study it. There is too much at stake to fall down in that or anything else. You are a soldier now, just as much as if you were in the trenches in France during the Great War, and must do your duty no matter how irksome or painful. West Point is no four-year loaf like college. It's a place for men with brains and guts. That's why when it is said of a man, "He's a West Point graduate," the argument as to education and training ends right there.

Your record as to skins this month is very good, and I know those you got were for reasons you would have prevented if you could. They seem to be along the line of making you more careful, rather than because of delinquencies.

I'll take some snaps of the family tomorrow and send them soon. I want to make another trip to Lassen Park as soon as possible, before it snows up there, but the last few days I have had no pep, lame back, bum kidneys, etc. Age will have its way, I guess. [He was 54 and lived to an alert 92.] I drove out to Steamboat today to see the silica sand mine, and although I enjoyed the trip I came back "all in."

This morning there was frost—the first of the season. Winter will soon be on us. [Dad always hated winter, as did I.] I think you will get about as much winter there as we do here and probably winter sports. [Winters were more severe at West Point than in Reno and in my day winter sports were minimal. A welcome ice rink was opened while I was there, and since then skiing has become popular with three lifts on the reservation.]

Much love from
    DAD

This is a letter marked "Thursday nite," date unknown.

Dear Folks—

Our first game is this Saturday with Boston University. The first game we (Plebes) play is with Perkiomen School on Drew's birthday [Oct. 15]. I don't even doubt the outcome of either, for we have some fighting hard teams.

The coach seems to think I'm pretty good now, for I've showed up well in some scrimages [sic]. I might make my numerals this year. [Numerals were a "1934" in grey felt to be worn on our black uniform sweaters. For plebes they were the equivalent of a letter.]

We had a military review today for a flock of Frog [French] generals.

One was covered with enough medals to make him at least a crown prince. "A" company got first line again—it's getting to be a habit. For about 5 successive times we've got it. Officers bet on which company will get first line. Once, back in the old days, A Co got first line for 12 successive Parades; a record which has never been equaled.

I'm right on the flank, no. 1 of the rear rank and first squad. I feel responsible for a lot of it because they see me first and then just a flock of rifles and kicking legs.

Sue is coming up to see me Sunday. Oh! But I'm going to enjoy those few hours with her. I can hardly wait.

Every nite in the mess hall the Corps gives an "A-R-M-Y — ARMY — ARMY—RAY-RAY-RAH-RAY—rah-rah-who-rah—West Point—Fight-FIGHT-FIGHT-FIGHT-FIGHT-FIGHT-FIGHT." There is no yell leader but everyone keeps together. It makes a fearful din, and at the end there is much cheering, whistling and napkin waiving [sic].

I weigh 204 pounds in uniform now; 194 stripped. I'm gaining slowly. Every nite after football I have about 5 minutes in which to swim. I spend it all on the diving board and am now learning to do a pretty fair jacknife [sic]. [Classmate Ken Kenerick* from Columbus, Ohio, coached me in this and we became fast friends.]

The airplane incident was interesting but I understand the way Dad felt. It's a risk but we should take risks sometimes even when they are unnecessary, just to prove to ourselves that we can take them when they *are* necessary. It will give the kids courage.

Lots of love,

DALE

The next letter came from Dad written on Monday, September 29.

Dear Son Dale—

Yours Thursday via air mail came today. We all went to the Nev-Utah game. There was a big crowd, 4800. Reno is growing so fast that each year sees bigger crowds. Utah trimmed us 20 to 7. They had a better

---

*A natural athlete, Kenneth R. Kenerick excelled at every sport he undertook, playing varsity football and basketball for four years and wearing the major "A." We were all astonished when Ken washed out of Flying School, but he went on to a distinguished career as a staff officer with the Joint Chiefs of Staff and was decorated with the Legion of Merit and the Commendation Medal. While commanding an artillery group in Thule, Greenland, he was killed in a helicopter accident.

backfield which brought them victory, altho Nevada's line was the stronger. Walt was put out in the 2nd half—a gash in his leg in which some stitches were taken at the hospital. I went in to see him after the game and told him he played well which pleased him. But he is far from satisfied.

I see W. P. swamped Boston University. Gee, how I would like to see one of the big eastern games, with say, Yale or Harvard. Those great eastern schools vastly outnumber West Point, but it is doubtful if they have any better squads because of the rigorous physical exams necessary to enter W. P. Still, they probably do some proselytizing and subsidizing which is hardly possible at West Point. I hope you beat Perkiomen School.

Jean and Drew had their airplane ride yesterday in an open biplane. They swooped around over the town and got a great thrill from it. Both were scared almost silly after they got in the plane but they enjoyed it. All of Reno's planes were taking passengers at 1 cent a pound.

I'm feeling better today, notwithstanding the heavy rain which has been pelting down steadily since early last night.

Drew brought home a very poor card from school today— His teacher, Miss Emma Smith, says he is "restless, inattentive, indolent." Mother does not hand her anything—says she just doesn't know how to inspire a child—says none of you did well under her. [Mother always stuck up for her own, even when there was some doubt about guilt.]

We are sending some prints. The old anti-photo complex is still working on Mother. Wants a better background, etc. She promised me she will have a real photo taken soon, tho.

Much love from
    DAD

In the same envelope came a letter from Mother:

Dearest Dale—
It was good to get a bi-weekly letter from you yesterday full of news. It may not seem like news to you but every word means much to us.

You are fortunate to be where they do everything the best way—even to football. You are getting the very best there is to be had. Dad has told you about our game. I can't say that I enjoyed it. Walt gave me a complimentary ticket. Was sorry he got hurt but he is getting along all right. We will be watching for the results of the Plebe game on Oct. 15th. We can tune in on Oct. 11th at 11:30 AM to hear the returns of the West Point game. Wonder if our set will be strong enough. Dad will have it well charged if he is home.

He is feeling better. Our days are certainly full and busy. We really enjoy both our roomers. Miss Moe is a lovely girl and we also like Miss Moody. We have received their rent now—teachers are always broke until their first pay day—and it has helped a lot.

Hope you are well and that your nose is giving you no trouble and that it won't be crooked.

Much love from us all,

MOTHER

I wrote home on September 30.

Dear Mother and Dad—

It certainly was a huge weekend. To begin with, we had the football game with Boston University. I suppose you've already read the score—39 to 0. The "Big Team" did a wonderful job on them and I never have watched such an interesting game. You see, I've never been to a big game before, and some of the things that happened, such as a 75 yard punt from behind our goal line, a couple of 40 yard completed passes, and a few runs of from 20 to 30 yards. The Big Team did much fumbling and tied up a few of the plays, but on the whole, they showed a quality of football that, I believe, will win ten strait [sic] games.

The "C" squad marched to the game so as to let those who were to walk tours or serve confinements could [sic] see it. We did plenty of yelling and the choir on Sunday was not as melodious as usual.

Saturday nite I walked guard in the 8th division. It was only an hour post, and I wasn't inspected, so everything was oke.

Due to the change from daylight to standard time we slept till 8 o'-clock this morning. At least some slept—I couldn't. At 7:30 I went down to the sinks and took a shower.

I was all spooned up for choir practice and Chapel, for afterwards at 12 noon I was to meet Sue. She had described her outfit and after the services I found her on the Chapel steps with her friend. We got in her car and I had my first auto ride in three months.

We found John, for the other girl, signed out, and boomed down to the Thayer for D.P. (Dining Permit)—the first time since the Big Day that I have been there.

After eating a turkey dinner for which the girls paid [cadets were not permitted to have any money—in a letter to his brother, John noted that "it cost the girl $10.00"] we killed time in riding around and talking. At 5 p.m. I had to stand Guard Mount and then Parade. Thus ended the day. We talked to them last out in front of barracks just before assembly for supper formation.

Lots of love,
DALE

There must be some missing letters from the folks. I wrote again on Monday, October 6.

Dear Mother and Dad—

Last weekend was too crowded for me to write, so I cut out my swim to get this off. I was pretty pooped last Saturday and spent the evening reading a story and going to bed early. The next morning, of course, was spent at Chapel. I am pretty low in French so I studied the rest of the day until Parade—then in the evening too, as we are supposed to.

My rank for the month is 63 in English, 152 in Math, and 284 in French, out of a class of 313. I'm not "dee" in anything but I'm pretty low in French. About 2.15. My sections are: 3rd in English, 6th in Math and 7th in French. There are 7 English sections, 12 Math sections and 7 French. I'm no. 1 in my French section and am the section marcher. It won't be long till I get policed to a higher section—I'm getting the swing of the lingo now.

We wore overcoats to the game Saturday. 54–0 was too big a score to be even interesting. [We played Furman.] It looks like we have another setup next week with Swarthmore. Two weeks from now we all go to Harvard. I'm going to have lunch with John at his home, and then see the city of famous beans. The week after that we go to New Haven.

I'm certainly enjoying football now. I don't care a bit for all the exercises but the scrimages [sic] are a real thrill. I only wish I were a better player.

No, we don't have to do much personal labor for the upperclassmen here. The most I did was to carry in a few trunks for the Cows when they came home from furlo. The best way is to keep out of sight whenever there is something to be done. If they call—I just pretend that I didn't hear.

I got the pictures you sent. All I need is one of Mother to complete the family in my locker.

Not having anything to buy with my boodle checks I spend them on football pools. I haven't won one yet but there is still a chance. If I do I'll make New York 50 dollars richer after the Illinois game. [There were ways to convert boodle script to cash but I've forgotten how it was done—we probably sold them to cadets who had ready cash. I know John had the barracks policeman (janitor) cash a check for him and John rewarded him with two cigars, but that was something else. We were permitted to buy from our Cadet Store account two "personal use" football tickets for $3 and six others at $4. These we would sell to our civilian friends who were always looking for tickets. It was our best source of cash.

[This practice was prohibited then as now. I also knew that a few of the more affluent cadets had their own checking accounts. The modern move to do away with script was a wise one. It was impossible to prevent cadets from having money.]

The upperclassman who marches behind me on the way to meals is a good egg. We make bets on the total game scores. Last week, if the Army game was odd I could fall-out for a week, but if it was even I would "Smell Hell." So I lost and am now bracing much. We have a similar bet on this next game.

Lots of love,

DALE

This secondclassman was Robert L. Scott,* who flew fighters with General Chenault out of China against Japan, became an ace, and wrote the best-seller, *God Is My Co-pilot,* which is now in its twenty-second printing. At the Point I began to believe his incessant hectoring was abusive, but it was probably because by always marching in front of him I was the most handy plebe to correct. I never could "fall out" even when marching to meals. Anyhow, as time went on I came to hate his guts. At the end of graduation parade I took my revenge in the sallyport, but more of that later. After Recognition we became friends.

---

*Robert L. Scott, Jr., from Georgia, was decorated with the Distinguished Service Cross, America's second highest award for combat action, three Silver Stars, four Distinguished Flying Crosses, and six Air Medals. He retired as a brigadier general.

On Saturday, October 11, Dad penned a letter.

Dear Dale Boy—
Your letter of last Monday came today to relieve the anxiety of ten days silence and made us very happy. You are all right—that's what we wanted to know. We read your letters over and over. Considering your numerous activities, especially football, you have done very well in academics. But I will be glad when you get out of the bottom section in French.

How grand it is that you are going to Boston, also New Haven, when the team goes! I still hope to see those towns some day. I suppose it's a complex hangover from unsatisfied youth longing, but it still seems to me, that if I were a boy again, I would rather be a West Pointer than anything else in the wide world. I know, too, there are many older men who feel just as I do.

Right now it's 11:30 AM here—about 2:30 PM with you—the Army-Swarthmore game is in progress. It's being broadcasted over KGO but I have tried and can't get it with our little set. Army seems to have the greatest team ever this year. It should be worth a king's ransom to see the Harvard game—you lucky dog!

I'm going to the Santa Clara game this afternoon and yell for Nevada. We'll probably lose as usual but I have a feeling it will be a real football game just the same.

You would surely be amused at Drew's doings if you were here. He has organized an army now, and he is the Captain. It's a sort of cross between a modern and a medieval army—some have shields, broadswords and daggers, with various devices painted on the shields. Drew has a recruiting "office" on the back porch. He has worked out examination papers they must pass—arithmetic problems, according to their school grades. It's an idea he got from hearing so much about West Point, as is the office of Second Lieutenant, one of his highest. He is the busiest kid ever, his mind works every minute. He has had some trouble with his work at school and once Mother went over to see about it. While Mother was talking with his teacher Drew said, "Well anyway, Miss Smith, I never have cheated in a single thing like a lot of the others." And the teacher said, "That's true, Drew, you never have. How I wish it were true of the others." Another West Point principle that has lodged in his little mind. He's doing fine now, since he brings his books home. 100 in geography yesterday!

Jean is more and more a wonderful girl with a fine record at school, a leader, and loved by all because of her fine disposition and great natural tact.

5 P.M. The big game is over, score zero-zero. It was a great game, well fought all the way through. One time in the 3rd quarter Santa Clara came dangerously near making a touchdown on a long forward pass. It sure peps us up to see the way Nevada played today.

Much love from
DAD

A letter from Mother came in the same envelope:

Dearest Dale,

We are a happy family this morning because your letter came. You were not to blame at all for our worry and concern—and I tried to tell Dad that it was only because you were so very busy that you had little time for writing—but I guess he was in a mood to worry and he really has because he wondered what kind of a jackpot you might be in. We are so pleased that you are doing well and will have two fine trips to Harvard and New Haven. It will make such a wonderful break for you and then, when you get back to work, you will work SO hard. I'm sorry French comes hard but it is all memory work and you will have to work very hard in it at all times. You are certainly doing well in English to be in the 3rd division and I am sure you will do even better—also in Math. I remember of hearing Albert Harris's mother say that there never was a letup to their hard studying—that Albert* had to work just as hard his Senior year as he did plebe year.

I know you would like to be on the plebe team and play next Wednesday but if you are not picked I will not cry about it. I would rather you did not play than to be injured and have it interfere with your other duties. So either way it is, one of us will be happy.

Good old Walt came over this morning and brought me a ticket to the Santa Clara game but I was afraid we would lose and was not anxious to go. I have asked Walt over several times but he hasn't come yet. I asked

*Albert E. Harris of Reno was one semester short of graduating from the University of Nevada when he entered West Point. He graduated in 1930 and served in Europe during World War II as commanding officer of an armored division combat command and was decorated with a Silver Star, a Legion of Merit, two Bronze Stars, and two Commendation Ribbons.

him to come when they let him out of the hospital. He won't play today unless someone gets hurt and they put him in for a spell. He is not in condition and looks white from being in bed so long. He says he is way behind in his class work.

You would get a kick to hear Drew play. He has been organizing an Army lately and is very important making all his plans and equipment. He wears the leggins you used to wear and has more belts and strappings—one across from shoulder to opposite waist, medals and more darned stuff. He and Lloyd are the bosses and they only take in little kids who will be bossed. He told me the name was N.B. Army and said that meant Nevada's Best Army. This morning he was loving the kitty and said, "Kitty, you should be very proud to be a mascot for a great warrior."

Much love dear,
MOTHER

I wrote a brief letter on October 9.

Dear Folks—

"That he has carried out his orders fully at the time and in the manner prescribed, or that he has reported himself for all violations or neglect of his orders." This is what is meant from an All Right asked of an assistant subdivision inspector, which I am tonite. I made 4 inspections between 7:15 and 9:30 to see that all room occupants were present or, in other words, get an All Right from each room.

I see you're not strait [sic] on some things. The Corps football squads are "A" the Army varsity, "B" the Army second squad or scrubs, and "C" the Plebe squad. Some Plebes have area tours due to excess demos and they are not excused from them to go to a football game—but they are excused to go to a formation. Thus the formation to march to the game so that all "C" squad men can see it—just a bit of red tape. [And a kind of quibble of the regulations that was condoned by the Tactical Department.]

I've been having some dental work done. They pulled that crooked tooth and are plugging up a lot of others. Believe me, if these Army dentists can't find holes, they make them. Have to study now.

Love,
DALE

A letter from Dad was written in Sacramento on October 16.

Dear Dale—

I am down here again for a few days to keep things hot on the job possibility. There is lots of talk about the Pyramid, and a reorganization is in progress, but nothing done yet—still, things look more favorable for a start on the mill than they did a month ago.

Yesterday your Plebe team played Perkiomen School. I have not heard the result yet. You may have had the honor of being on the team, but in any case, you have the honor of being one of the bunch. The big Army team is surely going through adversaries like a dose of salts this year.

The monthly statement of your grades and standing in the class were received from the Academy a few days ago. Considering your football and other activities they are very good. The French was pretty low as you stated but you will soon bring that up some. The English was very high and Math just in the upper half. It is really thrilling to see the machine-like precision and thoroughness with which they handle the academic work. What a Godsend it would be if a few of our countless universities could be so handled. They seem to be declining in value—the old earnestness of college men is missing. Is it any wonder that West Point opens doors of opportunity to its graduates that our modern universities do not?

Walt didn't get into the Santa Clara game. Still too weak. [Poor Walt Linehan never fully recovered from his injury so that he could play first-string football. It was a devastating blow to his ego, as he had started out so well and was captain of the squad. I kept in touch with Walt through the years. He became a successful executive with the Crown Zellerback Paper Co., raised a fine family, and died recently from heart disease.]

Much love from
DAD

And still another letter from Dad three days later.

Dear old Dale—

I came up from Sacto this AM got off the early train and sneaked home and into the house. It's cold and no one is awake yet. On the desk was your letter and also one from Mary. When I read yours and especially your grades, I could hardly restrain a wild yell of happiness. They are

grand—more, they are simply glorious. How proud of you I am. I'm so
set up that I'll be cocky all the rest of the month.

Yesterday I was in S.F. with the Hanleys [Dad's cousins] at 12:30. On
my way there I met a crowd in front of a Market Street radio that was
broadcasting the Army-Harvard game. I heard the great Army band—
the yells, saw in my mind the parade, saw the big H formed, and no
doubt heard your own voice. I arrived too late for the early Army touchdown that won the game, but I stayed until the second half began and
then hurried to my lunch date.

Much love from

DAD

In the same envelope came a letter from Drew.

Dear Dale

Thor and Mary sent me the best birthday present I ever got. It is a
light for my bike, and a horn that you squeeze a rubber ball at the end.
My bike is down at Oden's cycle shop. It has a puncture in it and I had
it fixed one day and I took it to school and after school when I looked at
it there was another flat and when I took it to Odens he said I would have
to get a new tube and I am anxious to get it and put the light and bat-
teries and horn on it. I like to work it. I wish you would write to me
often. I was using your shoulder pads but not the knee pads.

Your brother

DREW, S.

I don't remember sending Drew a birthday present. Maybe this was
a hint. I wrote a long letter home on October 19.

Dear Mother and Dad—

Things are certainly rosy and ace high again for me here. Geez, I've
got gobs to write about.

About Wednesday I was low. I didn't get into the Plebe game and was
sore as hell. I knew that I was better than some of the men in there for
I had played against them and this is a sure way of telling. It happened
that the visitors were late and the game was cut short. Only our first
string played. We won 7–0. I knew I hadn't been getting the breaks I
deserved—they had me on the 4th string. Well, I made up my mind to
wring the necks and step in the faces of a few of my classmates so as to

gain the coaches [*sic*] attention. It worked. Friday I was put in with the first string right next to an All American. I'm not sure of staying, but there's going to be some damn bruised classmates of mine from now on anyway.

Then Vacation.

Friday we "entrained" for Boston at 9:05 p.m. It was a great evening and the rally we had after dinner was a spectical [*sic*] that I've never before witnessed. The 1200 Mule Team [the Corps of Cadets] went mad—yes, just went mad. God, I never heard such yelling in my life, and that mess hall fairly rocked. We yelled for two days before the trip and this was the climax. A stunt that we pull is to wave our napkins after a yell. Captain Timberlake*—the best liked tac and a real man—gave a fight speech that should go down in history. "Gentlemen," he said, "we're not going up there to be tied." And we weren't tied!

I spent the evening before the formation listening to a classmate's phonograph. Did you know that we could have them? John is getting one for us. Anyway, the music was a treat and my spirits rose. It happens that at this minute I'm about 5 inches from that same phonograph which is playing "The Kiss Waltz" with Ruth Etting.

We entrained in a pouring rain that spoiled our shines and the press in our trousers. I had to sleep with Corley in a lower. There were 4 long special trains and 8 dining cars. Oh yes, we were "at ease" throughout—and even now because we won. The next morning we ate what we pleased in the dining car and formed at Allston. The clipping inclosed will give you the dope until we D.P.s [those on dining permit] fell out at the Common. John got a taxi and we boomed out to his house. The dinner was delicious but very confusing because everybody and his brother was busting in to see John.

We were taken by John's brother to the Harvard Yard where we formed before marching to the stadium. This was 12:45. Then we marched to the game. Harvard's stadium is huge and every seat was taken. It was the first time I had ever seen anything like it. Some 60,000 people. Well, anyway, we walked over Harvard so often that they were dizzy, and it was just lucky for them that we didn't put over 2 more touchdowns.

---

*Edward W. Timberlake, class of 1917, was promoted to brigadier general in 1943 and commanded several anti-aircraft brigades in Europe throughout World War II. His decorations included the Silver Star, the Legion of Merit, the Bronze Star, the Commendation Ribbon, and the Purple Heart. He retired as a brigadier general.

Army-Harvard game program.

Harvard's rooting section was supposed to stretch from goal to goal with seven yell leaders. They had the 7 yell leaders all right but the 1200 Mule Team made more noise than the rest of the stadium combined.

During the half the Harvard band pulled a clever stunt. They marched onto the field facing us and formed an A R M Y and played "Benny Havens, Oh" while we stood at attention. Then they marched around into a large block H facing their rooting section and played a Harvard song.

At the end of the game we gave a Long Corps Yell for the team and formed 5 minutes later on the grid for the march back to our train. The whole stadium remained in their seats to see us leave. Boston was nuts about the Cadets. If we could have staid [sic] over that night we could have owned the city. John's mother and some friends of hers came out to see us on the train. A newspaper man asked for a picture and the ladies were nuts about it. They fixed their hair and then the flash went off. Our pictures are in the Boston papers.

We got home at 6:00 A.M. this morning and feel pretty sleepy from two nights of berth sleeping with Corley. There wasn't room enough to get comfortable.

At Chapel this morning I slept thru my 4th consecutive service. I might be a hypocrite but I don't pretend to be interested.

Boston isn't much of a city. Though it has subways and elevateds its business section resembles that of Reno. It isn't pretty nor new like Los Angeles; it isn't majestic nor spectacular like New York; and it isn't cosmopolitan nor romantic like New Orleans; but it *is* historic. Some of the streets are interesting and I could almost imagine the Red Coats marching up them or seeing them shoot into a mob of people on the Common where we drilled.

I'm sorry to hear that you have a cold, Dad. Keep good care of yourself and don't, for heaven's sake, overwork.

Lots of love,

DALE

CHAPTER 7 FOOTBALL TRIPS

One tenet of the national service academies that separates them from other institutions of higher learning is the great importance placed on character development and personal integrity. Colonel Sylvanus Thayer, known as the father of the U.S. Military Academy, established this guiding principle during his tour as Superintendent from 1817 to 1833, and the other service academies have largely adopted the West Point honor system. Colonel Thayer wisely realized that a loyal and effective military establishment could exist only if officers were entirely trustworthy and honest. Only in that way could orders be carried out as planned and battles won. Disloyalty to the national government during the Civil War, moreover, revealed the necessity that the officer corps be imbued with obedience to constituted authority and dedicated to the support and defense of the Constitution.

The supreme law of the land as embedded in the Constitution is only as good as the traditions and customs of the citizenry and officials who accept it and abide by it, particularly the armed forces. The invidious example of the Soviet Union, whose enlightened constitution is so disregarded, illustrates this fact of life. Moreover, a military establishment that involves itself in politics can make a mockery of any constitution, as our neighbors to the south have so often demonstrated. Beginning with George Washington's example of removing his uniform when elected to the presidency, the code of civil control of the military has grown as a fundamental American military principle, and one never finds our officers resigning in a huff when they disagree with their orders. They carry out their lawful orders, no matter how onerous they may seem.

Such principles and traditions are at the root of the West Point Honor Code: A cadet will not lie, cheat, or steal or tolerate those who do. Thus he is honor bound by his oath of allegiance and ethically wedded to the principles which will make him entirely faithful to his service and his country.

The honor code can't be found in official regulations. It is administered by the Corps of Cadets through the Cadet Honor Committee. In my day a cadet found guilty would be automatically dismissed. Today the Superintendent may overturn the case or approve of the committee's findings and prescribe a lesser punishment than dismissal.

People are often confused about the "All Right" custom at West Point, which is a feature of the honor system. It simply means that when an "All Right" is given by a cadet, he intends to adhere to the regulations, and if for some reason he fails to do so, he will report himself for this infraction. Failing to report himself becomes a breach of honor and a major offense which could cause his dismissal, even though his infraction of the regulations might have been minor, such as going off-limits. Consequently cadets planning an escapade are careful to avoid giving an "All Right."

Dad's letter from Reno mailed on Wednesday, October 22, notes his understanding of the Cadet Honor Code.

Dear Dale—

Your letter of last Sunday came today describing the Boston trip and the big game. It was a great occasion, and a wonderful privilege to see it. The whole country likes to see West Point win because it exemplifies pure clean sport—it makes us feel good to know that one of the greatest national institutions is clean, straight through, and above corruption.

[I'm glad Dad didn't live to hear about the cheating scandals that occurred after the war. They put a tarnish on the Academy's honor system that will take generations to erase. Old grads like me still agonize over this fall from grace. However, the authorities must share the blame for placing too much emphasis on football and for relying on the honor system to ease administration. It is customary, as noted earlier, for brighter cadets to coach the dull ones. When assisting another it can be difficult for a cadet to determine whether or not he's revealing the content of an examination yet to be taken by the other. These pedagogical errors have been corrected, and today cadets are faced with fewer dilemmas as to what constitutes cheating.]

Too bad you didn't get into the Plebe game with Perkiomen but you have done exceedingly well to get on the squad and do as well as you have. You have the right idea about bruising up your opponents. If you hurt them every time, that and your unusual strength will generate a fear complex in your opponents, they will unconsciously dodge or flinch and you can go over them rough shod. I suppose "Get the other fellow *first* and get him *hard*" is as true of football now as it was in my day, 32 years ago.

So you drilled in historic old Boston Common. It must have given you an odd feeling to soldier on the ground where George Washington took command of the Continental Army. It is truly hallowed ground where our country was formed—even more so there than in Independence Hall where Washington's eventual victory was formalized.

Well, Thor & Mary are on the way up and should arrive some time tomorrow forenoon. The house is spick and span, and we will no doubt have a jolly visit, lacking only our Dale to be a complete picture. Yet we are glad you are there—another home town boy making good.

The "aluminiums" are beginning to drift in, big university doings this time no doubt. I suppose everyone will be too busy to write for the next few days.

Much love to you Daley, from us all—

    DAD

The next letter I wrote home was sent to Thor and is missing from the file. Mother wrote a long typed letter answering it on Monday, October 27. The letter reflects the joy she had with Thor and Mary there for the Nevada Homecoming weekend. I guess she wanted to share her happiness with me.

Dearest Dale,

Well, the big weekend is over and we have much to tell you. First of all, Nevada beat Cal Aggies 31 to 000—and we were happy to learn that Army tied Yale. We called the Gazette about 2:15 to learn the score. We pictured you parading in the Yale Bowl that morning just at the hour when we were enjoying the Homecoming Parade and wishing there were two of you and you could be here with us, too.

The weather has been the perfect fall that you know so well—not like the drizzling rain you had at Yale. The aft. of the game was marvelous. Clarence Mackay [the University of Nevada's great benefactor whose father, John William Mackay, made millions from the silver mines of Virginia City] and his party had places on the porch of the Training Quarters and during the half a bunch of the Sagers [a pep club] ran across the field to him and carried him on their shoulders over to the bleachers where they sang songs and yelled and honored him in every way. There were a number of shots of dynamite set off in the hills back of the campus.

Sigma Nu homecoming was certainly a grand affair. We all wished you could have been there. Thor had the time of his life—there were so many of his old friends and many of them with their wives. I gave an afternoon tea for Mary so that Thor's friends could meet her. I'm sure it was a success—the house was swarming from 4 to 6, everyone was happy to meet Mary, she looked so sweet and has such a gracious manner that everyone fell in love with her. Mrs. Jameson and Myrtle Conant helped me keep the teapot full and pour the tea with sandwiches, cookies, candy and nuts, and I had flowers, candles and decorations in yellow and orange, and Mary's dress was a deep orange.

Drew sings Hail Proud Nevada all the time—knows all the words— has carried words around in his pocket. When we were in the bleachers and everyone was singing, he was singing too at the top of his lungs and creating not a little notice from the older ones because of his piping high voice.

The leaves are falling so fast and everything is covered—all the doors are wide open and it is so sunny and bright. Thor and Mary left at 10 to 2—496 miles and I got a wire from Mary this morning "Arrived at 2.30 after perfect trip—lunch was great love Thor and Mary." What wonderful time they made. Could not have stopped for anything but gas. They averaged 39 miles an hour [in their Model B Ford coupe].

Much love from

DAD, JEAN, DREW AND MOTHER

On Sunday, October 26, I wrote to Thor on formal USMA stationery, to which I added the "D. O. SMITH" stamp (used to mark our books and everything else that would take it) on the letterhead. It was a weak effort at humor.

Dear Thor,

By the looks of the letterhead I own this here academy. Well, in a way I do an' in a way I don't. Y' see us folks here all has parents that is tax payers an' thus an' so we indirectly owns 'a place altho the gents 'round here don't as think so.

Well, Horse Face, I understand you had a pleasant trip back to old Alma. How was the Nevada likker in comparison with that distilled water you get in L.A. I would have liked to have been with you and to have sung Nevada songs in a gin haze—as I suppose you did. I'm glad Nevada beat the blank out of the Aggies for you. Nevada has a damn hard fighting team this year, don't you think?

The Big Team here got a bad break yesterday with Yale. We outplayed them but weren't lucky enough to win. If one of our ends hadn't been off side on Yale's try for point, we would have won. Incidentally, they got their goal on a break. The way our gang cut down the famous Albie Booth was something that did our hearts good. It was just like cutting down asparagus.

Yale is cocky. She's got too much guts and has the insolence to think she is just as good as we are. You can see how false this is, for no one rates us.

It was raining at Yale. The Bowl was a mass of color. Raincoats and umbrellus [*sic*] of all shades. The seats all have backs on them!

Yale is full of coonskin coats, and lousy women. Their campus is well scattered but the town is truly collegiate. I went on D.P. at the Travers Hotel in New Haven and it was ultra-collegiate.

Harvard has a beautiful campus. It even rivals those of the big western colleges. The buildings are mostly red brick covered with ivy. A river flows through their Yard and I noticed crews practicing on it.

I have big plans for the New York trip. I hope to turn the place inside out. From the stories of the upperclassmen, the place is so large that when the Corps of 1200 is turned loose, you don't see a grey uniform besides your own until the formation for return. Geez, but the Corps certainly rates. Everywhere we go, nothing is too good for us. We will be able to have most anything we ask for . . . even women! [The upperclassmen tended to exaggerate.]

My best to the wife and family. Drop in and see me sometime when you're down this way.

Love and kisses,

DALE

This letter from me to the folks was dated October 28.

Dear Folks:

Well, the Yale trip is over and Thor will send you his letter about it. Now we are piping the New York trip—the grand climax of all.

I'm on the third string now in football and we play a game tomorrow. I'm hoping to get in but my morale is low on the subject. I'd like to get a chance to sock somebody. All we do every afternoon is practice, practice, practice with about 10 minutes of scrimage [*sic*] a week. I get terribly griped doing nothing but blocking stuffed bags and tackling dummies.

I did well in French today. Made only one mistake. That means a 2.9.

Oct. 29—Well, we've played the game and I didn't get in. I suppose I should be happy that we won by 26–0 but I'm just griped as Hell.

John got in for the first time today. He caught a nice pass but got his face torn open pretty badly in a tackle.

Lots of love,

DALE

Dad wrote on November 3.

Dear Dale—

Tomorrow is election day and all the big hurrah. Mother will work checking ballots as usual.

Sorry you didn't make the string for the Plebe game, but you must not let the disappointment linger. Many a fine fellow does not make the team. The game's the thing—do the damn best you can with a cheer and a smile, and you are a man. Never mind the "breaks," and remember no one has anything but good will for you as long as you shoot square and don't grouch. The game's the thing. Play hard, and don't claim fouls. Do you know that some of the best coaches in this country never made a position on their own college team? That's the spirit—you just can't down them—no personal element in it at all.

[This was some of the best advice I ever received from Dad, but to my regret I couldn't follow it. My disappointment was so keen that I never fully recovered, and can feel the hurt to this day. I suspect that the coaches noticed my poor attitude.]

Well—ere long the football play will be lowered and other sports will be in the ascendancy at old W. P.—and the hard tang of eastern winter, too. But a full life is usually a happy one, and the weather will be incidental.

Bye, dear old Dale, and the greatest love.

DAD

Mother's letter came in the same envelope.

Dearest Dale,

Well, the first Monday morning of your fifth month at the Academy—
we will soon be receiving another statement of your standing. I think
you are doing fine dear—I will have no worry at all if you can keep up
the pace you have started.

I'm sorry that you were so low over the Plebe football game. I'm always sorry when that mood comes over you—but personally I'm just as
pleased to have you on the sidelines, even if you are low—and know that
you are whole and not broken boned or face smashed. The game Sat with
St. Ignatius (which name has been changed to University of San Francisco) was a rough one. Walt was hurt again early in the game and had
to come out for a rest and oh, he was mad. He wouldn't take any assistance, no blanket and just stormed around, pacing back and forth, talking to the coach and others—and finally got back in the game. They beat
us 20–13.

I know you will enjoy the trip to New York next weekend. Is the Corps
going to Chicago for the Notre Dame game? I saw Mrs. Sibley the other
day but we have not as yet had our real talk fest over our boys. She says
Alden is beginning to worry over his Xmas leave—financially. Said that
when he went to the Yale game he could have had a dollar, but if he took
it he would have had a day cut off of his Xmas leave. I had never understood that the Academy furnished you money for Xmas leave but she
says they do. And the parents can't send any money until the furlo at the
end of the second year. Well, we won't have that to worry about for a
long time yet. [Mother and Mrs. Sibley were a bit mixed up about all
that. We had to be out of debt to go on Christmas leave after the Academy advanced us a certain amount of cash from our account. As far as I
knew nothing prevented us from receiving more money from home.]

Much love—

MOTHER

The letter I penned on November 3 indicates I had recovered somewhat from my disappointment with football.

Dear Folks:

I hurried home from football tonite to get a letter off to my Mammy
and Pappy. It's been a crime the way I've neglected you. I get letters

from you or rolls of papers nearly every day. Those Homecoming pictures are great. Geez, but I would have liked to be there.

Well, Sue came up again yesterday and kept me busy until suppertime. We went on D.P. at the Thayer right after Chapel. She had her simple friend with her, but I managed to find a date for the wench. We got back just 10 minutes before Peerade and I had a taste of Beast Barracks days getting ready. I found out that Parade was in Overcoats and had to change all my belts. After Parade we drove around the Post in the Buick and managed to get in some hasty necking before supper.

John just came in and congratulated me on some "good work" I did at practice today. He said some of the backs were talking about me—said I was "underrated" and it was a "real job" to take me out. Well, it's true some days, but others I'm terribly off form. I'm not consistent. I would like to make my numerals this year but I doubt if I will.

I saw Mr. & Mrs. Seaborn [of New Rochelle] for a minute at the Yale game, and sat with the Loflands throughout the second half for they had seats adjacent to our rooting section.

I don't know for sure what I want to do in New York. Sue is beginning to lose her charm for me. It's quite plain that she cares more for the uniform than anything else. I threatened not to wear it in New York (it would, of course, be impossible for me to wear anything else) and she nearly had a fit. I would enjoy myself much more in New Rochelle having dinner with Ruth. That way I'd stay in training and keep out of mischief. I don't intend, however, to break the date cold, but will get some other brass buttons to show her New York on that night.

I've boned a section in Frog, and am now in the 6th. Last week my grades were 2.9, 2.8.

Lots of luck for you all back home. Love,

DALE

My battle with French had me more worried than I let on in my letters home. I wasn't at all confident that I could avoid being "turned out" for the final examination that decided whether a cadet could remain in the Academy. Twenty-nine years later my son Kort had the same problem except that he was deficient in all his academics and finally resigned.

I wrote home on November 5.

Dear Folks,

Tomorrow we have a review in Alg.—perhaps a writ—but I know it cold and have a bit of time now to do this.

The Plebes played McKenzie Military Academy today & won 20–0. I didn't dress because I had hurt my ankle in practice.

Everyone is hopped up over the New York trip—it furnishes conversation at the dinner table. "What have you planned for New York?" "I'm going to the Ritz Roof Garden to see Green Pastures. . . . dancing at the Astor. . . . just make the rounds of all the night clubs."

In tactics now we have finished the Browning Machine Gun, and the Automatic Rifle. Most of our time is spent with grenades, the French Mortar, and the 37 millimeter gun or one pounder. We have tactics from 3 to 4:30 on Tuesdays and Thursdays.

It's been raining for the last 3 days and looks like it will continue. When it rains the Hell Cats split up, each member taking one division. Our room, being situated where it is, gets a fearful blast of bugle notes at 5:50 A.M. I feel like yelling, "All right, all right—we hear you!"

The Albie Booth situation bothers Army none at all. [Some sports writers suggested that Army tackled too hard and hurt Booth deliberately.] It scarcely makes talking material. The tackle was just a typical hard Army tackle, and pure football. I don't know about Sasse [the Army head coach] but Bryan, our plebe coach, teaches us to play that way. Yale is a poor sport as far as I can see, because Army outplayed them hands down for the last 3 quarters.

The pictures you sent are great. I hope things are breaking well for you.

Lots of love,

DALE

A letter written on November 7 came from Dad.

Dear son Dale—

Your good letter was received day before yesterday and today I suppose you are on your way with the Corps to N.Y. for the Illinois game tomorrow. That the crowd will be enormous is a foregone conclusion. I see the radio hook-up for the game covers the nation completely with a multitude of stations. We are talking about going somewhere to see if we can get the game over a good set—it would be fun, for your voice would come to us in the roar of the crowd.

I was pleased with your well-thought-out analysis of your performance on the football field, and it is evident that you are not too downhearted at the prospect of not winning the numerals this year. It is my opinion that it would be little short of miraculous if you did make them. You were no great shakes at football here for two excellent reasons. First—in your early youth you grew so fast that you didn't have the proper physique. Second—Due to improperly developed physique, the hurts, pains and effort of the sport were too much for your mental poise—you developed a subconscious aversion and shrinking that you didn't overcome while here. It is evident now, as your body is approaching maturity and perfection, that your mental attitude toward football is changing and greatly improving, because of good coaching, and more maturity and experience in a most inspiring environment. It is a *man's* game, and takes both mental and body guts. Play the season all through, as hard as you can, as if the devil himself would kill you if you didn't knock the wall-eyed scrub opposed to you into the hospital with a wrenched back, cracked skull and broken rib. Give every play in scrimmage the utmost that's in you—be mad as *hell* but clear headed. Your reward will not be that you have made numerals, or the team, but in sincere admiration and respect of the squad and Corps for a man who can't be licked, and is game all through and never quits. Next year you will be older, tougher, and 100% better.

We are all happy here at home. And the crowning part of our happiness is our boy at West Point. West Point! The very name strikes a vibrant chord of pride in my heart. When I replied, too casually perhaps, to an inquiry by the Hanleys, as to where and how you were, the low "Oh"—and the pause, so significant of envy and admiration, was rich food for my bursting ego. And so it is with all who learn where you are, for countless men and women I hardly know ask me about you. Believe me, Nevada is proud of her boys.

Relative to your girl friends, we are very much interested, but you will decide those things, and they will come out all right if you are always the honorable gentleman. You will not be so susceptible or sentimental a little later, and have already learned that the "Brass Buttons" count for more than the man himself with the most of them—and their sweet mothers, too, who know too well that daughter is making no mistake and is doing herself mighty proud to hook a West Pointer. Of course we can draw only mental pictures but I think that I would enjoy Ruth more than Sue, yet both have been very kind and nice to you.

Must close this rambling missive and get it in the airmail.

Much love from us all,

DAD

I next wrote on November 9 after returning from the great New York trip.

Dear Mother and Dad,

Well the big time is over and we are back at work. Geez, but I'm happy. Everything broke right and the evening was a success. I'm in love again, that's me.

Friday night we had Saturday privileges and a show. I went with "Sib" [Alden Sibley] and we saw Richard Barthelmess in "The Dawn Patrol." It was a very good show—with a plot like "Journey's End"—not a single woman in it. For once the chumps who run the projecting maching managed to keep the thing going until the end. Last Saturday (week ago) it was a riot. Greta Garbo was on the screen and every time she'd kiss her man some nut would knock a whole row of dumbells off their racks. [Movies were in the gym.]

Yesterday we took a boat across the river to Beacon [John called it "a corker sail," but the wind kept us off the deck] and then entrained on the New York Central for the Big City. We were given box lunches and after arriving in the Bronx we marched directly to the Yankee Stadium. You've read about the game. [We won.] The Illini band was wonderful but they couldn't make as much noise as our band.

I phoned Ruth during the game but could hardly hear a word she said because of the noise. I did hear her say, however, when I asked her if she had a date, "No, I got rid of it." I saw the Seaborns and the Loflands. The latter took me out [to New Rochelle] after the game was over.

Oh, it was luxury [at Ruth's]. We had dinner and then turned on the radio while I rested my weary bones in a two feet deep davinport [sic]. Before long Ruth's mother had to go somewhere, and her sisters went to bed. Until nine thirty we had a delightful time.

While I was there Mrs. Seaborn phoned to ask if she might send something to me at the Point. "Anything," I answered. She asked me to come over for a horn of gin but I was being intoxicated enough where I was.

I took the last train in at 9:35 and succeeded in establishing an impression wherever I went. I taxied from the Grand Central. "Where are all the Kaydets," says I to the driver. "Well, most of 'em are at the Roosevelt Grille." So, "To the Roosevelt Grille!"

I got a seat at Bill Beard's table. He was with his father. [Bill Beard* was a secondclassman. He and his father, a major, were more than gracious to invite me to their table and Bill recognized me.]

What a band they have there! For an hour I danced with green, red, and black velvet backless evening gowns. Then down to the foot of 42nd street and home. But wait:

Wally [Wollaston],** the man who took Sue for me, tied it up gloriously by bringing Sue to the ferry. Wow, she saw me. Wally came over to me and said, "She's here and has seen you, you must come over and speak to her—say something." I thought it was a big practical joke and laughed, although when I looked, there she was. I was politely informed that I should make up better excuses. Anyway, Wally had a good time, and I now know the femme I really care for so what the hell.

Not one drink did I have. I was one of the minority.

Lots of love,

DALE

*William G. Beard went into the Air Corps and was killed in an aircraft accident in Hawaii in 1936.

**Pennock H. Wollaston was one of my good friends who was found from our class but returned the following year to graduate with the class of 1935. Recently we were reunited in Hawaii, where he lives in Pahala. Wally served with distinction in staff and command assignments in the Pacific Theater during World War II, being decorated with the Bronze Star and two Commendation Ribbons. Later, as an expert in security, he served as Army Attaché in both Iran and Jordan.

Mother wrote on Thursday, November 13.

Dearest Dale,

Your letter about the NY trip came yesterday. Glad you had such a fine time. Great for all the Kaydets to be taken and given liberty after the game. Hope every one of them were aboard when the train started—and all sober. What punishment is handed out to those who overstepped? What penalty if they did not return with the Corps? [It was dismissal in either case. After crossing the Hudson on the Weehauken Ferry we were formed by companies alongside the train that was to carry us up the Hudson River to West Point. Our tactical officers inspected us and those who had had something to drink kept their mouths tightly shut and held their breaths. Rarely was a kaydet late for the formation or found drunk.]

It is quite evident that you would accept your pin if Sue would return it. Well, that's the way things turn out. Many don't stand the test of time. I'm glad you found Ruth sweet and stunning—it was nice of them to have you out and nice of you to go. Who are the Loflands? [Mother forgot. The Loflands were friends of the Seaborns, whose son Jack introduced me to Ruth.]

We are having our first snow storm today. A great delight to Drew but he came home at noon cold and wet because of his low shoes, but glorying in having chased some girls with snow balls. He will meet me after school to get a pair of boots.

Friday morning— Didn't have time to finish yesterday. It was cold last night, the first freezing weather. Dad is having an awful time getting the car started—heating water to warm up the radiator. We have one of the apartments vacant and he wanted to go over there to look after it. Another tenant is out of a job. It will be tough on all of us if we can't keep the apts rented. [Dad and mother had invested some savings as down payment on low-cost apartments, but were having a hard time keeping up with the payments on the loan.]

Much love dear—we miss you a lot but can't wish you back. It is a most comforting feeling that you are so well established, doing so well, and cared for both mentally, physically and morally. You are a lucky boy.
    MOTHER

Dad's letter dated November 16 came in the same envelope.

Dear Dale—

Your letter of Nov. 5th descriptive of your trip to New York has been read and re-read and discussed aplenty. You must have enjoyed the brief liberty greatly. Things have a way of balancing up. After a period of work and restriction, freedom and play have more savor.

Your amors with Ruth and Sue are diverting, and the way in which you have wiggled away from Sue is perhaps as good a way as any. It's easy to say that the honorable thing to do is to tell a girl straight out, that you, or she, has been mistaken, how sorry you are, etc. and eat plenty of crow, and make her feel miserable, and yourself feel like a cad of the nth degree. But if you just sidestep her, as you did, and try to make it nice and easy at the same time, her pride is not as badly hurt, for she knows you care enough not to want to hurt and humiliate her. She will be mad enough all right, but in dear Sue's case it's only wounded pride—there is no love back of it.

With your little Ruth it is probably different. Of course she fell in love with the brass buttons at first, they all do. But she is kind of a wholesome kid, if we can judge, and will probably really lose both her head and heart to you, for you have winning ways. Of course you love her now, but will probably tire of her later—new scenes, faces and loves—the kaleidoscope of life.

We were very happy over your fine grades for October; they are splendid considering your other activities. Everyone who knows us is continually asking about you. Last night at Comus dance many asked and you can imagine the pleasure with which we replied.

Drew is doing fine at school now. One day he made 100 in each of three subjects; geography, arithmetic and spelling. He has a fine little head and I hope that some time, he too, can win an appointment to West Point. He hardly realizes it now but it is already his ambition. He surprised us a few days ago by his knowledge of military schools.

Love,

DAD

CHAPTER 8 THE CUBA GAME

General Douglas MacArthur clearly defined the rationale behind the extensive athletic program at West Point when he said, "Upon the fields of friendly strife are sown the seeds that upon other fields, on other days, will bear the fruits of victory. . . . " The program began in 1816, when a Master of the Sword was appointed, and consisted of fencing and military calisthenics. Fencing was on its way out even then, but there was a fascination with this ancient sport that gripped the military clear into my day at the Academy. It was somehow considered the mark of a gentleman, and, of course, we were all required to buy ceremonial sabers on graduation—and riding britches, boots, and spurs.

Intercollegiate competition began at the Academy in 1890 when Annapolis challenged West Point to a game of football. Cadet Dennis Mahan Michie organized a team and the first Army-Navy game was played. Soon the Army Athletic Association was formed and competition began in baseball and track.

I wrote home on November 13 with exciting news.

Dear Mother and Dad—
Geez! A great rumor! Army-Navy game in New York Dec. 6th! That's what Sasse* [Army's head coach] told the A squad tonite. [There hadn't

*Ralph I. Sasse from Delaware graduated with the class of 1916 and commanded a tank battalion in the First World War. He was wounded, and cited by the British. At West Point he was head coach from 1930 to 1933 and then was assigned to Mississippi State as Professor of Military Science and Tactics; there he became head football coach until 1937. He retired in 1940 but returned to active duty in 1942 and commanded an armored regiment at Ft. Meade, Maryland, retiring a second time in 1948 with a Legion of Merit and the rank of colonel.

been an Army-Navy game for several years and the country missed this classic athletic spectacle. The rift was over the eligibility of players. Navy objected to our playing men who had had more than three years of college varsity football while Army claimed all men who entered West Point were on an equal footing, and besides, Navy had about a thousand more students. Some clever entrepreneurs suggested that an Army-Navy game be played with the proceeds going to charity. Because this was during the Depression, neither school could refuse. This broke the ice and the games have since continued uninterrupted.]

Oh, what I could do with another evening in New York—New Rochelle. The only way I'd change my last evening would be to stay longer at 167 Coligini Ave. in New Rochelle.

Of course, rumors here are everywhere all the time. Once a year rumors come out that Plebes will get Xmas leave, but they never do. [Eventually the rumor proved true.]

I was almost certain that I'd get into the game Wednesday with Dean School, because I am on the second string to stay, but the tackle who is in my place on the first string played such a splendid game—much better than I could—that I didn't feel any self pity.

Dad, guts is the commonest thing, as Rockne says, on the football field. Not one man can stay out more than two weeks with eight coaches watching him and be gutless. My great fault is "going to sleep." Sometimes I am not on my toes at the split second that the ball is snapped, and that is half of it—getting the jump on the other fellow.

It's now after supper: [We had marched to majestic Washington Hall with light hearts in suppressed excitement. Removing our hats at the foot of the broad stone steps, we ran up through huge doors heavy enough to withstand a siege, entered the cavernous mess hall, and found our places. As always we stood quietly behind our chairs.] News travels fast here. When "Take seats" was given by the Cadet Adjutant from the "Poop deck" the Corps burst into a mighty roar—the loudest and longest I've ever heard. Perhaps we do play Navy.

I'm undecided whether to go out for Boxing or Basketball as a winter sport. If I get my nose fixed I'll never be able to box again, so I'll probably do that this year. Then too, the red comforter [issued to every cadet and thrown on the springs when one wanted to take a nap] beckons me, for I would love to deadbeat the winter and read novels.

Our Math P [professor] is a wonderful newspaper. He tells us everything from how Mendelson [sic] composed Humeresque [sic] to how to meet chorus girls and models from York. He's a great egg and we get along splendidly. I enjoy the class so much that I hardly care to bone a higher section.

Do you know a Lieutenant Drury?* He's an English P here and says he went to Reno High. He's asked me out to dinner in Highland Falls. He says we Nevadans must stick together.

Got hazed by my own classmates this afternoon while we were standing in the Area waiting for the command, "March off your sections," to go to class. All at attention, of course, and all conversation without moving our lips.

"What house [room] did the Woof-woof [Cadet Adjutant] announce were to be left for inspection by those Spicks [some visiting foreign officers]," I asked.

"A co. Where do you live?" from one.

"A co. first floor," I answered.

"That's it. Is your house in order?"

"Hell no, it's in a terrible mess." I wasn't beginning to feel so well.

"Your [sic] gigged. Violation of specific instructions," from no. 1.

"Five demos," says no. 3.

"Four more for room in disorder," from no. 6.

"Say, Smith, you might as well resign," pipes up no. 4.

It turned out that it wasn't A co. after all that was to be inspected.

Lots of love,
DALE

The next letter I received came from Dad, written in Sacramento on November 20.

Dear Dale—

I came down here yesterday to make some cyanide tests, gratis, for Al Blundell et al of Sparks, to show them what type of mill and process they should use at their mine, now shipping ore from near Rawhide, Nev. The tests are agitating merrily and it seems good to be among the old familiar beakers, bottles and smells again, and hear the hot hiss of a gas assay furnace.

*Frederick W. Drury, class of 1919, came from an Army family. He commanded a mechanized cavalry regiment in World War II, was wounded twice and taken prisoner in Germany. He was awarded the Legion of Merit and two Purple Hearts.

A letter from Mother this morning enclosing yours of the 15th. It sure warms me up like a shot of gin, old boy, to read those splendid grades of yours. Improved English is already evident from your letters, and your French by the scruff of the neck.

Hail big game, Army-Navy! That was glorious sport news, and makes every patriotic soul feel good. The game will be wonderful, the gate receipts over a million dollars, and of course, Army should win. Army has the edge, in that she can have players that have previously had 3 years playing experience in other colleges, because she enters men up to 22 years. Navy can't, as men must not be over 20 when they enter, is it not?

Much love from,
    DAD

Dad wrote again from Reno on Tuesday, November 25.

Dear Daley-boy—

Home last night at 10 pm from Sacto, my tests completed. It was like stepping back into old shoes to pull crucibles out of an assay furnace, to weigh infinitely small golds on a Keller balance, "poem in mechanics," once again. It may lead to a job, anyway, I must keep going. Sunday I drove with Mr. Macgregor through the famous Mother Lode district, Jackson, San Andreas, went through a new cyanide plant at the Central Eureka Mine, and an old one at the Argonaut, and learned of progress since leaving the game.

It made us all very happy, me particularly, to hear that you won a place on the line in the Kiski game. You had to be good to get there. And you had to climb a long way up from Nevada days in mental attitude and performance to do that at West Point. [My letter telling of this is not in the file. Probably sent to Thor and Mary.] I am inordinately proud of you. Whether you ever win numerals, or other insignia, matters not a whit to me. What fills me up is that you went in for a major sport, gave it the best you had, never quit, whimpered or complained, and the fellows and coaches admire and like you for it. Once again it's the way we work that counts, it's the game. It is evident that you have plenty of speed, and played a great game, for when a coach like Reeder* puts

*Russell P. "Red" Reeder, Jr., was one of Army's most admired coaches. As a cadet he excelled at all sports but had a difficult time with academics, being found and turned back two times. His sparkling autobiography, *Born At Reveille*, relates a colorful life full of en-

himself out to show his approbation, he feels and means more than he says in words.

[I remember making a good clean tackle in the Kiskiminetas School game, our strongest opponent, and being set up for weeks by Red's compliment. My hopes revived for making something of myself in football.]

Army has yet to play two mighty games [Notre Dame and Navy]. The outcome of both is in doubt, which makes them all the better. Too bad the Corps can't go to Chicago, but another trip to York for the Army-Navy lovefest will have its compensations. Old mother West Point may be Spartan, but she isn't niggardly. Those grim officers love all their boys—how much they never can show.

As to the relative merits of basketball & boxing I've nothing much to say. Boxing is a he-man's game, and your football record indicates that you might go a long way in the square ring, what with your great reach and height, strength and speed. Jess Willard became world's champion, yet most of the time he was too slow to get out of his own way. I really think boxing should be a mighty good game for a soldier. A good amateur boxer commands a heap of respect.

[Boxing is no longer a varsity sport at West Point because of a lack of opponents for dual meets. However, it is still taught in the gym classes and is an active intramural sport. Brigade champions have the option of entering the regional tournament, which is sponsored by the National Collegiate Boxing Association, and winners in the regional tournaments proceed to the Nationals.]

The Academy is an unconscious inspiration to Drewdy. He is all hopped up with West Point ideals, and the school's crankiest teacher, Miss Smith, frequently marks his papers "very fine," "splendid" etc. He thinks it's most despicable to cheat, but is not yet a real good sport—is inclined to quit and cry when beaten at games, etc. but he is improving in that respect, too.

Well Daley, I've rambled on some pages without saying much, and

thusiasm and dedication to his country. Red Reeder led his regiment ashore at Utah Beach on D-Day, June 6, 1944, was wounded, and lost his leg. A natural leader, for want of a leg he would have undoubtedly risen to high rank in the Army. Decorated with the Distinguished Service Cross, America's second highest award for combat service, the Legion of Merit, the Silver Star, the Bronze Star, and the Purple Heart, he retired as a colonel at West Point, where for several years he served in the Army Athletic Association and wrote books about cadet life which influenced many a boy to aspire to the Corps.

will close for the day, enclosing some clippings cut by Mother. We greatly enjoy the Pointers you send and read them from cover to cover.
Love,
DAD

I wrote the following letter on November 24.

Dear Mother and Dad—
Well, the days are passing by and it won't be long till the Xmas deadbeat. Come to think about it, I'm going to be in a bad way for giving Xmas presents. If Army wins I'll have bathrobes for Thor and Dad. It's a great stunt to bet bathrobes with Navy men—theirs are much better than ours.
Wednesday nite I'm going to dinner and a show with Lt. Drury. Alden and Shepardson are also going. On Thursday [Thanksgiving Day] we play our last plebe game—the undefeated Cuban Cadets. I believe it will be easy, however.
Last Saturday George "Showboat" Corley had 4 femmes up. Out of the lot there was one cute one and I managed to get her. We P.S.ed them to the game. Because John's femme wasn't so hot he became supernumerary room orderly [a purely fictitious duty] right after the game and left. My gal lives in Beacon, only 6 miles up the river, and she'll be down again.
The best fun of the weekend however was sleeping. It seems that sleeping is the greatest form of recreation here. Other places, a fellow would go to a show or get tight, but here he goes to bed.
I find myself beginning to draw pictures, so I guess there isn't much more to say. Practically every mistake I make, Frog included, is made by carelessness in class. It makes me very angry at myself sometimes.
Lots of love,
DALE

Four days later, on November 28, I wrote again.

Dearest Mother and Dad—
I hope you all had a very happy Thanksgiving. I wish I could have been home with you. Of course, we had the whole day off here, and it was a great deadbeat.
I've have a cold for the past two weeks (it's practically gone now), and

had been doctoring it with Listerine and not going to sick call for fear they'd break me into the hospital. You see, I wanted to play in the Cuban game. So yesterday I lay in bed till dinner and felt fit for a struggle with any eleven dark Caribbeans. We ate toast, lettice [sic] and lemon aid [sic] at twelve and were on the field at two p.m. Being on the second string I didn't start, but was put in just after the first two plays with instructions to "stress the kicking game." Like all good teams do (only this team as you will see didn't prove to be a good one), they attempted to run a play over me directly. Really it was a surprise. Three big swarthy interference men came driving at me but when they connected I thought they must have been made of cotton. Banging them out of the way was just like slapping down so many mosquitoes, and I got the ball carrier around the belly and threw him for a loss. Before long we began to smile at each other along the line and make determined efforts to keep from laughing. The great Cuban Cadets had nothing on the ball— no speed, no drive, no guts, no power. As soon as we got the ball we began putting over touchdowns as fast as we could call signals, till Lt. Bryan (our coach) sent a man in with instructions to "Come off it" (cadet slang), that we would cause a war with Cuba by disgracing them so. It happened that among the 5,000 spectators, was the Chief of Staff of the Cuban Army, not to mention our own Gen. "Bill" Smith.

So in the huddles, Johnson,* our star quarterback, would talk like this: "Let's see, try 36 on 2, and Craig,** you run for the goal line and get tackled just before you get there. We have to make this game exciting." But then when Craig got to the goal line he looked around and there was no one to tackle him—poor fellow.

I was taken out about the end of the second quarter and Bryan met me: "Get a blanket and keep warm, Smith, and forget—just forget that

---

*Paul E. Johnson, Jr., known as "Beanie" to his classmates, from Ashland, Ohio, was captain of our plebe team and played three years of varsity football for Army. After two years in the cavalry he resigned his commission and joined the Faultless Rubber Company in Ashland. During World War II he returned to the service, rising to major and later in the Ordnance reserves to lieutenant colonel. He became successful in business as owner of the Johnson Brothers Rubber Company.

**William H. "Bill" Craig gave up football after plebe year for soccer, at which he won two minor "As". A man of great vitality and infectious humor, Bill was a friend of all his classmates. After graduation he achieved outstanding skills largely in personnel fields. He participated in landings and subsequent operations in France, Germany, and Austria during World War II, was decorated with three Distinguished Service Medals, and retired as a major general.

that's a football game." Diplomacy entered strongly into the game—we were ordered to let them have a touchdown! They had travelled 2500 miles, why not? So by some star acting we let them get one over that didn't look too fishy.

[One reason why the Cubans played so poorly might have been the cold, which we were used to. It amused me that they wore gloves. Dad wrote that he couldn't help being moved by the gallantry of West Point as shown by the determination not to humiliate "the little dark visitors" and even to let them have a touchdown.]

In the dressing room where we had lain before the game in tense, suppressed excitement, we now began to have fierce battles with orange halves until a gruff order to come off it was given. I started the second half and had a hard time keeping my hands and feet warm. The game ended 35–7, altho it could have been in the hundreds to nothing. I was sorry it hadn't been tougher.

So much for the poor Military Academy of Cuba. Next year the Plebes play a return game in Havana. There is no justice!

The C squad ate its Thanksgiving dinner together at Supper and we certainly enjoyed ourselves.

Til [*sic*] the 13th of Dec. we will be kept out for practice—learning Navy plays and getting battered up by the varsity. It's a great game, and I wonder often if someday I might be good enough for the Army varsity—I'd hate to be a scrub for 3 years. I know how it feels. [I hadn't played enough quarters to win the prized numerals.]

The studies are grinding right along—I've neglected them this week but, of course, haven't gone de in anything.

If Army beats Notre Dame tomorrow I will have 15 dollars. I bet my total savings, $5, at 3 to one odds. Pray for victory or else you will get no Christmas presents from Yousmay College.

For my Xmas I can use black sox, handkerchiefs, boodle, razor . . .
[The letter ends here, subsequent pages are missing.]

Dad wrote me on Saturday night, November 29.

Dear Dale—

At 11 A.M. we went down to Conants where they have a better radio to listen to the Army–Notre Dame game over KFRC. While the rest ate a nice lunch I sat on the floor with my ear to the amplifier, and play by play followed that bitter struggle through the rain. What a game!

Nothing to chose between the teams, just a lucky break gave the game to South Bend. Hail, Army! The toughest game is over, and though lost—if one point is really losing—her brow is crowned with laurel.

Back home again and sounds of cooking as well as smells emanating from the kitchen. Drewdy is playing the phono & "On the Riviera" is blaring forth. Jean is at a show, and should soon breeze in to tell us about it.

This morning when I got up the world seemed kind of glum and cold. Approaching holidays held no cheer. I sat down and wrote this sonnet:

CHRISTMAS

Another milestone on the road to time.
We celebrate with gifts and words of cheer,
Send postcards 'decked with wholesome words in rhyme
To dear ones—and to others not so dear.
But half of those who celebrate today,
View with alarm another passing year.
Some quickly gather flowers on the way
Alas! Too soon to lay them on a bier.
What good to moralize in mournful vein?
Perchance 'twill make some few of us "play fair,"
Not wishing when we go too soon again,
To die unwept save by our kin. To dare
Undo some selfish deed before too late,
We're thrust, unwilling, through the outer gate.

But this evening in the pleasant warmth and bustle of our home, I wrote another:

CHRISTMAS

When I wake up on Christmas morn I'll hear,
Excited chatter in the kiddies room,
E'en with the dawn, and calls of "Papa dear
Will you go down and start the furnace soon?"
Quick from the quilts and still in bed attire,
I hurry through the halls and down below,
Yet 'ere the welcome warmth of winter fire
Spreads through the home, they ask if they may go.
Like deer they bound down stairs into the room,

Where decorated, stands the lovely tree,
With eager eyes they search amid the bloom,
For welcome gifts tied there by you and me.
Is there a joy in life to equal this,
The answering echo of our offsprings' bliss?

Sunday Night—

This morning Mother and I went to Baptist Church where Brewster Adams spoke on "The Impatience of Humanity." He spoke of the impatience of youth—a boy of his acquaintance had driven from Los Angeles in 14 hours. . . . Mrs. Humphrey in the seat ahead of us turned around and solemnly winked at Mother, being familiar with Thor's recent exploit.

We rented a vacant apartment again today, and feel much better as a result of it, altho the first month's rent must be spent for additional furniture and dishes.

Much love from
    DAD

Mother had written a letter dated Friday night.

Dearest Dale—

I saw Frank Brown's Mother and sisters this A.M. They say Frank is homesick again and complains that his Mother's letters are so infrequent— [Frank was a classmate of mine at Reno High and a neighbor. We were close friends and both aspired to Annapolis. Frank got Senator Oddie's alternate to my principal appointment, and when I failed to make it because I was one inch too tall, Frank easily passed the exams to enter the United States Naval Academy. He was a much better scholar than I but sort of a wild youngster, and he spent many days in "the brig" at Annapolis. Even so he graduated very high in his class.

[On two occasions Frank took me for dives in submarines to which he was assigned, and once I was able to take Frank and the crew of the *Seal* on a tour of the Hawaiian Islands in B-18 bombers.

[When the war started Frank commanded an S-boat which was reported missing in Aleutian waters. After the war it was determined from Japanese records that he had attempted to shoot it out on the surface with a Japanese destroyer and was sunk with all hands. For some reason, I imagine, he was unable to dive. Under the circumstances, with men on deck, I wonder why the Japanese took no prisoners.]

Do you remain in training for boxing? Or can you have boodle. I was tempted to send you a cake for Thanksgiving but you said not to send any until you told us to. But I didn't want to cause you to break your pledge. [Our last game with the Cubans ended our training obligation. We signed no such pledge for boxing.]

Tomorrow is the big game—I wish we could get it over Radio—but we are hoping the Army Mule will walk out with banners flying.

Much love dear—from your   MOTHER

I answered on December 3.

Dearest Mother and Dad

Well, your pot bellied son is plugging along and pushing the days behind him till Christmas comes. In academics I'm taking a rest. After analizing [sic] everything, I came up with the conclusion that it wasn't the studying that I did—it was how alert I was in the classroom. It doesn't take me long to master the lessons, if I can only keep from making foolish mistakes. Formerly I'd been staying up till second taps [11 p.m.] (we are permitted late lights always because poor Corley is so de) and felt dead every day—no more of that. [John and I worked diligently with George Corley but the lessons just wouldn't stick in Showboat's head.] I've boned a section in Math and French so I feel as safe and sure of staying here as I did of staying in Nevada.

Since Monday we've been learning Navy plays. It's been terribly cold and my feet are aching because the cleats in my shoes ram into my feet due to the frozen ground. It's like playing on pavement. Yesterday we practiced in the Riding Hall. A game of polo was going on in the other half! [The Riding Hall, a massive stone building perched on the bluff above the river, has been converted into a fine academic building called Thayer Hall.] It's hard to practice with no games to look forward to. We might get overnight in New York on the 13th because of our work, however.

I've had letters from Frank Brown and Al Edwards. [Al Edwards was another Reno High classmate who made it to Annapolis and did well there.] We plan to have a big time in New York. This time I will indulge in some of the lower pleasures of life because we are thru training.

There were big pieces in the New York papers about our Cuba game. One, a headline on the Sport Page! My name wasn't in them because I haven't a number on my jersey. The curse of working up from the scrubs!

Of course send me boodle. Mrs. Seaborn sent me a nice box of cake for Thanksgiving. I don't suppose we'll have to train much for boxing—we only have one match.

We've had a classmate's Victrola in our room for the past week and it certainly takes a beating. We have a stack of good records, too.

In gym we are having tests. I've fairly outdone myself on the horizontal bars. There is one exercise that over half the class can't do and I learned it on the alcove bar in our room during my minutes of relaxation from study.

In fencing I won my match and got a 3.0. I met my Waterloo in wrestling today. I weigh 202 lbs. now and was matched with a 207 lb. moose who plays short tackle. Up to now I had never been thrown and felt very confident—perhaps over confident. He dove for my legs and I hugged his waist and threw him over my head. For a second I almost had the match, but I didn't know what to do next. He managed to get away and break a half Nelson that I hadn't quite got on him and we tugged and grunted for another period. Finally we were up against the wall. I knew that if he once got his weight into me I was gone—I couldn't back up because of the wall, and he just hugged me like a big bear and put me on my back. I'd like to have another chance at him—I know I can throw him. Another alibi: He had a broken nose and I promised not to use a headlock on him. [For the life of me I can't recall who my opponent was. Perhaps Jim Walsh.

[One-eyed Tom Jenkins was our wrestling coach. He told us "The Terrible Turk" gouged his eye unfairly in a championship match. Tom taught us that "there ain't no holt what can't be broke," and that there was "a gart for every holt." He'd always ask our weight when setting up a match but no matter how unequal the figures were he'd order, "Close enough, wrestle!"]

To date this is all we've been tested in. I anticipate boxing. As for the apparatus, I'll fall down pitifully on the side horse and long horse. But the vaulting bars are duck soup because of my highjump work, and at the rings I'll do fair.

Well it's about time for supper. It takes longer to get ready now because of the overcoats and gloves.

Lots of luck to all of you. I'm glad Dad is again finding some mining work and some hot prospects. I enjoy his letters.

Love,
DALE

I wrote home the following week, dated "Saturday nite."

Dearest Mother and Dad:

Got your nice letters and have just read them. Also got one from the girl in Beacon. The little devil signed it "Flaming Mystery"—damned if I can remember her name.

The horizon for me looks clear and beautiful. This week I've been room orderly, mail dragger, and on a few other soirees, topped off with a guard tour tonite in the 3rd div. They're all behind me now. Looking forward: The only blot is 2 solid weeks of General Review Writs which have 50% to do with our grade. I've taken two of them already and maxed the first one with a cold 3.0. I did well in the other too, perhaps a 2.9. Then next week is the Big Game. Wonder of wonders, we (the C squad) are being rewarded for our extra work in football by staying out after our last game in order to run Navy plays against the A squad. We get the whole nite off in York and come home Sunday with the A squad. Additionally, some inspired woman has given all who care for them, tickets to the Follies, and after that we are invited to her home where she will furnish Follies girls to those who don't drag. This is just for us football men, of course. Not a bit bad, what! And then on the following week is Christmas with all its deadbeat, rest, 10 o'clock reveilles, and hops.

Someone else is giving every man in the Corps a ticket to any show he cares to see. Would you suggest Green Pastures, Lysistrata, The Vanities, The Follies, or another evening with Ruth? One thing I'm certain of, I'm not going to bed until I get on the train Sunday.

Yes, the Notre Dame game was hard to lose. I bet against Notre Dame, Mother. They sent a block of 3,000 dollars here at 3 to 1 and the 1000 bucks was raised overnight. Of course the authorities have nothing to do with this [and would have strongly disapproved had they known about it]. As for bathrobes, I can requisition them at any time.

What do you think of the Army team now that Notre Dame walked all over U.S.C.? I was glad to see that. We had a regular game yesterday with the first string A squad. I played against Messinger, King, Carlmark, Herb, Bowman, Humber,* etc. etc. of famous names. They were

---

*Edwin J. Messinger was commissioned in the Infantry and during World War II was operations officer of an airborne division. He also served in the Korean War as a regimental commander. Rising to the rank of lieutenant general, he retired with two Distinguished Service Crosses, two Silver Stars, three Legion of Merits, and three Bronze

plenty tuff [*sic*] but I got a big thrill out of seeing the ball carried once by a Plebe for about five yards on a 36 play which is the hole I open. We made about 3 first downs on them, too, which is nearly as many as Notre Dame made. They put over 3 touchdowns on us before it got dark. Then, too, we were using newly learned Navy plays which was a handicap.

[I have a vivid memory of playing opposite Dick King* one bitterly cold and dark night when the turf was frozen solid. Dick, a popular first-classman in A company, was an All-American end. His assignment on the offense was to take me out and on two or three plays I was able to slap him aside and get into the backfield. Dick finally lost his temper and on the last play he wrapped himself around me like a boa, effectively ending my drive. He wasn't made an All-American for nothing.]

Geez, I'm sitting on top of the world for boxing. There are 3 of us in the "engineer" half of the class which is my gym section—3 of us in the 200 lb. class. So the coach had the other two fight 2 rounds and after a rest, the winner was to fight me. The man who lost, Pete Kopcsak,** was Plebe end and a wonderful football man—he'll be All-American before he graduates. [And he was. A rawboned friendly man from Greensburg, Pennsylvania, Pete and I became good friends.]

The winner [of that two-round preliminary bout] was a beautifully built man, Bill Bunker,† who has already broken some academic swim-

---

Stars. Carl W. Carlmark graduated from Flying School and became a weather officer, serving in Alaska during World War II. He was awarded the Legion of Merit. Edward G. Herb was commissioned in the Engineer Corps, served in Europe during World War II, and retired as a colonel with two Legion of Merits and a Bronze Star. Wendell W. Bowman earned his wings at Flying School and commanded a communications wing in Europe during World War II. He retired as a major general with a Legion of Merit. Biographical sketches of King and Humber are noted elsewhere.

*As commander of a B-29 group flying out of Saipan in 1944, Richard T. King, Jr., was shot down over Japan but luckily survived prisoner-of-war camp. A classmate who was with him, Bill Brugge, didn't make it. Dick was decorated with a Silver Star, a Legion of Merit, and the Purple Heart. He retired as a brigadier general. Byron E. Brugge died of malnutrition in the Japanese prisoner-of-war camp at Fukuoka. He was a colonel with two Air Medals and a Purple Heart.

**Peter J. Kopcsak led a Negro tank battalion in General Patton's Third Army and in a violent three-hour action soundly defeated the German opposition, thus being awarded Silver and Bronze Star Medals along with a Purple Heart for a serious leg wound.

†William B. "Bill" Bunker, from a proud Army family of West Point Bunkers, won letters in swimming and participated in numerous extracurricular activities. After graduation he served in the Cavalry, Engineers, and finally the Transportation Corps, rising to the rank of lieutenant general. Decorated with two Legion of Merits and a Commendation Ribbon, he is known as a promoter of the Army helicopter.

ming records. But I had boxed with him in practice—knew that I could beat the tar out of him. So we got in the ring, shook hands, and were off! It might sound like boasting—sure it's boasting, but I can boast to you—the first round was a massacre. Not one blow did he land, and I pounded his face to a glowing pulp. Soon the round ended and we went to our corners puffing. Then I got a funny feeling—felt like I was being a bully and pounding him up for nothing but a 3.00 in the test. In any real match they would have thrown in the towel for him, but that was impossible here. So next round I took it easy. In doing this I got a good sock in the puss which let me see stars for a second, but the round was nearly over and I didn't have time to K.O. him after that. We were allowed to use only our left hands to hit and our rights to guard—otherwise Mr. Bunker would have been knocked into the middle of this week.

Well, you can imagine how I felt when old hard-man Billy Cavenaugh [the boxing coach], onetime middle weight champ of the world, called me over and asked, "Are you going out for a winter sport, Smith?"

"Yes, Sir, I'm coming out for boxing just as soon as football is over."

"That's fine, you'll be good at it."

I don't know whether it has happened to me or whether it's the place I'm in—anyway, West Point has done me a world of good. For some reason unknown to me, I'm almost a big shot here, while at Nevada I wasn't worth a tinker's damn.

For one thing, I've gained lots of weight—now about 202 lbs. stripped and I have worlds of self-confidence—something unique to me.

Back to academics: I had the highest mark in the 5th section in Math, and it was my first week with it—a 2.6 ave. Not as hot a mark, however. In Frog I made a 2.8 & 2.7—in B.S. [English] I made a 2.5 & 2.6. Sunday—

Glad to hear that Dad has some hot prospects in the mining racket—I hope they materialize.

For a Christmas present, please get my calling card plate and have United States Corps of Cadets put down in the right hand corner—same kind of printing—and then some cards. I need them badly!

Lots of love,

DALE

CHAPTER 9 THE NAVY GAME

At reveille on the morning of the Navy game when our ranks formed in the Area of Central Barracks we found about half the windows festooned with hanging sheets on which were printed boasts and exhortations such as "Beat Navy," "Go Army," "Sink the Navy." Cadets in one room demonstrated considerable originality by hanging a black poncho out of their window. Printed in white on the poncho was, "ARMY WILL WIN AND THIS IS NO SHEET."

School spirit was at its highest. At the great rally the night before, Major Timberlake, one of our favorite tacs, toasted, "Here's to heart and nerve and sinew; here's to a gang that's never licked; here's to the fighting Army team!" If we didn't yell ourselves hoarse then, we did at the game in New York's Yankee Stadium. And Army *did* win.

But the excitement of the game was overshadowed by the glamour of Broadway. New York society turned itself inside out with hospitality. "Ziegfeld's Follies" and "Earl Carroll's Vanities" were competing musical revues on Forty-second Street and each tried to outdo the other in entertaining the Army and Navy football squads. We plebes on the C squad were included and were treated no differently from the varsity.

My next letter home told of some of this excitement. It was dated December 13.

Dear Mother and Dad—
Won't have time to write much, but I just wanted to tell you that I had a very wonderful trip.
Saw Frank Brown, Al Edwards and Bill Parsons on the 50 yard line after the game. [Bill Parsons was a Midshipman from Reno who had been three years at the Naval Academy.]

Met Sue—by accident—in the Astor. [The Astor Hotel on Broadway and Forty-second Street was a traditional cadet hangout. It has long given way, sadly, to a modern office building.] I spent the first part of the evening at the Hollywood [night club] with her.

Later, after barging around in general, I went to the St. Regis with some pals. Wow! They served us champagne and scotch. Delicious! [A particular treat during Prohibition.] A hot band, beautiful girls from The Vanities and everything delightful—I didn't see The Vanities but these girls put on acts for us in evening clothes. [The fan dance was all the rage then. Seminude girls holding large ostrich feathers in each hand teasingly managed to cover their most attractive parts as they pirouetted across the stage. At the St. Regis party the Vanities girls used menus for fans.] Wow, what a party. Very informal and all—some of the Middies and Kaydets would even be so bold as to break up a chorus by trying to dance in it. I'll give it to you later in detail.

Love,
DALE

Dad penned a letter to me on Wednesday, December 10.

Dearest Dale—

Your fine letter of Saturday night arrived this morning and your achievements and good fortune in various activities have made us all happy and light-headed. Your academic grades and records in the writs are a joy—a Nevada lad making good,—*our Dale.*

C squad must have done very well indeed this year to be rewarded with so much liberty and distinction. But mind your step and keep your head. Like myself you are greatly swayed and led by your emotions, and emotion is a fine servant but a deadly master. I think, though, that you are most likely to spend the evening with little Ruth, who will keep you well in hand. Shows are merely shows. Next day we wonder what it was all about. They are worth little except when in good company, to heighten emotionalism.

As to whether it's the place you're in that enables you to do well, that's easy to answer. It is first yourself, and secondly the place. Up until now you have put forth your best, for the place demands it. And we very often get out of a thing what we put into it. At Nevada you were too young, and had not yet found yourself. Now you are more of a man,

Brothers in Arms.

Naval Academy cadets enjoyed liberty in New York City after their West Point counterparts had to depart by the New York Central ferry at 42nd Street for the train ride back to the USMA. Cartoon in 1934 *Howitzer.*

physically and mentally, and if you keep striving (which is the only *true happiness*) you will be twice as good a man in every way next year. I can preach to you without fear of reproach from you because I have not done anything remarkable myself. I had a poor start but managed to catch up with some of them.

We enjoyed the story of the wrestling and the boxing. Truly men's— and soldier's—sports. Sports knit together the modern armies, and the officers who played football, boxed, etc. are just twice as much respected as those who did not. Hence the emphasis on sports at W. P.

I am surprised at your gain in weight, despite the football. I didn't weigh 200 until over 25 years old. Good food and regular habits account for that gain in your case, I think. [The last page is missing from Dad's letter.]

Mother also wrote on December 11.

Dearest Dale,

Your good letter of Saturday and Sunday came today. Oh, you don't know how happy Dad and I were as we read it and we laughed aloud many times. Seems as though you have gained wonderfully in every way since you went there.

Dad started a letter to you this aft. but since then has been "in conference" with several men. There may be a vacancy at the Mackay School of Mines. The Curator, Mr. Oliver, is ill and must take a leave of absence—and Dad is trying to get the appointment. There will be no appointment unless the Nevada Legislature appropriates some money for the work—and so Dad's first work will be to influence the newly elected assemblymen and senators to promote the measure when the Legislature meets in Carson in Jan.

There are lots of things in the wind but they move so slowly. However, it keeps Dad interested and helps him to make new contacts all the time—and so keeps him in good spirits.

I know Thor will be crazy over your letters—will send them on tonight. The children are getting enthused over Xmas—Drew bought a few of his presents tonite. He is now up on the University pond trying to skate. Jean is at Junior High at a rehearsal—the Gayety is this Friday night.

You make us all so happy, dear. Jean, too, just thrills at your successes. Tell us how much money they give you to spend on your trip.

Much love dear from us all

    MOTHER

My next letter was dated the fourteenth.

Dearest Mother and Dad—

Well, I'll start my long narration.

Friday nite was a riot here. Such a rally I have never dreamed about. We had supper half an hour early so that more time could be had for the speeches. The Supe gave the first talk, and set the Corps wild when he announced that the Area Birds might go on the trip also. So they gave him a Long Corps Yell, which is a great honor. It was the first I had ever heard given for anyone. Later we gave one for Coach Sasse and another for Humber, the team captain. This yell is given at attention and is the greatest honor the Corps can bestow.

We had 7 o'clock reveille and took the boat for the other side of the river at 8:15 [where we caught the New York Central to New York.] We marched directly to the Yankee Stadium after the trip, and you know all about the game. I took the subway to the Astor and began the evening.

Strike me pink, I felt a touch on my arm and there was Sue—looking stunning. Of course, she said she hadn't expected to find me there, and tried very hard to make me believe it. She had written a note forgiving me, so what could I do?

I got a date for her homely friend and after cleaning up we went to the Hollywood for supper. Wow, what a place that is. Just two steps from Times Square, and the most naked chorus in the world. The climax of one of the acts was to display a completely naked girl! Even I was shocked. What is this modern generation coming to? To boot, they had a beverage menu on every table with martinis 'n everything, and an open bar. This isn't a speakeasy either! Wonder what a speakeasy is? Suppose they're going out of existence. Say, Reno had better wake up— it's a backward village. And the bill, it was so reasonable that I helped pay it. $8.70 for 4 people, and we had a chicken dinner! No cover charge whatever. The drinks were only 50 cents apiece. We danced some and enjoyed the wonderful band. Everything was in honor of us. They had an Army-Navy review. The Navy chorus girls would ask for cheers while the band played Anchors Away and every Navy man would yell. Then they would play Slum and Gravy and the Army men would yell even louder for the army girls. A great time.

We left about 10 and Sue took us for a taxi ride out to Central Park and around till 11. Then we returned to the Astor and said goodby.

Things were running high at the Astor—a party in every room. I spent the next hour there and then went with a gang to the St. Regis.

They fixed things up brown for us there. The acting host and I became bosom friends before long and he promised to get me the best chorus girl. And he did! Earl Carroll was the master of ceremonies and the girls put on various acts from his Vanities. It was very informal—we even cut in on Colonels.

A man came up to me in the St. Regis lobby: "I guess you don't know me, but I'm Colonel Hoggis. I used to be Com [Commandant]." Wow, I snapped to with a bang, but he recognized me! [Shook my hand.] He wanted me to meet his party. I don't remember many names—a flock of Colonels and a Mrs. Chrysler. All very very nice people.

Oh yes, some debutants gave us a fashion review.

This host [a Mr. Doyle] called me Captain and his personal body guard. He insisted upon my meeting the best looking women present. He said to look him up next time I was down and he'd get me any date I wanted in the whole city. [I never followed through on this generous invitation, more's the pity.

[Classmate Ralph Bucknam* had more foresight than I. After the Illinois game he suffered with a dull blind date and resolved not to waste any more precious free time in New York. He came across a picture of a beautiful ballet dancer in a New York paper, Vivian Fey, who was performing in Earl Carroll's Vanities. With no preliminaries he wrote her for a date after the Navy game. And to his astonishment he received a brief, perfumed reply indicating that her mother thought it would be all right. She gave him a first row center ticket for the Vanities and Ralph found himself in the show with a spotlight on him and the cast making much over him.]

Well, all the upperclassmen [on the football team] recognized the plebes [on the C squad] and everything was a complete success.

Next day as we were walking down 42nd St. on our way to the ferry, I saw the posters in front of the various shows. Here were pictures of the girls I had danced with.

And now I must study English.

Lots of love,

DALE

Mother wrote Wednesday night, December 17.

Dearest Dale—

Have sent you a little Xmas—not very much—but you know we cannot do much this year. It will be very quiet with you and Thor away.

Have ordered your calling cards but they haven't come yet. Dad got

---

*Smiling Ralph E. Bucknam, Jr., from Long Island, New York, worked his way up from seventh string on the plebe football squad to first-string center on the Army varsity, winning two major "As". Feeling himself unsuited for military life, he resigned and took a football coaching position at Harvard, where he studied law. He became a successful international patent lawyer but returned to the Army as war approached. Our paths crossed at Langley Field, Virginia, where he conceived the idea of equipping an airplane with a magnetic submarine detector and I assisted him in modifying an old B-17 with his invention. It worked but was superseded by a more advanced device. At Langley Ralph met the comely Ruth Barlow and I stood up with him at their marriage in Williamsburg. After the war he returned to the practice of patent law.

a couple of new records to send you. They may not be new to you. Jean and Drew especially like Betty Co-Ed but I'm betting that you already have it. We haven't bought a new record since you left, as you can guess.

I have been working this week and Dad has been the housekeeper. Weather is turning colder tonite. Wonder if it will be a white Christmas. All the merchants have Xmas trees lighted in front of their stores and it makes the town look very gay. I will have to do the rest of my shopping between 7 and 9 P.M. or else during my noon hour. Dad got Drew a Bebe gun and a tool chest. Guess that will be enough for him.

Didn't you see Ruth at all on your trip? Will she be sore or just disappointed! More next time, dear.

Much love,

MOTHER

On Sunday, December 21, I wrote home.

Merry Christmas Mother and Dad—

I'm writing this on my back in bed. It's great to get a well earned deadbeat. The writs are over. It was a terrible strain. I'm glad that in June we won't have football thru half of them. I'm afraid I lost a lot of files, but I'm not turned out. Many of my class, however, are. That means they will have to take the final examination in whatever subject they are turned out in, called the turn out writs, and if they fail in one of these they are found. Poor Corley is turned out in everything. He is almost sure to be found but the poor guy studies constantly. The other Plebe room on this floor has 2 of 3 turned out, and I believe one will be found. They have a good system here. If you are found in only one subject it is possible to take a further writ about 9 months later, and then join the class one year after yours. These "turn-backs" are recognized if plebes. Of course they are out of school for a whole semester and the summer. There are a lot of turnbacks in our class. Corley is one. But he was turned back for reasons of health. I doubt if he'll get turned back again this time.

I've been getting a taste of the area. During August I got an excess of 6 demos and haven't been able to walk the 6 tours of an hour each until now because of football. It's pretty hard for a lot of the fellows, but I didn't mind it much [truthfully I hated it] because of all the walking I've done with Dad in the Sierra Nevadas, although my arm got a little tired holding the rifle. A slugoid has anywhere from 11 to 22 tours [hours] to walk off. This is bad because they have no time left to play. For him this place is ten times as bad as Sing Sing prison could be.

John and I have a vic now. It's a portable and a pretty good one. The Plebes down the hall bought one and then got another as a Christmas present. They sold it to us for 10 dollars. What a bargain.

I got your picture, Mother, and like it a lot. I don't know what the other folks want, but this is o.k.

I sent a flock of Xmas cards—not like yours but very West Pointish and clever. It's getting bad when I have to send a Xmas card to the folks at home, but I'm flat broke and won't be able to send much even later. You see, the only way we can get money is by selling football tickets and then having the tickets taken out of our Cadet Store account. I had to use all of mine for my evening in N.Y. and for the vic.

I didn't get any Navy bathrobes. Those I asked to bet wisely neglected to answer my letters so I'm bathrobeless.

To Thor and Mary I'm sending a subscription to the Pointer. You will get a clever calender [sic] (that we could buy) in a few days.

Last nite we all saw the Marx brothers in Animal Crackers. It was a riot. They take all prizes.

On the York trip I didn't see Ruth at all. She had another date. I guess I didn't rate enough to have it broken this time.

When on leave the upperclassmen wear cit [civilian] clothes. It would be a pleasure for me to get into the old suit again. I wonder if I've forgotten how to tie a necktie.

It hasn't snowed here yet. I hope we will have a white Xmas too, for a lot of the fun is tobogoning [sic]. We have a wonderful new skating rink and everyone is skating now. John is out for hockey. It's an interesting sport—something like lacrosse, only on ice.

Christmas spirit is everywhere here. After chapel they gave the choir each a box of candy, and when I got home John had the room filled with boodle. His box had come.

We have one more day of school and then 10 days of vacation. It will be a wonderful rest.

Drew's papers are fine, and I'm glad to hear that Jean is doing well too. I hope you all have a Merry Christmas and I'm sorry that I can't be there.

Lots of love to you all,

DALE

P.S. I'm sorry you had a cold, Mother, and I hope you are well now. DOS

I wrote Thor and Mary on December 22.

Dear Thor and Mary—

I received two damn fine letters from you, so I'll have to write this instead of studying tonite. I don't want to study anyhow—tomorrow is the last day and we won't get graded.

I'm back on the Company table for meals now and have to put up with a lot of nonsense—just like Beast Barracks. Tomorrow is the last day, however, for next semester I will get on the boxing training table.

Tomorrow afternoon our big time starts with a reception at the Supe's house. All the other classes go on leave. Tomorrow nite will be my first military hop. I'm dragging blind—the femmes from York won't be up until later.

The room is full of boodle. I'll get sick if I don't quit eating. Christmas makes its mark even in this isolated hole. We have already hung up our socks on the fireplace mantel.

The Navy game was a wonderful trip. We managed to do everything possible in the time we had free. The fem I had was a 3.0—some show girl. I didn't see much of her, however, there were too many others.

Geez, what a gripe. They're going to make us go to Chapel on Xmas. Next thing you know they'll be asking an All Right at taps to see if we've said our prayers.

It would be great to see you crazy people. Geez, but I'd like to go on another party with you again. You know I've spent many sad hours thinking about what lousy gin we had on that last one—we could have done things brown with 10 more percent. I wish I could have sent you that pint of rye which I left at the Astor. I bought it and then didn't take but two drinks out of it. There was too much better likker everywhere else.

I don't see how I could get home next Xmas. If I could fly that would be the nerts, but first Dad would have to find a gold mine. For Furlo, I'm thinking of getting a job on a boat thru the canal. Then I would jump it at Pedro, see you for a while and then go home. But that's a long way off.

Well, I hope youse people have a very Merry Xmas and a tight New Year. For me it only means a flock of seven o'clock reveilles.

Lots of love,

DALE

Mother wrote:

Dearest Dale—

Well—here it is Xmas Eve—and I wonder what you are doing! We put up our tree on Sunday—it is a pretty one and we have 3 strings of lights. I have been away from home all day for the past week and a half and I am glad Jean & Papa could look after things for me. Preparations for Xmas have all been with Jean. The tension is now at its height—she and Drew would like to go to bed early—you know!

We are sorry you can't be here but we know you will enjoy the day with your pals. Glad you have a Victrola. I know you will keep it busy all this vacation. During classes are there any restrictions on when you can play it? [Indeed there were.]

Frank Brown's mother phoned today. Dad answered. Frank wrote his mother how fine you looked—your shoulders erect—you were proud of your height—and how W Point had improved you.

So glad you got all through your writs—but I knew you would. The poor devils who tried and failed—I am sorry for.

We have much to be thankful for. I hope you will be well and happy thru the vacation. If you get all the boodle that has been sent you will end up in the hospital. But you always did know when to stop!

A Merry Xmas dear—hope you have plenty of good times this week..

Much love from us all—

MOTHER

And from Dad, also on Christmas Eve:

Dear Daley boy:

Your fine Xmas letter arrived this afternoon and we were so glad to hear that you got through the "writs" all right. Too bad for Corley and for others who did not pass them. Their system is fair and tested by many men and many years. I would hate very much to see you a "turnback," but from now on there will be no more danger. Still there will be no let up on the academic work. The place could not be what it is if it did not demand and get a lot of work out of the cadets.

Everyone continues to ask about you. Today a boy delivering special mail, a girl in the public library. "How is Dale getting along?" [I worked in the library while going to Nevada.]

A special delivery letter came from Thor today, he is as cheery as usual and I hope he will like his new job. You will enjoy the great box Mary and he have sent you. Isn't it too bad we can't be together tomorrow! But such is life, and I have no doubt but that we will all have holidays together sometime again.

Later home, supper over, cooked and served by Dad—kids touchy and hard to handle for excitement—Drew has been begging to go to bed—and other nights it's a fight to get him to bed before 10. Tonite he wants to turn in at 8. Uncle Cash* was here with Vallard—says I might get a job as a federal mineral appraiser, or else in the Gen. Land Office. Am going over to Carson in a day or two to get out some letters on it.

Merry Xmas, Happy New Year and much love from

    DAD

Enclosed with the above two letters was an undated one from Drew.

Dear Dale

I am just saying Merrie Xmas to you. We have our tree up and it is about nine feet and we have three strings of lights. I think thats a great many don't you! We have lots of ornaments too. We opened one package and I got two pencils. I looked at a Navy book over at Gills and it was shoing pictures of the goat laughing and the army mule crying. And it showed other things and I had a notion to put the book in the fire or throw it outside. I did not have much to say.

Much love from your brother

    DREW

I received a warm letter from Sue written on Christmas Day, accepting my invitation to visit. Said she and her friend would be up Saturday afternoon the twenty-seventh and stay at the Thayer. There was no word from Ruth.

On Christmas Day I was on duty and typed a long letter home.

---

*Uncle Cash Smith was Dad's younger brother. Vallard was the middle one of three boy cousins. Weldon, the eldest, became an Army Air Force flyer, fought with distinction in the South Pacific where he was badly wounded, and later retired as a full colonel. Vallard had a distinguished career in the Army Signal Corps and also retired as a colonel. The youngest, Lowell, went to West Point, became an Air Force fighter pilot and saw much action in Europe during World War II. He retired as a colonel with the Silver Star, the Distinguished Flying Cross, and eighteen Air Medals.

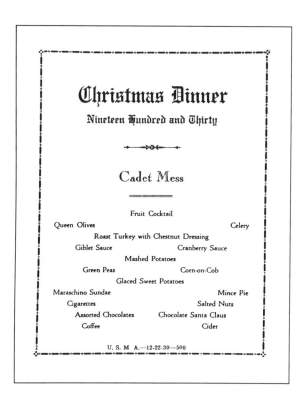

Christmas Dinner

Nineteen Hundred and Thirty

⊷⊷≫✠≪⊷

Cadet Mess

Fruit Cocktail

Queen Olives   Celery

Roast Turkey with Chestnut Dressing

Giblet Sauce   Cranberry Sauce

Mashed Potatoes

Green Peas   Corn-on-Cob

Glaced Sweet Potatoes

Maraschino Sundae   Mince Pie

Cigarettes   Salted Nuts

Assorted Chocolates   Chocolate Santa Claus

Coffee   Cider

U. S. M A.—12-22-30—500

Dear Mother and Dad:

Merry Christmas to you all! I'm CCQ today, which means Cadet in Charge of Quarters. It sounds big but it's a terrible soiree, especially on Xmas day. I went on at noon and won't go off till noon tomorrow. I have to make a flock of inspections and stay in the orderly room [answering the telephone and locating cadets for their visitors]. Outside of this and the fact that I will miss the tea dance and the hop tonite, I don't mind it.

We've been having a whale of a time lately. Tuesday most of the upperclassmen left—enough stayed to make up the Guard detail and be the company officers. These are those who have special punishments, too many demos, or are in debt.

[At reveille that morning we were astonished to hear the carillon in the Cadet Chapel that dominated the hill behind Central Barracks peal out the notes of "How Dry I Am" and a few other tunes even less respectable. An upperclassman had found his way to the carillon keyboard and was advertising to the world his exuberance at going on the long-awaited Christmas leave. Unfortunately he was caught and suffered a slug, but the legend of his escapade still lives.]

Tuesday aft. all of us in the plebe class went to the Supe's reception. It was very nice and I was fortunate in meeting a 3.0 fem. She is the daughter of Colonel Scott, a medical officer. I attended my first West Point hop in the evening, and dragged blind—very blind—through the aid of Mrs. Rogers [the cadet hostess]. The fem was about a 2.0 for me, but others thought she was the nerts; so I managed to get plenty of hops for her and enjoyed myself cutting in on the few fems I knew. I had about a 2.0 time too. My hop shoes were tight and there was no possibility of necking a girl anywhere. The balcony—the famous balcony was wind swept and covered with snow.

[Even so some braved the cold and a cadet was skinned for "kissing a young lady on the balcony at Cullum Hall." His B-ache to the tac read:

1. The report is believed to be incorrectly stated.
2. The young lady kissed me and I was powerless to resist her.
3. No offense was intended.

[I don't recall whether he was awarded demerits for this but under the Draconian policies of the Academy he probably was skinned again for being "facetious."]

The next morning we went wild with our freedom. It was a wonderful sensation to saunter around the halls and sing and yell as much as we cared to. John and I went over to the gym to try to get some skiis, but they had all been taken. Next we tried for some skates, and they were all gone too. I was about ready to go home and pile into bed when an amazing idea sprang into my head. I had read in the "Blue Book" about the hills where coasting was allowed. We looked up Pop, the barracks policeman, and obtained a bobsled. A gang of us dragged it up to the stadium, and started down the hill towards the Thayer Hotel. Wow, but it did travel! I just managed to get it around all the curves but one—the last one. Here it got away from me and we went over a curb and into a stone wall. It broke in several places but we mended it with rope and went down a few more times. We never did get to the bottom of the hill, however.

I slept throughout that afternoon, and in the evening we were soireed to go to Chapel. This shot one evening for us.

Last night Santa came around to every plebe and left him a box of candy and two oranges. Dear old Santa. I heard him curse when he stumbled over my shoes, and John said, "Thank you, Mr. Claus, Sir." Because we forgot to hang up our socks we will probably soon read: "Socks not hung on mantel in violation of general orders, 25th inst."

This morning I borrowed a pair of skates and a gang of us went up to the rink. It is a wonderfully modern place to skate. They even have music. I did pretty well, and with a little practice it won't be long till I won't be noticed. Many of the southern men could hardly stand on their pins.

The dinner we had was a huge success. Everything and all we wanted of it. I'll send you the menu.

The boodle and presents you sent me were very nice. We made short work of the cakes—the first *home* cooking for me in a long time. I only wish I could have got a package off to you. When I get my next boodle book this will be attended to. I sent home a sweat shirt that Jean, Drew or Dad might use. I hope this letter beats it there so you won't be disappointed.

Poor Shepardson is still here. He didn't make his original deposit and so is still in debt. I'm only $53 in debt now, so it looks like I'll be all right for next year if I don't buy anything.

Sue is coming up in a few days. Ruth and her Mother both said they would be up but I haven't heard a word from them, even though I wrote and asked them up for today and tomorrow. It's well that they didn't come today, but I'm griped in several new places that they haven't wired, phoned or at least written a letter. Can it be that I'm aflicted [*sic*] with the curse of halitosis?

[I wrote Ruth on the twenty-first, inviting her up for the New Year's Eve hop, and she responded with an apology written on December 31. She said she had a date for New Year's Eve and besides her mother had been ill.]

I've received many nice cards and Mrs. Seaborn in New Rochelle has been exceptionally nice to me. She has sent two boxes of boodle and a dollar bill (which I immediately lost in a game of 21 in an attempt to make a million). Thor and Mary gave me a year's subscription to the New Yorker. It's a very popular magazine and full of all New York gossip and information. It will come in handy for I have two more trips there soon. One on the 16th of next month.

I hope you all had a happy Christmas. Thanks to Jean and Drew for their presents and to you and Dad,

Lots of love,

[It was unsigned.]

CHAPTER **10** THE GLOOM PERIOD

Despite my disappointment with Ruth's defection, the euphoria of the Christmas deadbeat still lingered and I was unprepared for the widespread depression that would soon grip the Corps when the foundlings left and the long dreary months of winter seemed to drag by endlessly. After the Christmas holidays there wasn't much to look forward to. June Week and Recognition seemed so far in the future as to be little more than dreams. Again and again I thought, "What am I doing here?" Was my goal so all-fired important that I had to put up with this deadly routine and demeaning existence day after day, week after week, month after month? The upperclassmen seemed particularly grouchy and took it out on us plebes.

I think Dad anticipated my emotional letdown from his own college experience, which, with his numerous jobs, had kept him on a rigorous routine even more demanding than mine. (He worked his way through the University of Nevada running a dairy, which meant that he started his day at 4:00 a.m. He also played football and edited the school newspaper.) This is indicated in his letter of December 28.

Dear Dale—

For an hour I have been reading the "Howitzer" [the West Point yearbook], which gives a good cross section of Cadet life. I learn that Yearling year is the hardest in academics and sends a good many down the hill to the station, and that 2nd class is easiest, yet proves hard for some who take it too easy and get behind at the last. Yet none of it can be too hard for the boy with two college years behind him if he does an ordinary amount of work. No doubt you enjoyed the holidays, the Christmas trees in the mess hall and at Cullum, and the bright hops at the Thayer, the long sleeps, reads, and relaxation. Vacation over, you will take up work again with new zest, the months will drift by, and before long the green leaves will come again. Summer—Yea Recognition!

Much love from us all,
DAD

An undated letter from Drew came with the above.

Dear Dale;
I want to thank you for the penent. Dad and I thought it was going to have army on it. But I am glad it had West Point on it. We got your picture and this is the way it looked——O——the line is other boys and the highest is you. The one that shows all the boys exercising. There is a little hill at a boys house near by and it is covered with snow tramped down. Every day after school I get out our big sled and it is lots of fun to go down it. I went to a free basketball game today at the high school. The girls against the boys. The boys beat 14 to 3.

Much love,
YOUR BROTHER DREW

I wrote home on December 29.

Dear Folks—
Today I got three more boxes from you. I thought my Christmas was about over but this was a big surprise. We all like the records, and my calling cards are the nerts. Merci beaucoup.

I managed to get a box off to you—went down to the Thayer and did a little shopping. "Dinty" Moore, the cute girl who works in the gift shop is a good friend and I spend time with her B.S.ing and playing with the silly toys.

Sue came up with a friend last Saturday and stayed till Sunday. We went to a Tea Hop at the Thayer in the aft. and to another hop at Cullum in the evening. Also saw a show—Follow Through.

Spent most of Sunday at the Thayer with her.

[I took the greatest risk of my career that rainy Sunday afternoon with Sue. We were talking intimately in a secluded corner of the Thayer balcony when she invited me to her room. For a cadet to be caught above the balcony of the Thayer was a most serious offense, probably resulting in dismissal. But this was an invitation I couldn't refuse. Sue left first to

Hop card kept "on the cuff" by cadet.

open the room. Fortunately there was no one else on the balcony and I ducked into a stairwell, sprinted up the two flights of stairs, peeked down the hall, found it empty and ran to her room. I was mortally frightened that someone had seen me and the dangerous prospect of getting back unseen haunted me. There were no preliminaries. We both knew what we were there for and our union was brief and rather unsatisfactory. Afterwards I didn't tarry but escaped to the safe balcony as soon as possible. Understandably this performance didn't endear me to Sue. After we said goodby I never saw her again. Some months later I received an invitation to her wedding.

[I must confess here that Sue Williams wasn't her name, and to set any minds at rest that might be disturbed by the consequences of this escapade, she did not marry in desperation.]

We are certainly enjoying our freedom. This morning we played a game of polo in the sinks—they run under the divisions and comprise the locker rooms, latrines, etc. We wore P.J.s and polo helmets.

An order came out on the D.B. [daily bulletin] that we would coast no more except on a toboggan slide which is over a mile away. And having no skates, I spent most of today reading and deadbeating.

The boys are having a hard time with the turnout writs. Corley hasn't passed one yet and he studies constantly. Funny custom: they wear white gloves when they march off after breakfast to take their writs. I suppose someone did it in the dim past and now it is a tradition. There is lots of cheering and yelling of encouragement from the Corps when they march out of the sallyport. None of the turnouts B-ache. They take their ordeal with smiles. It's a good quality to be able to laugh in times of disaster, and everyone here seems to have it—perhaps it's a universal quality of youth, but at least it makes us proud of them. I'd like to see them all stay. There are close to 60 turned out from all classes—most will be found—some few will be turned back.

Sometimes I picture myself being found—walking home and into the house. Not disgraced, but with a feeling infinitely more uncomfortable. And many of the gang will have to do it. Albert Wilson,* down the hall, the son of a Major—what dreams his father had for him!—will be found, poor fellow.

There is a hop tonight at the Thayer and I'll stag it and look for a 3.0— the hopeless quest. Lots of femmes here—and beautiful gowns, but it's

---

*But Albert T. Wilson, Jr., wasn't found. He beat the turnout writs, stayed with the class, and graduated. When Japan surrendered, Al and his brother Jack, both of whom had been flying B-29s against Japan, went to General Curtis LeMay and asked if they could borrow a B-29 to look for their father. Their father, an infantry officer, had survived the Bataan Death March and was imprisoned somewhere in China. General LeMay readily agreed and had "AL-JACK" painted on the underside of the B-29 wings. After buzzing one prison camp after another, they observed a commotion in one with panel signals being laid out. Landing at a nearby airfield they found their father, put him aboard their B-29, and flew all the way home to Southern California.

very hard to get to know them. Never a chance to talk for long or be alone with one.

Old Cullum Hall is very picturesque. If the grounds were of a different design one could imagine himself in the early 19th century, so ancient does the hall appear.

I hope you all had a good holiday season. Did Drewdy get a football from Thor? Wish I could have sent him some toys.

Perhaps I can fly home next Xmas. If I could figure out some way of raising gold around here. A thought! I might write a story of this place—send it to Thor for correction, have the Supe O.K. it, and in the end, sell it.

Love,
DALE

I worked from time to time on a short short story for *Collier's* magazine but never submitted it. It never seemed quite right.

I wrote home again on January 1, 1931.

Dear Folks—

Happy New Year! Our vacation is over, but for me it has been successful and I'll feel ready to get back to work. There's still a lot to pipe. Five months to recognition, June week, yearling deadbeat and summer camp! Recognition! What a milestone. I hope the months pass as fast as the last five. Then there is boxing and track to pipe, too. I hope to do big things in boxing for I have worlds of self-confidence and feel as strong as a moose—many others can hit harder than I but they have a hard time getting by my guard. Thank the Fates for my height and long arms!

Funny thing, I ranked *second* in my section in gymnastics—there are about 25 in the section. The fellow who ranked me is Bunker, a very graceful gymnast, who has been at it for several years. He isn't so hot in the downstairs work, however, for I beat him in fencing, in wrestling, and in boxing. If I do as well this next semester I'll rank pretty high for in the downstairs work I have won in everything but one wrestling match.

In academics I boned a section in math and frog but lost one in English. This makes me 4th, 4th, and 5th respectively out of 12, 6, and 12. I'll have to do better this next semester. The grading is very strict—in frog, for instance, they take a tenth off for every mistake when we only

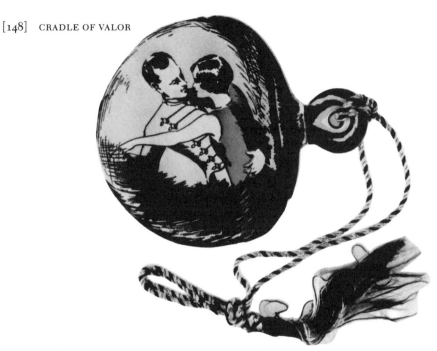

have 30 tenths and the possibility of 300 mistakes. No percentage basis at all, you see.

Ruth hasn't been up and I'm angry. I asked her especially to come for the New Year's Ball of last nite but she wired that she had a date. So I went to a show and slept the New Year in. I had stagged to enough hops and didn't feel like bumming more dances from my classmates.

Many Washington, D.C., girls were up. There is a new style of dancing which is the rage down there but seems very ugly to me. They press their breasts and cheeks against their partner's coat and stick their tails way up in the air. I can't see it at all and neither do any of the other Kaydets. The girls appear stooped and far from graceful.

We get much pleasure out of our Vic. During this vacation we have had access to hundreds of records and we play the best of them constantly. Nothing can make me feel more contented than a very good record.

I certainly did enjoy all the things you sent me. The sox are twice as good as those we buy here, the shaving brush is a pip, and I am now writing with Jean's lovely pen-pencil. I hope my box to you has arrived by now. I wish I could have gotten something better for Drew. The statue I sent is ver' rare. I've had it saved since the day I entered—is the only one in existence or something.

Well, I must get to writing my many thank you letters. This is my last day of freedom for a long time.

Lots of love,
DALE

This letter from Mother was written Friday evening, January 2.

Dearest Dale,

We all enjoyed your letter today telling of how you have been spending your vacation. I know you must be enjoying the freedom even tho you can't go tobogganing any more.

I do feel sorry for the boys who are out—oh, how sad we would feel if it were you—and all those mothers and fathers will feel the same.

That was a famous idea of yours—to write to earn money to come home on. Start right in writing on any old subject—work hard in your English—for we are all looking for you to do much of that and gain recognition for it. Of course, it is not the most practical idea to think of coming so far for just a few days—but wouldn't it be grand? We can dream of how wonderful it would be to have all of you home for Xmas.

Sort of sorry you tried to send us a box dear, we did not expect it of you. We realize everything you get at the Gift Shop means just so many checks against you for your future trips. As Dad says, we want a fine photo of you some day in your uniform. Am sure they are very expensive—and so you may not be able to get it soon. Explain to us about the rules against sending you money occasionally—such as you say Mrs. Seaborn did. For instance, just before your trip to NY if we sent you a bill you wouldn't have to ask for money for the trip. You need something for taxi fares, etc. Frank Gill [at Annapolis] told his folks that the eastern boys had never seen silver dollars—so when he went back in Sept. he took several extra dollars to sell to the eastern boys.

Very much love to you from us all—and success to you this coming semester—

MOTHER

A short letter from Dad also written on January 2 was in the same envelope. It covered pretty much the same material as did Mother's letter although his thoughts on the foundlings are interesting.

Dear Dale—

.   .   .   .

Poor boys on the turnout writs—how sorry we feel for them. Some of course did not have the stuff that makes soldiers, did not work, and are of course unfitted. Others, not very bright, or not having had enough preliminary academics, just can't cut it, although they work hard. I suppose Corley is one of the latter, and it is too bad for him. There is something very sad and tragic about being handed such a glorious break only to lose it because of insufficient mental equipment. We are not afraid that such a disaster will happen to you, for you have a good start now, and thoroughly realize the great benefit that will come with steadily sustained work.

Much love from
    DAD

My next letter home was dated January 3 but it might have been written on the fifth.

Dear Folks—

Well we are all back at work now. There isn't much to pipe anymore, and things seem so far away. This is what is known as the "Gloom Period." It will settle down hard when the Foundlings leave. None know until that day whether he failed.

I have some pretty good news. It might mean that I'll get made for summer camp. [Being "made" meant being promoted to a cadet rank on the "make list." New yearlings in summer camp could rise as high as acting corporal with two chevrons on their lower sleeves. It was a highly prized distinction.] I rank 17 in gym out of the whole class. Lawlor ranks 150 and Corley in the 200s, so you see 17 is pretty high ranking. I hope I can do as well this semester. This ranking amounts to a lot in yearling makes for they take into account leadership and military bearing. We graded each other in these qualities.

Saturday was a big day. I'd only been out for boxing one day, Friday, and was informed that I would fight Smoller, the other plebe heavyweight, on Saturday. For some bad reason I was very sick Friday night and Saturday morning, and would have backed out but I figured it would take more guts to do that than it would to fight him.

So I went over to the gym at 3 P.M. for the bout. Imagine my surprise when I learned that the fights were to be held upstairs! When we walked into the room it was packed with spectators—even the Supe was present. There had just been a basketball game with Princeton and everyone remained to see these try-out bouts of the boxing team.

My heart was beating hard and I was doubly excited when a second began to shove gloves on my hands—for mine was the first bout. There was nothing else to do but climb through the ropes, listen dully to the announcer, hear the referee's instructions, shake hands, go back to my corner, and jump out when the gong sounded.

My arms were so stiff from Friday practice that I felt certain I couldn't use them, but when I felt the old dukes waving around I forgot all about the stiffness—all about everything but the desire to dominate those two dukes of mine. It was a setup, the fight. Poor Smoller could have been on the mat in the first round had I been cold hearted, but he was a classmate and I hated to see him go down in front of so many spectators. Don't, however, think that I got by unhit. Far from it; my puss took a number of healthy smacks. About in the middle of the last round I was getting damn tired of it, and decided to put an end to the fight there and then. I took a left to the body in order to get the opening and a split second after his blow hit I had sent a right square to his jaw which dropped him to the mat. For a second I stood with a hand on my sore stomach and then turned to find a neutral corner. But the fight was over before I reached it—the referee called it off. Smoller* wasn't out. Just knocked down pretty hard.

Well, I must get at my Math now.

Lots of love,

DALE

I wrote again on January 7, 1931.

Dearest Mother and Dad—

Today is foundation day. Corley and about 38 others in our class are rushing around now turning in what they can and getting their clearance papers. We will miss Corley; I hope he finds something more suited for him. There will be a big time tonight for the foundlings in

---

*Likeable John F. Smoller played varsity football and track, winning major "As" in both sports. He was made the cadet captain of A company his firstclass year and graduated with a fine academic record. Serving largely with the Field Artillery, he held combat command jobs in World War II and retired as a major general with a Distinguished Service Medal, a Legion of Merit, a Bronze Star, and the Commendation Medal.

New York. They will try to drink away their bitterness and enjoy their freedom.

Because of the new entrance system 39 is a relatively small number to be found. Some few over 60 Plebes left last year.

The list of foundlings was read by the woof-woof at lunch, and they all got up and left the Mess Hall. Tonite they will be gone. Sort of sad getting found from this place. [John wrote that the empty bunk gave him a sinking feeling.]

Have you read about the revolution in Panama? Arosemena, the abducted president has a son here in our class. We call him Rosy.* All the trouble his father is in doesn't seem to bother him much. Sorry they overthrew the old man. We were going to visit the presidential palace on Furlo.

Boxing is plenty tuff. Yesterday I walked into a sock that set the bells ringing. I didn't even see it coming—didn't even see the cow-catcher, but I surely heard the wheels. [Trains used to have grilled cow-catchers out in front of the engines.] I would have gone down had there not been a wall nearby to lean against. My opponent was a varsity heavyweight who had a lethal left hook. I'll have to practice a lot before I can beat him.

Now I must go over to the Kaydet Store and get measured for my new white uniform. It won't be long now . . .

Lots of love to all of you,

DALE

Dad wrote an upbeat letter dated Wednesday, January 7.

Dear Daley boy—

I have spent the greater part of the day writing two letters, one to the Commissioner of the General Land Office in Washington asking for a job, and the other to Sen. Oddie asking him to help me get it. That

---

*Bey Mario Arosemena and I became good friends. We were both on the boxing squad and roommates on several trips. I saw him for the first time since graduation at our fifty-year reunion and met his charming wife, Chicha. He has been eminently successful, but it hasn't been easy. He started as a boiler fireman for the local power company at $75 per month. Then he won a Rockefeller Scholarship to Harvard and earned a master's in sanitary engineering. After Pearl Harbor he was appointed by the government of Panama to the Inter-American Defense Board in Washington, D.C. Following the war he went into private business but continued to serve on top-level government assignments.

makes 4 live lines out for jobs, so things begin to look better. I saw Sam Durkee, State Highway Engineer, the other day and he promised me a job as a resident engineer sometime in the Spring—said he would have it, that he was going to look out for his friends. So that made me feel better. However, I may get something better than that before Spring; here's hoping!

Your last letter made us all walk on air, dear boy. We have not recovered from all the cheerful good news in it yet. Every once in a while Jean will wiggle and say "Oh boy!" and when asked will merely explain, "Dale." Your box arrived yesterday and the cute little West Pointer stands beside your picture on the piano; the pennant is fastened across the top of one of the French doors. We are all glad it says "West Point" instead of "Army," and Jean is crazy about the little compact with the crest; she will be the envy of all her set.

But it is not gifts that we want from you. Nothing in the world you could have sent us, no matter how rare or valuable, could have made us half so happy as the knowledge of your achievements at the Academy. You have rounded the half-way pylon of the dreadful plebe year; you are among the leaders in the great race—on to higher honors—greater efforts—to Recognition, to Yearling year—I can hardly suppress a desire to yell, in the ancient Army style. "Yea, Dale!"

We greatly enjoy the photos you sent and already they have been scanned by many even under the magnifying glass—to see how your nose looks—and if you seem older, etc. I see a straighter, stronger, more determined Dale; a little older, a little less carefree, but with more purpose and more contentment. We can never have enough pictures.

The grading is indeed strict there and I can easily see that the man who has not had at least one year of good solid college and got away with it with credit would have a tough time. The percentage in Frog is so arranged that your recitations must be well nigh perfect. But then they are not teaching merely an average bunch and are certain to demand a lot.

Well, as usual, Dale old boy, my letter is full of moralizing and short on news. Tonight it snows—for two hours great flakes have been falling—we should have a foot in the morning. Drewdy is looking for his sled. After supper I go down to lodge to rehearse "John Brent," a soldier play of Colonial days, with Washington, Hamilton, Lee, Lafayette and other good Masons who made our country. I will be Col. Gridley, a prosecuting attorney at the court-martial of John Brent. We will probably visit several other Masonic bodies in Nevada and put on the play. It will be given here on Washington's Birthday. Imagine me, if you can, shaking an impassioned finger at the unhappy John Brent as I histrionically thunder, "*You* shot him, did you not?" We will get a lot of fun out of it.

Mother just came home in the twilight and softly falling snow.

With much love from

DAD

I answered this on Sunday the tenth.

Dear Folks—

I was on guard in the 8½ division and read your letter while walking my post. Very daring, but I wasn't inspected once.

I have a good time at meals now—a full table of plebes in the training area. I don't know what this place would be without athletics—a hell on wheels I imagine.

This is considered the Gloom Period but we plebes don't mind it too much—it's all the same for us. We never have had much to pipe but Recognition. We take a beating all the time anyway.

I don't know about the photos you want. I'm too much in debt. I thot of getting them made for Xmas but the cheapest is about 15 bucks. So we'll leave it till next Xmas—they will be good gifts.

You can send money any time but I don't want you to. Considering the condition you're in, I have plenty.

I haven't a Kodak but will try to borrow one and take some snaps for you.

Boxing is a big grind. We have to run to North Gate and back every nite now—road work. [And Billy Cavenaugh required us to run with our fists above our chins, punching the air. By the time we staggered home our arms were like lead.] We spar three rounds each nite also.

Spent most of today reading Red Book and boning red-comforter. [Napping on the narrow cot.] My grades were pretty good this week.

Lots of love,

DALE

Dad wrote another upbeat letter on the same day, January 10.

Dear Dale— We were glad to get your usual graphic letter, descriptive of the boxing tryouts, in which you undoubtedly demonstrated considerable prowess. It will furnish you excitement and plenty of athletic training, will also develop self confidence—self reliance. A sense of bodily ability makes other men instinctively respect you, even tho they know your prowess will never be used against them. It certainly is a great thing for a soldier and officer, who must demand absolute obedience of his men.

I have good news this time. You know I have had an application in as Curator of the Mackay Museum, and Assistant Engineer in the Nevada State Bureau of Mines. Yesterday I was assured by Director J. M. Fulton that he would recommend me for appointment as soon as the State appropriations of funds are made, which will be sometime toward the end of February. The pay will be $2400 a year to start—with a promise of more later sometime if I prove worth it and funds are available. My work will be in helping with the geology of a topographic map of Nevada—field work with the Bureau of Mines and in cooperation with the U.S. Geological Survey. I shall have to study again for a while and get up on geology, and am going to take up work at once under Prof. Jones.

I have seen each Assemblyman and State Senator and left each a typewritten copy of the two laws to be renewed, upon which my job depends, and all are strong for them.

It will turn out well for me, if I have the ability, and am not too old to still learn. Mother feels good at the prospect of breaking into the very select Faculty Woman's Club. I think she always felt she belonged there! The salary though small is almost as good as was the S.P. Co. job, and should enable us to save enough money to come back to see you when you graduate.

Much love from
    DAD

At last, after being out of work for over seven long months and in the midst of the Great Depression, Dad had all but landed a job. He never lost heart, never lost his spirit or his self confidence, and never let up in his drive to find work. Neither he nor Mother ever complained of being poor or asked for a handout from the government or anyone. They simply economized to the limit and survived, taking every opportunity for making a buck here or there. But now the long dry period was about to end. Dad didn't note in his letter that he had been working at the Mackay School of Mines as an unpaid volunteer for some time before he was offered this job by Mr. Fulton.

My answer was dated January 16, 1931.

Dear Mother and Dad—

I'm very happy to hear of Dad's big break. Will I soon have to call him prof?

Perhaps there is no place in the world so uninteresting and solidly the same at this period—the Gloom Period—than is West Point. But I must write you for I know you look forward to even an envelope.

[The Gloom Period was no joke. Although we plebes were living in a sort of purgatory anyway, the Gloom Period accentuated our misery. We sprinted to reveille in the dark, five minutes before assembly, and stood shivering in the bitter cold. At least we could get by with donning only trousers, shoes, overcoat and cap. It was still dark when we dressed and marched to breakfast after again standing in ranks five minutes early with a brace. The short days meant that it was pitch dark again when we marched to supper. And always the biting cold, sometimes with ice underfoot.

[But it was the seemingly endless and grinding regimentation that dragged down our spirits like a heavy weight. Thoughts often jumbled through my head, "Must I march to meals in the dark forever with up-perclassman yapping at my heels? When will it ever end?"

[Yes, it was gloomy, all right, and the authorities knew it. Rumors abounded of cadets resigning and even of suicide, although I never knew of this drastic escape actually happening. The Supe had the band play in the mess hall during supper. It helped some. At least there were no parades, and Saturdays were spent in the gym cheering Army teams competing in basketball, boxing, wrestling, gymnastics, and swimming. It was the bright spot of the week.

[One doesn't hear of the Gloom Period today. The more relaxed regimen of the Corps, the more freedom to leave the reservation, the presence of women, and the existence of ninety-two extracurricular clubs do much to enhance morale.]

I seem to be holding my own in the 4th section of Math even tho it is full of hivy [smart] men. I should be going up in English soon, but in French I'll probably stay where I am—it's about the best I can do—I can learn pretty well, but I think very slowly, and they speed up French—time limits and all—more than anything else.

My fem Ruth is in love—but not with me. Nice of her to tell me at least. No chance to keep a gal in a place like this. One remarkable example is of a cadet who got slugged for kissing his O.A.O. [One And

Only best girl] in a public place. He received an invitation to her wedding with a civy [civilian] before he had finished walking off his slug!

However it worries me little. [The hell it didn't!] I can get a date with a fem who will spend all the money and show me a wonderful time—some wealthy debutante. [Sour grapes.] Mr. Doyle promised me this, all I have to find is his address. [I never found it!] He was the St. Regis host, if you remember. I wouldn't have enough money to take Ruth out anyhow.

I hope everything is going well at home.

Lots of love,

DALE

Obviously the boredom of the Gloom Period combined with Ruth's change of heart had consumed me with self-pity, and I failed to appreciate fully the enormity of Dad's wonderful success.

The "dear John" letter from Ruth is not in my file, but one she wrote on January 16 was conciliatory. This is it:

Dear Dale:

I didn't try to be mean in my last letter, really I didn't, I was just being frank. Of course I realize now that I might have used more tact.

Now that that question is settled, I really would enjoy seeing you on Saturday. Get in touch with me Saturday when you get to N.Y.C. and let me know if you can possibly come out here for supper. In your answer to this letter let me know your plans, if any, and if you have none we'll find something to do when you get out here.

[The rest of her letter dealt with a trip to a boat show and the Chrysler building—nothing at all personal, which was not unusual for her rather boring letters. I graded it 2.0—barely passing. And she ended it "Votre ami toujours, Ruth." Big deal.]

The choir trip was for January 30. I'm sure I informed Ruth of this change.

Sister Jean wrote on January 17.

Dear Dale,

I am so sorry I haven't written you sooner but the last couple of weeks were surely tough. . . .

I want to thank you so much for that lovely, lovely, lovely compact. It's just a *dream*! The crest is so pretty and the color just matches my dress (good one) and it is loose powder and I can have it always. Everybody just loves it.

Mama will send you the good news from Thor and Mary.

Peggy Gill, Aldene Branch (Emory Branch's sister), Norma Jensen and I have a club called the "D4" (dirty four). We've been having lots of silly fun and our sign is the skull and bones. We are going to have a meeting tonight.

Some of those jokes in the Pointer are swell. We have changed some of them around and used them in the "Prospector."

Love from your sister,

JEAN

And Mother wrote a loving letter the next evening, Sunday, January 18.

Dearest Dale,

A few minutes ago it occurred to me to pop some corn. We are still munching. Wish you were here for a handout. Drew had gone to bed before I thought of it but I could not resist calling him down to have some.

I am mailing a couple of Sagebrushes [the University of Nevada newspaper] to you—also a copy of Time which Thor sent to Dad for the year.

Drew has a new chum. Russell Trathen, our new Sheriff of Washoe County lives just above Boardman's and they have taken a nephew to live with them and Drew finds it very attractive to play with him and ride down to the Sheriff's office and play with the handcuffs, etc. Today they started off early to ride around on their bikes, only coming home long enough to read the Sunday funnies. They rode out Purdy Highway to a turkey shoot—Russell is quite a shot—and while there he gave them some money for a treat. So they came down to the College Inn and bought some candy and then went to a show—all without our knowing where Drew was. Time came for Sunday dinner about 3 and Drew could not be found. When we finally located him at the Trathen's I gave them both a talking to. [Mother could do it, too!] Now Drew has to stay home for the evening—an awful punishment.

You will be interested in Thor's letter—a memorable one, he calls it. [The letter is not in my file.] And so it is. It will be a turning point in their lives, a readjustment in thoughts and living. They will be very happy I'm sure. So when you step off at San Pedro on your furlo you may be greeted by three instead of two. [As you have guessed, Mary was pregnant.]

If we could raise the steam for a new car we would like to drive back and take in June Week next year and then you drive us home. Wouldn't that be some fine plan. [Mothers can dream, too.]

It's quite late and everyone has gone to bed but me. So I guess I will say good night to the best plebe cadet at West Point. Dad had a nice letter from Sen. Oddie saying he had written a very strong letter to the man to whom Dad applied for a position in the Gen Land Office, same as Uncle Cash. Sen. Oddie was glad to hear of you but said he had heard from others that you were making good. Do you see much of the boy who was a friend of theirs? [She was referring to Tom Foote. He was not in A company and there was little opportunity for a plebe to go visiting.]

Mrs. Seaborn [in Reno] tells me that Paul [her brother-in-law in New Rochelle] wrote his mother in Boston all about you and she wrote her that you must be a fine young man from what Paul had said. You have a lot of contacts to keep up, haven't you, with all your other work. Hope you are fine and fit and not getting punched over the cliff in boxing.

Much love dear and good-night.

MOTHER

CHAPTER 11 CHOIR TRIP

Dad was in one of his dark moods when he wrote the following letter. His life was a series of optimistic highs and pessimistic depressions, but Mother understood him and knew how to handle his emotional swings. I've been told that I inherited Dad's cyclical moods, although I consider myself very even-tempered. But it did appear that Dad was getting the shaft from the Mackay School of Mines and he certainly had just cause to be depressed over it.

As for me, the Gloom Period was ending. The choir trip and boxing lifted my spirits and I continued to improve in academics.

On Monday evening, January 19, Dad wrote:

Dear Dale—

Mrs. Sibley was in today, bringing news of West Point and Alden. She had a program of the opening of the new indoor skating rink to show us. Yes, the plebes do take a beating all the time, and often are sick at heart, and hunger for the love and comfort of home. The men of the Army must first learn to obey, and take what they get without complaint, before they, too, are fitted for command. But what a wonderful place it is! Ideals of duty, honor, patriotism; cherished, taught and lived. One big white spot where greed and future wealth are not looked forward to as the goal of life. You come out only a 2nd Lieutenant, but with a fire in your heart, a ring on your finger, credentials of a training before which the greatest men bow with admiration.

Sometimes when things look dark to me, the thought comes that I have a son at West Point. My head comes up then, and my eyes shine. My honor is greater than that which comes to many. I have had a wonderfully good piece of luck in my checkered existence. I have a son . . .

I am not hopped up over my prospective job at the Mackay School—
They are an odd sort of school-teacherish bunch headed by Dean Fulton, a solemn old owl, whom I knew as a very wild boy many years ago.
And I am to start at $2000 and work up! I'm too old to work up at any-
thing now—time's too short for me. [This reduction in his promised salary no doubt soured Dad.]

.   .   .   .

Jean today acquired a new white satin gown, to wear to Rainbow—
she is growing up. Drew spent all day yesterday with young Robert
Trathen, didn't come home to dinner—he was in bad here, but not pun-
ished, little rascal. He is all hopped up over guns, cops and bandits now.
Mother has gone to Eastern Star, I may go later myself.
Much love from
      DAD

Mother wrote the following Thursday. The letter is undated but it was
probably the twenty-second.

Dearest Dale—
Just recd. your nice letter enclosing a new West Point sticker. Thanks
a lot—we all like it—but wish we had a new car to put it on. Just recd.
Thor's (enclosed) telling of his new car. I said "Thor should have this
sticker" and Dad bristled up and said, "No, he can get his own sticker!"
Glad you like the photo of me. Thor and Mary like it too—so I guess
the rest of the family will have to agree.
I sent you another box of boodle—a cake Jean made—learned it at
school. Am afraid it will be pretty dry by the time it reaches you. Let
me know.
Surprised about the all-American football men being found! Guess
wherever they came from the college was for football instead of studies—as so many are. I feel so thankful every day that you are there
where there is an inspiration to study—for I do not know what you
would have accomplished here.

.   .   .   .

When is 100th night and what celebration do they have and are the
plebes in on it? [Besides being 100 days before graduation and the traditional end of the Gloom Period, it was the night when the cadets put
on an original stage show and had a chance to make fun of their superiors
and the system.] 3½ months till June is a short time. Just 2 years ago this
week when you took your first exams [for Annapolis] that was a "gloom

period" for all of us—only we never gave up hope. [An administrative mix-up forced me to take the exam three months earlier than I had expected and I wasn't prepared. My flunking it was a low blow to the whole family. Dad was incensed by this Navy goof and wrote everyone he knew in Washington. I'll have to say this for the Navy, they recognized their error and I was permitted to take another exam later in the spring. But the Navy had the last word, and now required me to take a three-day exam in six subjects as opposed to the one-day substantiating exam in only English and math that I had failed. I dropped out of college and the whole family cooperated while I immersed myself in high school textbooks for the next three months. It surprised me when we received word from Bill Parsons at Annapolis that I had passed. Next year the Army accepted this Navy exam for my appointment to West Point.]

Dad goes to the University as regularly as tho he were on the pay roll. Much love to you dear. We are with you all the time.

MOTHER

I wrote home January 22.

Dearest Mother and Dad—

I received your letters last nite with Thor's enclosed. Very good news—plenty good news; and I won't see the little rascal till he's a year old.

We enjoy our weekends around here now. Saturdays are especially interesting. All afternoon there are sports of competition with other schools. Swimming, fencing, wrestling, boxing, gymnastics, (Alden has developed into a remarkable gymnast) and basketball. They call it the 3-ring circus but it's more than that. We never know what to watch.

I've been here in the hospital for a couple of days with the flu but I'm breaking out today. We've had a lot of fun in this ward—everyone has been raising old fashioned hell. You wouldn't think a sole [sic] was sick, but that's the way with men in this man's army—as long as they can breathe they wise-crack.

A negro orderly went to sleep in a chair yesterday morning and one of the yearlings turned the clock up 3 hours. In about 5 minutes the orderly woke up, looked at the clock, and nearly went nuts.

We aren't far from a room where they're expecting an army-child any minute and, of course, there are countless grinds about that. Last nite we pretended to post a guard so as to get immediate news of all developments.

We haze the poor nurses too. The night nurse is greeted by a thousand coughs whenever she enters the ward.

Some of these men have been here for weeks. I'm getting out right away before something happens to me.

A lot of boxing men are here. Woodward,* the A squad heavyweight is in this ward with the flu and others are downstairs. Quite a flu epidemic going around.

I enjoyed Jean's letter and will answer it soon. Hope things break for you Dad and everything goes well.

Lots of love,
DALE

I wrote another letter home on January 24.

Dear Folks—

Well, it's another week finished. We are all pushing by the days and piping spring. Too, it's just another week before the choir trip. I haven't any definite plans for that yet.

Today I got skinned at S.I. [Saturday Inspection]. My first skin at S.I. since beast barracks. My overcoat was dirty. I'll B-ache it tho because it is the only one I own and I can't get it cleaned for we wear them all the time. I've got too many quils [demerits] for this month already. (This isn't a bit important; just something to put down on paper.)

I'm pretty much out of condition and will have to work hard to get back into shape for our match next month. It means my numerals if I get to fight. You never can tell, those prep schools might not even have a heavyweight.

.   .   .   .

I'm going to have to study some frog now because I must bone a section or two in it if I ever expect to be made [promoted to acting corporal in the summer].

I'm glad Dad has such fine prospects. Then maybe you could come back for graduation.

---

*William R. Woodward served in the southwest Pacific during World War II as G-3 of the Eighty-first Division and was awarded a Legion of Merit. After a distinguished career he retired as a brigadier general.

We have a new record called "Love for Sale" which is very hot and has a beautiful chorus—the Waring sisters. This piece is the rage around here now. It comes from "The New Yorkers."

I'm sure powerfully homesick but I suppose I'd better come off it for I won't be getting home for a long time yet. It wouldn't bother me much if I could just see one or two of you and my old friends.

Lots of love,
DALE

Dad wrote on Sunday, January 25.

Dear Dale—

I supposed you felt a little low over the news Ruth wrote you, but such things often happen. It was decent of her to write you about it, though, and the sporting spirit of the West Pointer no doubt dictated your gallant reply.

. . . .

Young Desmond Jeffers, the freckled boy, is out in the kitchen where he has been for an hour or so watching Jean's every move. Well, Jean *is* turning into a mighty good looking young lady and is even better than she looks. She is becoming active in Rainbow, and was asked to be their organist, but declined and went into the choir instead.

Drewdy just arrived; had made a trip up to the U. to find me, but failed because the doors to the building were locked and I was on the second floor.

Much love, dear Dale, from all of us. We will not often be so busy that letters will lag—and some fine day we will all come to see you, and some other day you will come to see us—and what a reunion that will be!
DAD

Dad wrote again on Monday the twenty-sixth.

Dear Dale—

Your letter from the hospital came today, and we are all so sorry to hear that you are sick with flu. And we don't know whether to believe you when you say you are getting out—you may be like the others there and not get out so soon. Still, your letter is so cheerful we have hopes that you are getting out.

As for the University appointment I have heard nothing more about it, but as Dean Fulton has promised it, I suppose it is reasonably sure, when the state legislature makes the appropriations. However, I am not sure I can fill the bill on topographic surveys and hope I can work it out so my work will have to do with geologic reconnaissance and mapping. I'll not worry about it. . . .

Mother overdid and was indisposed today but is better tonight and is going out with Jean to Rainbow initiation. The girls have a little dance afterward. Desmond is to take Jean. And Jean just came down stairs to show me her new white satin dress. It's quite beautiful, and so is Jean & all grown up, a finger wave, high heels. We've lost our little girl and found a lovely young woman. And she is wearing Mother's long string of crystal that Thor gave her. She is very happy.

Lovingly,

DAD

I wrote home on January 29.

Dear Mother and Dad—

Well, seeing I made a 3.0 in Math today I can take time out to write this note. It will be the last one till after the big trip because I'll be very busy.

We leave at 12:05 Saturday and altho we don't go to SI we have to exhibit our brass and gun in the morning (leave them on the bed). We're free as soon as we hit York, and from then till 3:30 p.m. on Sunday. We leave for home at 6:30. The service is at the St. Thomas Church on 5th Ave and 53rd St.

I'm going to dinner at Ruth's after all, and will bring her into York for the evening if I can afford it. I'll do my best to win back the "lost love."

Boxing is coming right along. I didn't lose much of my condition in the hospital and hardly any weight. My cold is about gone too.

It's been warm here for the last few days but it turned cold again today and snowed. We had been going to meals in Dress Grey. The Hudson is about all frozen over.

It won't be long till spring, recognition, and Yearling deadbeat. We all live for that.

Lots of love,

DALE

Thor wrote a letter on *Los Angeles Examiner* stationery dated Saturday, January 31.

Dearest Mother, Dad, Dale, and the kids:

I apologize for not writing, but I have a good excuse. I don't know whether Mary told you the details but what seemed to be bum luck for me turned out to be a real promotion. They have divorced the two Promotion departments again, and have put me down here as Classified Promotion Manager. Thayer has made $70 down here and the fellow before him $75, and so in a few months time I ought to be making at least $55 or $60. [He was writing about a weekly salary.] So much for outlook. Another thing is that I'm now a big executive (noise of clearing throat importantly) for I have a department of 3 people. An artist and a copy writer besides myself.

Mary is going to quit work on March 15th. She told Mr. Waite in confidence.

.   .   .   .

Will ring off now and write more promptly from now on. Thanx for the nice letters.

Love

THOR

A perceptive note from Dad was on the back of Thor's letter:

Dear Dale:

Will write you a personal letter soon. Don't be low, old chap. It seems to me that West Point is run on schedule even to temperament. It's Gloom Period, therefore you must be Gloomy! Bunk!

And also a typed note from Mary:

Hello Uncle Dale: I am stealing a few jumps on Thor who has just gone upstairs to submit some copy for approval. I wait his arrival so that we can journey homeward together.

Tickled you approve. Of course we'll send him to West Point to be an officer like his Uncle Dale. Do you think we could keep him away? [Thor and Mary had three girls!]

Well, don't forget we like those letters often. Much love from

MAMA [MARY]

I wrote home on February 1 with a report on the Choir trip to New York City.

Dearest Mother and Dad—

Well it is all over and wow, what a success! After getting my room, I went with Wollaston to see Sweet and Low with Fanny Brice and a lot of other nuts in it. It was a review, and about the wildest, most risque [sic] thing I have ever heard of. Wow, what's been going on in the world since I left it?

I left early in order to get to New Rochelle for dinner but got tied up in the theater crowds and didn't arrive till about 7:00 p.m. I spent till about 2:00 a.m. with Ruth and certainly did enjoy myself. She is sweeter than ever and I'm going to win her back if it takes 4 years.

When I got back to the Astor I found many parties in session and therefore didn't get to bed till 6 a.m.—reveille time. The bed was so soft I almost hated to go to sleep.

About 11 a.m. a second-lootenant [sic], friend who had been with us, came down and woke us up. We spent the rest of the morning in song and B.S., having breakfast at noon.

[There were some risqué barracks room ballads that we enjoyed singing with great harmony. Notable was "O'Reilly's Daughter," which became popular in the Army Air Forces during the Second World War and was sung with gusto at every drunken party. At our fiftieth reunion I asked a cadet if it were still sung and he'd never heard of it. *Sic transit gloria mundi.*]

For the rest of the time, till 3:30, I walked around N.Y. and saw the sights. This new Empire State Building makes Chrysler Tower look like a church spire!

The service and a large dinner at the Astor ended the weekend. We arrived home about 8:30 p.m. and sang "Alma Mater" and "The Corps" in the Area. This is a pretty old tradition. Everyone threw up their windows to listen and clapped and yelled when it was over. The O.C. [Officer in Charge of cadets, who rotated daily along with the cadet O.D. or Officer of the Day] came out on the poopdeck with the Supe and stood at attention, uncovered.

Lots of love to you all from a happy Kaydet.

DALE

P.S. I boned another section in Math. Now in the 3rd. John Lawlor, who was in the 3rd came down to the 4th and now I boob him royally. D.S.

John wrote home: "We had a good laugh over Dale. He was skinned for studying in the mess hall. He says a guy can't study in peace around here."

Dad wrote on Tuesday, February 3, 1931, using his business stationery with heading: ALFRED MERRITT SMITH, MINING ENGINEER, 229 MAPLE STREET, RENO, NEVADA.

Dear Dale—

When this reaches you your N.Y. trip with the choir will be over, and routine will again prevail at W.P. I hope you had a good time, and that it was a pleasant break in the rigid discipline of the Corps.

Yesterday I went up to the apartments and put down some "battleship" linoleum in the hall. It took me all day to level up the floor, cut and cement it down, and I am sore in every joint. Can't do such things as well as I used to.

I went again today to the U. to work on the mining book—am getting into it a bit better now. I think my appointment is coming on all right— it seems that the appropriation will surely be made. I see more or less of the profs, of course. My report on the Colorado River area has gone about, and I am to address the Faculty Science Club on March 5th. Whoops!

.   .   .   .

Much love from us all,
     DAD

My next letter home was dated February 4.

Dear Mother and Dad—

Well, just 117 days till June. 100th night will soon be here, and that ends the Gloom Period. It's been warmer lately and spring is even now in the air.

The 3rd section in Math is full of hivy [bright] runts. I'm certainly out of place among them and haven't many hopes of staying there long. I don't yet see how I got up this high.

Perhaps I can tell you something of New York. We came down on the West Shore of the Hudson and detrained at Weehawken, N.J. Here we were freed. The ferry across the Hudson is an old affair—so is the station—everything wooden and ancient, it seems, but on close examination the buildings are found to be stressed with steel. The ferry, however, certainly makes knots even if it does appear to be falling apart—as do all means of transportation in York.

The ferry lands at the foot of 42nd St. This is in Upper Manhattan Island and is now becoming the business center of the city in place of Lower Manhattan. Upper Man. comprises the theatre district (almost all of 42nd St.), Times Square (where the Astor Hotel is), and the new towers such as the Chrysler and the Empire State.

Lower Man. contains Wall Street, the financial section, the used-to-be tallest buildings, such as the Singer and Woolworth, and a few new towers, one of which is the Bank of Manhattan.

From the ferry we could just see the skyline of Lower Man. but it was too foggy to see the Statue of Liberty.

Taxi fair [*sic*] in York is very reasonable. People travel everywhere in them and there are thousands of cabs. Many of them look like huge limousines with very snaky designs.

The people, however, who one sees on the streets are pitiful. There is truly a depression here, and it has put its mark on thousands. They are proud of New York, though, for not once was I "touched." And people all try to dress well even tho their clothes are shabby.

From Times Square York looks much like Market Street and one of those streets which cuts into it at an angle, save that in York there are no—or rather, very few—street cars.

(To be continued)

I have 10 minutes to get to bed.

Lots of love,

DALE

Dad's letter was written from Reno on February 4.

Dear Dale—

Yours of the 1st, on your return from NY received today, a happy letter, that left us happy in turn. We are so glad you had a good time. However, don't be too sure about winning Ruth back, keep your heart under your breast bone and remember about other fish in the sea. Most of all we were moved by our mental picture of the choir singing the age-old songs in the Area of Barracks upon your return. We would have given much to have seen and heard that.

Whoops we gave over your postscript: up another section in Math! Grand old kid, you. Writers refer to "the terrible math" of W. P. which weeds out the lazy and unfit. And now you are in the 3rd Section, notwithstanding all the athletic activities.

The Days—the days march by, swiftly. Only 4 months to Recognition; which we await with a considerable degree of our own eagerness.

It has rained and snowed here all day long. As usual I went to the U. and worked on the book data, they are getting used to seeing me around. I will be glad to get on the salary roll again, when that time comes.

Much love from

DAD

I wrote home on Saturday, February 14.

Dear Folks—

Bayonets have many uses—they are used in war to kill, and in peace as screw drivers—but their best use is in cutting delicious cake from home. I've never tasted that brand before—it was certainly tasty—merci beaucoup.

Today I slept. Had intended to go see the fights at least but slept through the whole afternoon. I needed the sleep badly because for the last week I haven't once let down and boxing was pretty strenuous. Tuesday, of course, was "bloody Tuesday" [bouts that would determine who would fight the following Saturday in the meet]. There was some real fighting, and Wednesday we plebes had our tryouts. I think I made out all right—we'll see in a few days. I hope very much that I get to fight next Saturday.

I stayed in the 3rd Math section. Expected to get policed [upset—a cavalry term for being unhorsed] because I made only a 10.8 last week. But made a 13.1 (only 2 in the section higher) this week so I stayed. Went 2 tenths pro in Frog (not good) but haven't seen my B.S. [English] grades.

Lawlor just came home. Army won the fights but lost the B.B. game. The boxing squad hasn't lost a meet yet. They fight Penn State next Sat. A very tuff meet.

Well, I'd better get ready for supper. Ice cream tonite.

Lots of love,

DALE

On February 13 Mother typed a community letter.

Dear Thor, Mary and Dale,

Guess it will be easier to write all three of you. I haven't written to Thor since receiving his nice long letter last week. I am glad you are finding your work so interesting and that it is keeping you so busy. True, I benefited from your leisure hours in that we had more letters from you. . . . I hope they are through with their shakeups and that things will go along smoothly from now on. . . .

I am too envious for words that you have a new little Ford. . . . I can't imagine tho that you will have the space for the special cargo you will be carrying along. . . .

Yesterday Mr. Russell took the Cub Pack that Drew belongs to on a hike up near Verdi. Cars took them to the old red bridge then met them at 3 to bring them home. They had a grand time—Drew too tired to eat his supper.

Dad is down at a rehearsal tonite. They present the play next Sat. . . . Dad has taken so much interest in it.

Everything is rather quiet in Reno. In driving around we notice nearly all the apartments have Vacancy signs hanging. So we are no worse off than other people who are wanting to rent apts. We now have two vacant.

We got the statement from the Headquarters at West Point giving Dale's rank as of Feby 1st. Out of a class of 290 members and 1 absent, Dale stands in

Math   80
French 211
Eng.   108

On Oct. 1st his ranking was Math 151, French 284, Eng. 63.

I hear Dad coming now—so will close. Much love to you all and good night.

MOTHER

A typed letter from Dad was written Wednesday, February 18, 1931.

Dear Sons Thor and Dale:

Last night I walked around the house; it was cheery and comfortable, but something seemed to be missing. Vaguely I wondered what it was. Suddenly the answer came: Thor and Dale were not here, and the thought was succeeded by a feeling of loss and loneliness. The mood was fleeting, however, and soon passed, as do all moods, as well as pains and joys, gently erased by the moving hand of Time. It had the effect of making me realize that I had not written to Thor for a long time, and the result is this letter, such as it is.

Day after day I walk up to the U and ensconce myself in a comfortable chair in the Mackay Research Room and review files of the Nevada Mining Press, making notes therefrom on a bunch of cards embracing Nevada's 330 mining districts. I rather enjoy the work, but after a few continuous hours of it the monotony monots. . . .

I may have to do some work in the field and it sure scares me; I am reading Nevada geology to beat the band, and hope to absorb enough to be able to drive the outfit cook-wagon next summer, which is about all I can qualify for. All I want is to be able to stick on the payroll. It is also planned to send students out to do field work and perhaps I may be detailed to superintend some of that. I am not going to worry about any of it though. Either I can, or cannot do it, and will let it go at that, but I will surely try as hard as I can.

Dale, you are rapidly approaching your 20th milestone. Plenty young to also be approaching Yearling year at West Point. You are to be congratulated on your splendid record thus far, and you will go a long way and be happy if you continue to put out in the fine spirit of the past year. You have found the secret of happiness. It is Work, coupled with a desire to be generous and cheerful. There must be a lot of it at old West Point. I have repeatedly read pp 46–47 in Bugle Notes, by Cadet Swofford, First Captain.* If this country is going to survive a lot of leaders with that sort of spirit are the ones who will save it.

Well, Mother is out on the front porch calling the long loud call for Drewdy. She used to send it out for Thor and Dale. As of yore, it means supper is ready and nothing must delay. Perhaps she will add a line to this before I close it up.

Lovingly,
DAD

---

*Ralph P. Swofford, Jr., wrote of the spirit of West Point and its opportunities. He graduated fifth in his class of 1930, served with the Allied Airborne Army in the European Theater in World War II, and was awarded two Legion of Merits and two Bronze Star Medals. After the war he was Chief of Staff at West Point and later commanded the Air Force Institute of Technology. At that time I was Director of Education at Air University and fortunately became acquainted with him—a truly great Air Force educator. He later commanded Air University and retired in 1965 as a lieutenant general.

Hello—my dear boys—and Mary—

Really nothing to add and if I had there is little time for it now because supper is over and Dad is getting into his coat and hat to go to the last rehearsal for their Masonic play. He has enjoyed it so much, that he says "What will I do when this is over?"

Much love from us all,

MOTHER

CHAPTER 12 PLEBE BOXING

One of the reasons I went out for boxing was because I had secret lingering doubts about my courage. I was puzzled that I hadn't done better in football and wondered if it was because I hadn't been aggressive enough for fear of being hurt. I knew for sure that at Reno High and again as a freshman at Nevada I had gone out for football and after a few days had quit because I couldn't take the pummeling and the resulting aches and pains. Oh, I rationalized that I had to work after school in order to have some spending money, but I couldn't fool myself about what the real reason was. And Dad saw through my excuses but made no comment at the time.

The success I had had in boxing as a part of the gym class led me to believe that I might make something of myself on the plebe squad, but I had no taste for the beatings I was sure to get when boxing with the upperclassmen on the varsity. Because of my height I was pretty sure of making the basketball squad and I had had some limited experience with the sport at Nevada. But I wanted to prove to myself that I had the guts to compete in a rough body-contact sport. Moreover, Dad's letters indicated that he believed boxing would bring me more respect than basketball. So boxing it was.

I wrote home on USMA stationery (a signal that the letter was important) on Wednesday, February 18.

Dearest Mother and Dad—

Things have been going along smoothly lately. I've been training like the very duce [*sic*]—thinking boxing all the time—and therefore don't get very griped at things. I'm in very good condition now—never have been in such good shape. However, I'm very nervous and can't do much studying. I've read a novel by Kipling—Captains Courageous. We've been having Trig for the last month and so I can afford it. I know most of that stuff backwards. Tomorrow, we start spherical trig and I'll have to bone that—never studied any of it.

We've had several boxing tryouts and I believe I'm on top for the heavyweight class. Now if this prep school will only bring up a heavyweight—

The varsity fights Penn State at Penn this Saturday, so our meet will be the main event in the gym. Truthfully, I'm scared to death, but I'm sure that once the bell rings I'll feel like murdering someone.

Yesterday, Bloody Tuesday, I fought Walsh, 207 lbs. and I think I won on points. I hit him with all I had but couldn't knock the big moose out. I'll have to bone up a better right arm.

By a stroke of good luck, we got the money back which we bet on the Notre Dame game. [The Commandant had found out about it.] So part of my five bucks is now invested in new records. I have: "Reaching for the Moon"—Ruth Etting—"Overnight", "Sweet and Hot", "You Said It", "Blue Pacific Moonlight" and "You Didn't Have to Tell Me".

All in all NYC can't compare with L.A. for entertainment. I haven't yet seen the equal of George Olson's in Hollywood. No band can surpass Earl Bennett's and no trio can equal the Biltmore trio. Altho New York is plenty wet, it closes up everywhere after 2 o'clock and there is nothing to do but go to bed—a terrible place for Kaydets who want to stay out all night.

Inclosed is a picture of my friend Colonel Hodges,* whose wife I danced with at the St. Regis. I tore it out of the Tribune.

Say hello to Jean and Bud. [I thought the nickname "Bud" very attractive and tried to hang it on Drew but no one else would call him that.] I'd surely like to see you all. I'm very glad to hear of all the things Dad is doing. Sounds like Thor in college [who was always busy with a string of extracurricular activities].

Lots of love,

DALE

Dad typed a letter on Tuesday, February 24.

---

*Campbell B. Hodges, class of 1903, was Commandant of Cadets at West Point from 1926 to 1929. I never saw him again after that football party at the St. Regis.

Dear Dale:

We got your letter today with the news about the fights and training and all the enclosures. Also the big book about the Army-Navy game, which mother has been polishing with her nose for the last hour—she didn't even read the Gazette tonight which bespeaks phenomenal absorption.

You did well to win on points with 207 lb. Walsh. As to your ability to "hit", that will come with more age and experience. I judge from what you have told me that you have pretty good sock when you get a chance to place it.

Pretty nice for you to get the Notre Dame money back. How come? Army lost that by a mighty slim margin, though.

I contend that no one's education is complete without having climbed up the Statue of Liberty. You might consider that next time you get to N.Y. Of course, places of entertainment were not quite so gay and numerous in those "Gay Nineties" when I visited there. You live in a much more wonderful age.

When I'm so old I have to walk with a cane and six-inch steps I'll let Major Dale O. Smith take me there sometime when his grand old Alma is having a football game with Navy. [I regret this never happened.]

Still you are a Westerner. It's in your blood and you will always love old Frisco and L.A. and Reno. We can't get away from it and we don't want to.

We both admire Col. Hodges. Such a fine, splendid face. The great string of medals across the broad breast. There's a man for you. How fine that he recognized you and you had the pleasure of dancing with his wife.

Well, we put on our big play, John Brent, and it went over big if we may judge from the comments. Very gorgeous colonial uniforms and much grease paint. It is rather significant that all the big men among the founders of the U.S. were Masons. Tomorrow night we put it on again for the wives and families.

I am still working at the U. on Lincoln County mineral resources book. The bills have been introduced at Carson, one has passed the Senate. I have never ceased to study since the prospect came up and find that I can still use my mind, though it's not as flexible as it used to be. I will be able to tell Henry G. Ferguson, of the USGS (a member of the American Society of Economic Geologists) that I agree with his hypothesis that the granitic batholith of late Jurassic or early Cretaceous of the Sierra Nevadas and that of the early Tertiary (Eocene) of the Rockies meet and perhaps overlap in central Nevada, etc. and all about the association of certain Miocene and Pliocene lava flows with certain types of ore deposits. But when it comes to fossil flora and fauna and microscopic work I will be sunk.

And now I've run out and will let Mother finish this. Love from Dad.

Mother added:

Dearest Dale,

It is 9:30—have enjoyed reading the Army-Navy program you sent, and all the little clippings and souvenirs. We will keep them in a box I have of other things. I would like to have a book to put them in—but feel sure you would rather fix it up when you come home summer of 1932. [Mother was wrong about that. All I could think of on yearling furlo was chasing girls.] Would like to have a book to put all photos you have sent for fear some of them may get lost—we show them so often. The Sibleys have all of Alden's pictures in a book.

Hope you had your boxing bout last Saturday but we are thinking the chances are slim for a prep school to send a heavyweight such as you.

So that's why you got into Section 3 in Math—because you had Trig here. Wonder if you will be able to stay there with Spherical Trig. I don't like to have you training so hard that you are nervous. Jean says she does not know of the records you speak of. Suppose they will come along later. Just now she likes Sweet Jenny Lee—You're Driving Me Crazy—Crying Myself to Sleep and the Kiss Waltz.

I keep busy hurrying through my work each day in order to get out and enjoy part of the day. This aft I agreed to be here at 3 waiting for Drew who was to come straight home and go to town with me for a new pair of shoes. We want to take him tomorrow night to see Dad's Masonic play and he must be all spiffed up. Well, I waited till 4, then started out to look for him and found him spinning tops over at Kenneth's—forgotten all about his date with me. So he and I spent the next hour downtown. He found 4 nickles on the floor at one of the stores and then he searched for a "Sallywalker" but didn't find one and bought carmels instead and still has 10 cents left.

Hugo Quilici came across the lobby of the bank to ask for you. Every day there is some one who asks—but we won't have any writeup in the home town paper and let it be sent to an upperclassman.

Well dear—it's bed time—and too late to mail this tonight. We all send you much love—and good luck.

MOTHER

My next letter home was marked Monday with no date. It was probably February 22, George Washington's Birthday.

Dearest Mother and Dad—

Today is a holiday. It's great to have nothing to do. We slept late this morning—reveille on Sundays and holidays is now at 7:40. At ten we had boxing practice and a run to North Gate. It is a beautiful spring day.

I didn't get to fight Saturday. It was a great disappointment because I really believed that I would. Jim Walsh fought instead and was defeated. Billy—the coach—thought that Jim was the best man. However, I'm sure that I can beat him. I've done it but the time Billy was watching us Walsh had the edge on me a little. I'm to fight next Saturday, but I'd rather have fought both of them.

Gee, I'm getting left in the cold all the way around. Sue has announced her engagement and is to be a June bride. A Princeton man who lives in Calif. I'll be getting my pin back any day now. My own fault, I suppose.

I've an idea. How would you like me to call you up in April? We take the Choir trip on the 26th. I couldn't do it from here for many reasons. Will you find out how much it would cost? And at what time it would be best to do it?

I did pretty well in academics this week. Got a 2.9 in an English writ and a 2.8 on one in Math.

I've spent quite a bit of time in the Libe lately. It's a wonderfully interesting place. Many old letters written in 1784 etc. Old prints and maps. Most everything about West Point. Looked at some old Howitzers. Except for the dress hat the uniform hasn't changed since 1893. The place looks little different. They have a letter here from Frederick the Great—a Washington by Stuart, etc. etc.

In gym now our work is changed a little. We have graduated from the foils and now are slashing each other with the saber. In other departments the work has advanced also.

Today they gave a 21 gun salute and pulled up the large Garrison flag at reveille. This is 20 by 36 feet and is very beautiful. There are 3 flags; the Storm Flag, the Post Flag, and this one flown on special days.

Yesterday was 100th night. The show won't be till next week, but this ends the Gloom Period. Only 98 days till June.

"——and then when you're a general you'll be mean and treat me like Napoleon did Josephine."

Cartoon from *The Pointer*.

For my birthday I would care for only some cit [civilian] underwear and P.J.s. Some black sox would help too. Anything that looks like summer awning is what I wish. It's the fad here to have the loudest shorts and P.J.s that can be found.

I'm glad to hear of Thor's new car and of his good luck at work. I'm sure things will break for you, too, very soon.

Lots of love,

DALE

Dad wrote again from Reno on Saturday, February 28.

Dear Thor, Dale, and Mary:

Today things opened up quite a bit and good breaks are in the offing. Dean Fulton advised me that the bill, which is for joint work with the USGS, had passed, and that the appropriations for the Bureau of Mines bill was also sure to pass, all had been agreed upon and the bill was with the appropriations committee. Therefore, some sort of place for me in the yet nebulous plans of operation is assured. But I do not know when it will begin.

Dean Fulton has also recommended me for a mine examination to be made of the Nevada Douglas Mining Company property 6 miles W. of Mina. The client is in New York, so I suppose it will take some time for correspondence to go and return in regard to it.

This morning I was agreeably surprised by being looked up by Prof. Hill, who asked me to repeat my talk on the Colorado River to the Lions Club next Thursday, if I would be so kind and had the time. He said he had heard it was very instructive, and he was sorry to have missed it at the last meeting of the Faculty Science Club. Needless to say I accepted with much pleasure.

.   .   .   .

I like boxing because it is entirely a man's sport and calls for everything there is in an athlete. I am glad Dale is doing well in it. It proves he has both skill and "guts", something very essential in any undertaking in this world.

Wish we could see you all. But separations have their compensations, for won't we all have a marvelous reunion some day! Thor and Mary and little Skeeziks, and Dale the soldier, to say nothing of Jean and Drewdy.

Much love from

DAD

I wrote home on February 27.

Dear Folks:

I've got two nice letters from you recently. The Choir picture was very interesting. Shame, shame, that you could not recognize your very own son! He is certainly in plain view. The arrow marks the spot. Those in white are the regular church Choir. In our Choir there are over 120 voices—only a few men are included in this picture.

Something I've never remembered to write you: This 1st classman Read* from Nevada is the prince of heels. He didn't recognize Sib his whole plebe year which is a pretty low thing to do being from the same

*John William Mackay Read commanded a Field Artillery battalion in China during World War II and was a liaison officer with the Chinese army. He retired as a lieutenant colonel in 1953 and returned to Reno. He died in 1973.

podunk. Once I was in his div on an errand. For no reason at all he began to haze me as no flanker ever has, and I wasn't used to it. I soon became hugely griped—particularly after I found out who he was—and walked out on him. So don't ever say anything about him to me.

Well, I fight this Saturday for sure. I'll have to get plenty of sleep tonite and not think a thing about the fight.

I was glad you sent me my rankings. We can see them on the bulletin boards but I never get around to doing it.

Yep, I'm soon to be 20 years old. Gee, I feel like I'm at last a man. The number of years is always the mark of manhood whether a fellow thinks he is grown up or not.

I've just finished a long Victorian novel by Thomas Hardy called "Desperate Remedies." He certainly deserves to be a famous author. He can keep the reader interested with the simplest occurrences.

I was glad to learn that Jean is doing so well in her work at Junior High. Also glad to hear that she is doing so well in her work outside of school. Rating a boy with an Austin is doing exceptionally well. I wish I could rate a girl with an Austin—that is if I could get in one.

The records Jean likes are all good. They most all start from New York, however, in musical comedies and such so we've been first to wear them out.

Mother, be careful what you tell people who ask about me. Remember, a word from you is just like a word from me, and some things I tell you in letters I wouldn't like to get out. For instance, this athletic stuff. I haven't done anything special yet and perhaps never will (but I'll keep on trying) and I don't want people to think that I'm doing wonders when I'm not. Elsie Seaborn [my contemporary in Reno and sometime girl-friend] thinks I'm a big shot. Maybe I will be some day, but until then I'm just working hard and enjoying myself. You understand.

I'll get out of S.I. again tomorrow, have an early dinner of steak and egg-nog, and then tumble into bed until 3:00 p.m. I'll fight about 5:30.

We have finished all of plane and spherical trig. We took the course in less than 2 months which would take a year to cover in an ordinary college. And we *know* it too—believe me—not only how to work the problems but how to derive the formulae. Analit. will be the next course.

Lots of love to you all,

DALE

I wrote to Thor on February 28, 1931, just before the fight.

Dear Thor:

I haven't a thing to write about but I haven't a thing to do right now either so I might as well scratch along. This is my big Saturday—I fight the heavyweight bout in the Plebe meet with Augusto Military Academy (wherever in hell that is). I don't suppose they are very tuff but then one never knows—I might get the hell beat out of me, but let's not think about that. Let's think about spring or something. Geez, the spring weather is surely on us here. About all the snow is melted and the South Area is completely dry again. It reminds me of last summer, but let's not think about that either.

The less I study the better grades I get. I'm spending my odd hours reading novels now and do as well if not better than I did (in my studies, of course) when I used to spend all my free hours in a text book. I'm well up on all the New Yorkers and Collierses.

Truthfully, I'm sure tired of athletics. All I've done since September first is run and exercise every afternoon. And train too. Tonite after the fight I'm going to buy a tin of Camels and smoke them all—one right after the other. This ends boxing season. Yet the best thing a plebe can do is stay on a training table and athletics is about the only racket that permits this. My name has already been put on the track squad list so I guess I'm sunk for another 3 months.

I haven't written a thing for the Pointer in ages. I'd like to sit down and try my luck sometime again.

I have a good plot for one of those short-short stories, Thor. Maybe we (mostly you) could write it together. I think West Point stuff would be bought quickly if it were written even fairly well. N'est-ce pas?

It goes like this (I tried to write it but got in a hundred jams. I don't know enough about narration.): A first classman with his O.A.O. dances last hop at Cullum Hall—"Army Blue" is always the last tune. He must, by regulations on his All-Right, walk with her to the Thayer. But since she is so sweet and because she lives far away and can seldom come up he decides to take her there in a taxi. To get out of his All-Right he "signs in" from the hop and then rides to the Thayer with his O.A.O. Very accidentally a tac sees him get out of the taxi with his fem. The tac lets him know that he saw him, and a few days later he is very dramatically slugged. He must walk the Area for 4 months and also be in confinement that long—a truly hellish torture.

When he at last walks off the slug he gets a letter from his O.A.O. telling him that she is to be married and how sorry she is for him.

This is a true to life story. Do you think it a good plot? It is too complicated for a S-S story?

You see, I have to make some money so we'd better try it, what? I'd like to raise enough to be able to take a fem out in York on the April Choir trip. If we don't do this, I'm going to have to borrow some from you, because I already have the date.

I know you are very busy, but write me what you think about it anyway.

Now, I'd better hop to bed and get some precious shut-eye. I'm certainly going to have to be on my toes in about 2½ hours.

Give my love to Mary,

Your useless brother,

DALE

My next letter home was written Saturday night, February 28, on expensive USMA stationery with the Academy crest.

Dearest Mother and Dad—

I feel great tonite. Boxing is over. Funny, I never realized what a perpetual strain I was under until now the pressure has lifted. This afternoon we won. Army varsity and Plebes, too. I won my bout also, and can't help but feel good about it. I fought a man much smaller than I and knocked him out in the 3rd. I hated to do it because the fight was too one sided—he was much too small—but that was the only course left open for me.

I'm glad for one thing that I have checked a sort of yellow streak that I always feared I had. This was the main reason I went out for boxing— because I was afraid of it. And now I believe I'll go out for it next year, because I might have a good chance. I still can stand a lot of improvement on handling my dukes.

I'm going to the show now and will finish this later.

Sunday nite: The show was a wow. A comedy called "Up the River." The prison scenes drove the Corps wild because of their striking similarity to the life at West Point.

That's about all that has happened this weekend. This afternoon I read and slept. Tonite I'll study some.

I hope everything is going well at home. Give my love to Jean and Bud.

Lots of love,

DALE

Mother wrote a long newsy letter on Monday, March 2, 1931.

Dearest Dale,

I have had a very busy weekend. Dad wrote you about Tommy Landrum's mother being with us. Bob [Merriman] had arranged for her to stay here and he met her at the train. She is a very dear little lady—and the kind that just fits in and is happy and appreciative and pleased with everything. Sunday Bob came after us and took us to the house for lunch.

Last night we went to the Hospital and Tommy is getting along fine. He is afraid he will have to quit school because this will put him so badly in debt. I told Tommy he could come stay with us after he left the hospital and until he could take up his work again. He works in the laboratory with Deac.

Your account about Read was interesting — I am not surprised — because I thought it strange that he had not recognized you. His mother and I were in High School together—so you see I have known her so long — I have talked with her frequently about West Point. After you had been in academics a month or so I met her one day, asked her if her son had seen you and she said, "Yes, he knows about him, but you know he cannot recognize him until he has been there a year" and I said "Oh I know all about that, but he can recognize him if he wants to—all the other boys from Nevada have." And I haven't seen her since.

I understand how you feel about the things I might say about you— So many people ask—and I always say you are getting on fine and like it a lot— Have told the boys about your being out for boxing and choir.

When I read your letter aloud today at the dinner table, Jean was embarrassed to think I had mentioned anything about her and the boy friend with the Austin—but she should know that we tell you everything that would be of interest.

I sent a box today for your birthday. If the shorts are not the right size send them back for exchange. Could not find any material in town quite loud enough to make you some pajamas but I was thinking I might ask Mary to pick out some material in LA. Would not have had time to make PJs for your birthday even tho I had found the gayest "summer awning" in the world.

Much love dear from all of us—we enjoy your letters so much.

Many more happy birthdays,

MOTHER

CHAPTER 13 SPRING COMES

As one of the following letters indicates, my class was learning the hard way about the Cadet Honor Code and system. The code, "A cadet does not lie, cheat, or steal or tolerate those who do," and the system for enforcing it, were officially sanctioned as a cadet-administered tradition by General MacArthur shortly after World War I when he became Superintendent.

Each cadet company (there were twelve in my day) had an Honor Representative and the twelve sat as a committee that judged all cases of honor violation. Those found guilty were invariably dismissed.

Today, each of the thirty-six cadet companies has two Honor Representatives in addition to a number of Honor Representatives at higher levels of cadet command. Members of the Honor Committee conduct investigations and submit findings and recommendations to the Vice-Chairman of the Honor Committee for Investigations. This cadet will consult with the Honor Committee Chairman, the Office of the Staff Judge Advocate (an officer), and the Special Assistant to the Commandant for Honor Matters (also an officer) before determining whether to dismiss the case or recommend that the Commandant convene a full honor investigative hearing. This body is composed of four members of the Honor Committee and eight members from the Corps at large. A vote of 10 to 2 is required to sustain a finding of guilty. The Commandant then reviews the case and forwards it to the Superintendent, who has three options, as I have noted earlier: concur with the findings and forward the report to the Secretary of the Army to separate the cadet, overturn the case, or find reason to retain the cadet with punishment short of dismissal.

Although considerably more detailed than the honor system of my day, the present system undoubtedly is more fair and even-handed. Prior to its creation there had been several instances of cadets being dismissed for honor violations that hardly seemed warranted. One such was when a cadet, filling out an application for Ranger School, noted that he could do twenty push-ups when he actually did only eighteen. Pangs of conscience caused him to report himself for having lied, and he was dismissed.

Another instance was of a cadet who visited an off-limits pizza parlor in civilian clothes. The Honor Committee judged that he had an "intent to deceive" by wearing civilian clothes, and he was dismissed. Today's honor system would never sustain such twisted reasoning.

I wrote home on Wednesday, March 5, 1931.

Dear Folks,—

I received your long "birthday" letter today. I have a little news to answer for it.

A Co was inspected last noon on the stoop of barracks for Scarlet Fever. One man has it. It was just a formation, and some other companies yelled out "A co's unclean." No one else has got the disease yet, however.

Read recognized me after the fight Saturday. So did a lot of others. I accepted Read's recognition since it was he who pulled up the flag of truce. Till that day last Sept. in the 13th div., I've ignored him—didn't pay any attention to him whenever he spoke to me.

No, I haven't written to any of the gang in a long time. You can tell them, if you care to, just exactly what I do, but don't make it seem more important than it really is. I must write to them soon—even then I won't tell them anything about my "accomplishments."

[My one bout in plebe boxing wasn't enough to win numerals and I was still without the prize I so valued.]

I stayed where I was in Math and Frog last month, but I gained two sections in B.S. We have theme work now and I shine. I could be in the first if I spent more time on the assignments, but I always put it off until an hour before class.

Three fellows have been after me to come out for track. It seems foolish to start it so early and I haven't any desire to run around a board track every afternoon. I'm going to deadbeat now until I am policed to a company table—then I'll go out for track. Another man wants me to come out for Lacrosse. I think I'd have a better chance at track.

Hundredth nite show is called "The Corps Has Gone to Hell." I wish

Cartoon from *The Pointer*.

you were here to see it with me. It is going to be in the Gym. They're building a stage for it now. Perhaps Cullum is too small a hall.

Tell Jean to keep up the good work with the fellas. I laughed when you said she was embarrassed that you told me the low-down. For a while I imagine that she will be very Victorian and even later keep enough of it to make her charming.

Lots of love to you all

DALE

Another from me was written on my 20th birthday, March 7, 1931.

Dearest Mother and Dad,

John and I have just finished the delicious birthday cake. The shorts you sent are unrivaled in the Corps for colors, and, of course, I can make excellent use of the soxs. Thanks for the works.

The little "ironies of life"—I'm on guard tonite. I'd planned to see a show but don't suppose it's a good one anyhow.

John and I must move tomorrow. They're making our room into a trunkroom and putting us upstairs in 223. This is an area room and we will be able to see the uniform flags [the flags which signified the uniform to be worn that day] and the clock from our window. It also is a southern room. Not a bit bad except for the moving. Usually only first classmen get second floor rooms. [They were prized because they were far enough from the division entrance door for us to hear the tac coming for inspection, yet without too many stairs to climb.]

Enclosed are a couple of marksmanship attempts. Our first work on the sub-caliber range.

Golly, I rank 66 in Math now. I'm doing no more studying than usual but I guess others are doing less. This certainly makes me an engineer in this subject at least. [Engineers were those ranking high in academics; goats were low ranking.]

The hazing isn't a bit bad now. It's only the lack of entertainment, freedom and women that is hard to endure. I haven't spoken to a fem, save on the Choir trip, since Christmas. John went on his Catholic Choir trip this weekend. He is in York now, the lucky cuss! Still, I feel sorry for the poor devil, he'll come back a disillusioned man. I don't think he'll have much fun. Perhaps you laugh at the contrast—a puritan Catholic living with such a deep sinner and pleasure lover as me. I've tried, not offensively, but only when he broaches the subject, to show him the "light" of truth and realism. But it's a useless task. We get along day after day without the least of hard feelings nor ever a quarrel.

[I was dead wrong. John could have as much fun as anyone. With a broad smile and ready wit he was always a welcome contribution to any group. I was indeed lucky to have drawn him as a roommate and he helped me often with academic problems.]

Well, it won't be long. Three months till Recognition, Summer Camp, and getting to know my classmates better. Perhaps I'll find a pleasant fem at one of the hops and drag her to another. And perhaps I won't. Although it's always best to think that I will.

Lots of love to you all,

DALE

I wrote again the next day, Sunday, March 8.

Dear Mother and Dad—

You've been awfully good to me. I've gotten lots of letters and two packages this week. The boodle was delicious and Mother's picture is beautiful. It is before me now.

I've enjoyed a good deadbeat this weekend. Yesterday I went to the fights. They were very exciting and Army won as usual. They're not as gentle around here as they are at Nevada. If a man goes down they count him out—most places they stop the fight. One of the bouts yesterday was certainly a slugging match. McAleer,* the Army man, was knocked down in the first round but got up on the count of 9. In the second round he recovered amazingly and succeeded in putting his opponent on the mat twice—once to the count of nine. But in the third round Mac took a beating and was put out cold—flat on the floor with arms out-stretched. It was a thrilling fight.

Alden is a marvelous gymnast. He took first place on the horizontal bar in the first meet. Yesterday he had hard luck—fell off at the beginning of his exercise. Reason: He had torn a huge piece of skin from his palm in practice a few days before. I'm surprised at his success. This place has done wonders for him. He matured slowly at home, and didn't begin to grow up until he started college. But in a town like Reno a fellow hasn't a chance. His reputation is always with him. This is similar to my case.

In the evening I went with Alden to see Clara Bow in "Her Wedding Night." Very funny.

There was a lot of snow on the ground this morning and sleet is falling now. Is this spring?

I must write a letter to Thor now. Lots of love to you all and thanks lots for the presents.

DALE

Mother wrote Monday afternoon, March 9.

Dearest Dale—

We have two short letters from you since I last wrote. Good letters—because you were happy and had won your bout and boxing is over for

---

*John H. McAleer, class of 1931, served as a regimental commander of infantry in World War II as well as in the Korean War. He retired as a colonel in 1955 with a Legion of Merit, a Bronze Star, and a Commendation Medal.

awhile. So—the yellow streak is downed, is it? Well, I don't believe you had any yellow streak—if so—it was a pale cream color. I suppose all those conquests are fine for a real he-man to experience—Dad and I are amused over your intention to dead-beat it until you are policed to a company table—perhaps you need that experience too. But not too long of it, eh?

Hope no more scarlet fever has developed. So, Mr. Read recognized you when he found you could box. Tell me, what did you earn when you won the bout? You spoke once of not having earned your numerals in football—does this give you your numerals?

Jean has just phoned for us to come for her—she has been at Rainbow—so I will close—Much love from

MOTHER

Dad wrote on Wednesday, March 11, 1931.

Dear Dale— Yours of the 7th received, a nice chatty letter. Your roommate, John, is undoubtedly a fine fellow and your differences in philosophy & religion may have served to make you tolerant and respectful of each other. . . . Happily for this country, American Catholicism has undergone some evolution for the better.

I think, so far as such as thing can be accomplished in this age, you and Thor grew up without a religious bias. With your advancing years, you will adopt your own philosophy, which will undoubtedly be based on personal knowledge that such happiness as we may have, such peaceful content in life, comes from knowledge of duties well done, to others and ourselves. That's simple enough, and we know it's true by experience.

Your shooting targets are simply marvelous. I had an idea that you would eat up that rifle and pistol stuff. But you have a great advantage over so many of those fellows who have never handled a gun before.

Yesterday aft I went up to the U. but didn't do a tap of work, just "bull sessions" all the aft.

We have passed a gambling bill—Pay a license and set up the wheels, anyone, anywhere. It isn't good but since no attempt has been made to enforce the existing law, the police and officials graft off the games. It will at least stop that. I wonder how long before they get around to the fact that liquor grafting can now only be stopped in the same way! The liquor business has become a very controversial subject, almost everywhere now, and I'll bet it's made a national issue next presidential campaign. [It was, and Prohibition was repealed.] It really was to some extent the last time, and but for Al Smith's religion, and the fact that Hoover was a sort of popular idol, Smith might have been elected. And now—after Hoover's miserable showing, his slowness to take any definite action in anything, and his apparently lining up with the cussed corporation kings of the country—there is bound to be a powerful reaction next election. [There was, and Franklin D. Roosevelt was elected.]

This land is rapidly getting ready for a dictator who can stop grafting, gang law and corporation greed, it seems to me. [F.D.R. was hardly that, but he wielded tremendous power in bringing the country out of the Depression.] What a silent laugh I get out of these poor deluded fools who think there will be no more war. There are several hundred men with families in Reno out of work and wondering how they will get along.

And now I guess I've rambled on enough for this time, so Goodnight, Dale-boy, from

DAD

I wrote home on March 11, 1931.

Dear Mother and Dad—

There isn't much news. Just the same old grind. I'm looking forward to June when I can walk out of this room like a free man instead of running and hiding from upperclassmen like a rabbit from hounds.

The plebe system might be all right for awhile, but a whole year is too much. Many hates develop that are never settled throughout the remaining 3 years. We have decided to give a certain heel 2nd classman a royal beating right after recognition. Not that any one of us hasn't the guts to do it right now, but a plebe is *always* wrong and he would lead a life of hell until June. It's the same way with calling a man out (challenging him who treats you unfairly to a fight). I thought of doing it many times, but finally gave up because of the consequences. It is only a fable that a plebe has the right to defend himself against one who affronts his honor. Before I entered I believed this fable to be true.

There isn't much to the uniforms. Lieutenants, 3 chevrons and up, wear red sashes and one white belt (a sword belt) and high plumes on their FD hats (tarbuckets). First sergeants and supply sergeants also wear the red sash and sword belt, but do not have the feathered plumes. Other sergeants wear a sword belt and a white waste [*sic*] belt. All others wear cross belts with a white waste [*sic*] belt and side arms (bayonets) and carry rifles. We only dress this way when under arms, at some sort of ceremony or on guard. The daily guard is made up of 5 firstclassmen: Senior and Junior Officers of the Day, Senior and Junior Officers of the Guard, and a Sergeant of the Guard. The SOD and JOD are the only ones who ever wear a red sash over their sword belts.

The small diagonals on the cuffs are service stripes. One for a yearling, two for a second classman, and three for a first. All the FD coats have three buttons on the cuff. [It is said that Frederick the Great of Prussia put buttons on the cuffs of his soldiers' uniforms to prevent them from wiping their noses with their sleeves. We carried handkerchiefs tucked inside the stiff white cuffs that were pinned to our sleeves.]

A custom around here is "dragging". Lately they have been dragging in the mess hall all the new corps squad (athletic) captains and managers. Of course this is against regulations so it is done in a hurry in order that the OC (Officer in Charge) won't see. A gang grabs the man, puts him on the floor and pours a pitcher or two of water on him, usually up his trouser legs, but they're not particular. In summer camp they do it with all sorts of messy things such as liquid brass shiner and shoe polish.

[In spite of its discomfort, being dragged was something of an honor. When the class of General of the Armies John J. Pershing held its fiftieth reunion at West Point, the class of 1936 invited the general to make the graduation speech. General Pershing accepted and requested that, when he and his classmates came to lunch in the mess hall, arrangements be made to permit his classmates to drag him because he had never been dragged as a cadet!]

In the training table area there is always a lot of rough house. They throw everything from food to table ware.

[While making one of his noontime walks through the mess hall, the Commandant, "Nellie" Richardson, noticed a glob of butter on the wall. He stormed up to the poopdeck and had the battalions called to attention. "Gentlemen," he began, "I have just observed one of the most outrageous acts I have ever encountered. Someone among you has thrown a pat of butter which landed on a beautiful wall of this magnificent building. Some of you have failed to realize that your generous government has given you every advantage. Why, you live in palaces and yet

you treat this place just as if it were nothing more than a cheap chop-
house. . . . " He was right about it being a beautiful building. On one
vast wall was an unfinished mural depicting twenty of the great battles
of history, a truly fine piece of art.]

I take a couple of laps around an improvised board track every night
now. The rest of the time I spend in boning fiction—studying, and
trying not to think about West Point.

One of our classmates resigned yesterday. He was in my Math section
and in the first English section. Said he didn't like it, well, who does?
It's always best to finish anything you've started, regardless.

Lots of love to you all,

DALE

Dad wrote a letter dated Saturday, March 14.

Dear Daley-boy:
Your letter with a note of discontent and homesickness came today.
Ah, well, we all have those times, when we wish to change the "scheme
of things entire," but we pass through them. The sun shines and happiness comes again. Your troubles, and mine too, are after all pretty
small things. Death, with its attendant misery and despair has not come
into our midst, as to so many of our friends. We have good health, and
good luck. You, yourself, have the most splendid opportunity that could
have come to you—there is nothing I would not give, or do, if I could
be in your place.

As to your grievances with upper classmen—forget it. Large men do
not pack around little grouches. You can't afford to be touchy and thin-
skinned. After you are recognized, only a few days from now, just put it
all out of your mind. There is no one among those who have offended
you that you can "give a beating." You are a heavyweight fighter, and not
one of them would be your match. It would be most unfair, and if you
did beat some boy up, the Corps would surely dislike you for it. You will
not be so easily affronted when you get out of the Plebe class.

As to the defects of the plebe system, you will judge it more impar-
tially from the upper classes. It may be pretty tough at times, but it goes
without saying that there are a good sprinkling of cocky lads in every
4th class. They have to be good to get in there, they know it, and their
egos are pretty well inflated by many friends and parents telling them
so. If you don't like it later on you can make it easier for a bunch of
plebes by recognizing them. It's the Cadets themselves who carry out

these things. [But not today. The Tactical Department has published Circular 351-1 entitled "The Fourth Class System," which says, "Upperclass cadets will not recognize a fourth class cadet unless there exists a prior friendship or a corps squad/activity social relationship."]

We had a big boxing show here last night. Nevada vs. Cal Aggies, and they cleaned us plenty. We won only 2 out of 7. But Jack Dempsey was in town and came to see the bouts, made a speech after being introduced from the ring, and refereed the last bout—heavyweights—which we won. Theis is a terrible mauler, and nearly killed his opponent. Rather sporting of old Jack to come up and take part. I was on the program as a timekeeper and again rang the bell. [The last page of this letter is missing.]

Mother wrote the same day, Saturday evening, March 14.

Dearest Dale, and Thor and Mary—
This week I had to lay off about three days with a bad cold but I'm fine again. Nothing goes very smoothly around home when Mother is not up and coming. We have been having springlike weather but oh, there is so much sickness. So much flu and pneumonia.

The report from the Supt. of West Point came today for Feb. Dale is 66th in Math, 217th in French and 66th in English. Mighty fine, isn't it fellas?

.   .   .   .

We would love to be close enough to see you oftener—but we are like Dale—we try to keep busy and not think about it.

So Dale has moved too—hope you like the new room—and the view. Dad and I like your letters so much and are glad you give us your opinions on things in general there. I almost count the days with you and I'll be glad too when June comes.

Much love to all of you and write soon again—
    MOTHER

I wrote home on March 17, 1931.

Dear Mother and Dad—
I'm lieing [sic] on my stomach and writing this in bed. Have a half hour till taps—a half hour between tattoo and taps.

It's getting warmer here now and we wear dress grey very often. It's

Joseph Cleary. From 1934 *Howitzer*.

great to be rid of those heavy overcoats which require an extra minute to put on and another to take off.

Track is now in full swing. The track is over at the summer camp site. It runs all around Camp Clinton. If you can imagine 3 rows of tents put lengthwise in Mackay Field with many large oak trees here and there, you would have a fair idea of Camp Clinton itself. Of course there are no tents now. It is all an athletic field. When the leaves come out it will be beautiful.

Today the sun was shining brightly and Joe Cleary* and I took an easy workout together. Afterwards we played around with the shot and discus, were in some newspaper pictures and walked back to the Gym across the Plain. We swam for about a half hour before coming home.

*Affable Joseph A. Cleary was one of the best-liked men in our class. His roommate wrote, "He could be depended upon to brighten any situation with his ready Irish grin and suitable joke." Joe chose the Cavalry as his branch of service and was assigned to Ft. Stotsenburg, Philippine Islands, when war broke out in 1941. As a major, Joe was given command of a battalion of the Philippine Army and was in constant action covering the withdrawal to the Bataan peninsula. He was killed while defending a bridge north of Bataan, the first USMA graduate to be killed in World War II. Joe was posthumously awarded the Silver Star for gallantry.

One of my classmates got found on honor today. It was for plagiarism in an English theme. He was a keen file and I liked him lots. It was a foolish stunt for him to do. The Court Martial [it was the Honor Committee] has been going on for several days. He was convicted today. I feel very sorry for him.

Another is resigning, and another who tried to resign without success got himself found by intentional plagiarism. The class is thinning out. [These were rumors. The Corps was never advised as to exactly what happened.]

I'm glad Thor is doing so well. I received a letter from him today. I hope he has a good supply of home brew on hand when I come that way on furlo.

I have an awful suck in the Gym department. I don't know how I ever got it, but it is certainly too great for me to ignore. Upstairs especially, whatever I do is oke with the officer instructors, but others catch hell. It's embarrassing for me sometimes, because they show their partiality so plainly. Once I was drilling the section (as we all do at times) and, of course, was on my mettle. I gave the section many movements and yelled my commands out pretty well, if I remember rightly. But in giving an odd number of "to the rear marches" and then commanding a squad movement I got the whole section inverted and reversed. Each one kept his respective new position in his squad, however. (It's dark now but I'll finish by using lots of paper and writing large.) To go on with the story, when I had finished the instructor said, "One thing about Mr. Smith, he didn't invert the section" and he meant it. You see, he couldn't tell whether the section was inverted or not without me being in my squad. It was a laugh.

Explanatory note (a suck is a drag or pull). [Favoritism.]

Well, I'm almost asleep now. This is a funny thing writing with my eyes closed. I'll see tomorrow if it is legible enough to send. Lots of love to you all,

    DALE

I wrote another letter March 23, 1931.

Dear Folks,

This is just a note. Nothing important has happened.

I want you to send me a box of books. Most important is my math books. I'd like my Calculus and Advanced Algebra. Also my two French texts. I'm sorry I didn't bring them with me. If I don't get a good Analytical Geom text soon I'll be down with the goats. The one we use might just as well be thrown out the window. It gives no answers and no examples, so that I wouldn't know if my answers were correct even if I could work them. Send me any other texts that I could use here, you know the subjects—no Philosophy or Psychology, however. I'm sorry to inconvenience you but it really is essential that I have them.

We're writing military reports in English now. Quite practical, what?

I saw "Hook Line and Sinker" last Saturday—a very good comedy. I don't know what I'd do without my weekly show.

Sunday afternoon I rated a blind drag but it was a disappointment and I wished I had stayed at home with Don Quixote (I'm reading it). I had thot, since I've been womanless for so long, that anything with skirts would excite me, but I'm just as fastidious as ever. I'd never be content to live on a tropical island with only native women around. Since I've seen and known smart, well-built and handsome fems, I'm content with nothing else.

Well, I must go out and mail the letters now, and this with them.

Lots of love to you all,

DALE

I wrote home on Saturday, March 28.

Dearest Mother and Dad,

I'm sorry to have neglected you. Had the time to write many times, but I wasn't in the right mood. I decided that no letter would be better than one with a lot of griping in it, for no matter how hard I try, letters I write always tell what I'm thinking at the time—what else would there be to write about? But now I feel fine even though I have all my equipment to get ready for SI which will be two hours hence.

Last week I had a bad time with math. Our book on Analyt. is terrible as I have told you. I did fairly well in class—ran on luck, but in a writ I went very dee—got a 1.2. Everyone else got nearly as poor marks. The next day, yesterday, I ran in the luck again and maxed it cold [got a perfect grade] at the board while none of the others in my section came near to maxing it. Today I did well too, so I'm not worried. By asking many questions I have begun to understand it.

Oh, yes, Ruth sent me a very nice letter and this raised the spirits much. She is a fickle little devil but as truthful as can be found. A fine girl in any event. I hope to take her out when I go to York. It's time I did—she's entertained me always and I haven't repaid her once.

I swiped a few grains of explosive—I think it's TNT—from the Artillery class this morning. I lit just one grain of it and the small explosive shot about a foot into the air.

This Artillery class is a riot. A sergeant is our teacher—we rank him, we know it, and he knows it—so we have a big time. But we do learn a little, as much as is possible, I imagine. The class is held in a room which contains a 75 mm gun and a caisson. We have gun drills and get our good Dress Grey all dirty.

Track is coming OK. We have our first meet on May 2nd. The varsity has a meet next month. It is getting warmer all the time.

We're having tests in Gym again. I've won one wrestling bout so far. I won't rank as high as last time, I think, because the upstairs work is too much for me. We have a lot of upside down exercises and I'm not too graceful, although I can do them all. I am really surprised at myself, however. 9 months ago I wouldn't have attempted or dreamed of doing some of the exercises. [These were gymnastic exercises such as kips, hand stands, rope climbs, etc.]

After these tests we will specialize in whatever we please until June week, when we will give an exhibition—the whole class, mind you. "Every man an athlete" is the motto here.

Well, I'd better get to my cleaning and polishing. Everything must be in *perfect* condition for S.I.

Lots of love to you all,

DALE

I wrote again on March 29, 1931.

Dear Folks—

I just received Dad's long letter. I surely do enjoy them. They're the only ones I receive that make me go to the dictionary to look up new words. [Too bad I didn't go more often to correct my spelling.] I'm glad things are going well now.

Today I've done some sewing and cleaned up my desk drawers—not to mention having folded my laundry which is a regular Sunday duty. Then I read the Herald Tribune—New York's best paper. I miss Jean and Drew a lot. I wonder if they miss me. I suppose not—not much at

(Form 17).

WHITE. J*

CADET'S LAUNDRY LIST.

West Point, N. Y. ..... Sept. 19 193

ORIGINAL

I certify that this list is correct, to the best of my knowledge and belief.

Signed ......

Cadet ...... Company ...... Class ...... Floor ...... Division

Sent	Item and Cost per Unit	Received	Returned	Amount
	Bathing Suits.....02			
	Belts, Shoulder....01			
	Belts, Sword.....01			
	Belts, Waist......01			
	Blankets, single...15			
	Blankets, double...25			
	Cap Covers......05			
	Coats, white......15			
	Clothes-bags.....free			
	Cloths, wash.....01			
	Comfortables.....20			
	Collars...........01			
	Cuffs, pair........02			
	Drawers..........02			
	Gloves, pair......01			
	Handkerchiefs....01			
	Jerseys...........05			
	Pajamas, suits....05			
	Pillow, cases......02			
	Sheets...........02			
	Shirts, white......03			
	Shirts, colored....03			
	Shirts, night......03			
	Shirts, grey......05			
	Shirts, under......02			
	Socks, pair......02			
	Supporters.......02			
	Sweaters.........10			
	Towels, bath.....02			
	Towels, face......01			
	Trousers, white....10			
	Union suits......04			

Duplicate Laundry Lists shall be sent to the Laundry   See Par.
22.08, Orders. U. S. C. C.

least, for I got used to having Thor away very soon, and didn't notice his absence. I must write Jean soon. It's sweet of her to want to work. That's right, give her her noble gesture.

The math grades came out O.K. for me this week. 12.4 At least I am still in the 3rd section—one got policed.

In my last statement, I'm $63 in debt, but we got lots of new clothes last month and I think I'll be out of debt by summer. I'd like to buy a tennis racket and a set of golf sticks. I could use them plenty during Yearling deadbeat.

The new clothes were: A dress coat, pair of trou, and eight white coats for summer. They all run into plenty of money. I'll be permitted a $5 boodle book when I get out of debt.

Less than a month till the next Choir trip, too.

I'm awfully glad, Dad, that you got the new position and will soon be at the old grindstone. I know you'll enjoy the new work.

Lots of love,

DALE

P.S. Sue sent back my pin. Pretty good of her, what?

CHAPTER 14 DAD GETS A JOB

Before coming to West Point I had wasted many odd hours dreaming of becoming an aviator. My high school economics notebook was pasted over with pictures of Orville Wright, Billy Mitchell, Admiral Byrd, Eddie Rickenbacker, Frank Luke, the Red Baron Von Richthofen and his conqueror, Captain Roy Brown of the Royal Canadian Flying Corps. It was also adorned with pictures of famous airplanes clipped from the aviation magazines I poured over: the French SPAD, the British Camel, the German Fokker triplane that Richthofen flew, and the American DH4.

At the Academy I was puzzled at how little interest our officer-instructors evinced in aviation, and I was only dimly aware of the animosity then existing toward that upstart arm of service, the Army Air Corps. The ill feelings caused by the General Billy Mitchell court martial still lingered. But not all instructors were so inclined, and in first class year I took a chance and wrote a monograph arguing how a modern attack plane could have changed Napoleon's fortunes at Waterloo. I was given a high grade for it.

I didn't have much desire for a career in the Army at this time but I knew that my chances of getting into the Air Corps Flying School at Randolph Field, Texas (the best flying school in the country), would be pretty good after graduating from the U.S. Military Academy and being commissioned a regular officer. And I also suspected that a regular officer with wings would have a better chance of advancement than a reserve officer. Such a commission was offered to flying cadets who graduated from Randolph and Kelly Fields. Consequently I was determined to stick it out at West Point. With each passing day these dreams seemed to take on more meaning.

The good word from home raised my spirits even more. Dad wrote from Reno on Sunday, March 29, 1931, with the wonderful news of his final appointment. He had been ten months without a job but with Mother's loyal help had found ways to cope with the Great Depression. They had suffered, all right, but the family never went hungry and was still able to enjoy the simple pleasures and closeness of family life. I never heard them complain of the Depression, except about how it affected others. Dad had actively kept many irons in the fire, had been optimistically patient, and was eventually rewarded. It must have been a time for great rejoicing at home. I wished I could have been there.

Dear Thor, Mary and Dale:

Mother is busy recovering a quilt for me to take with my bed out to Scossa, and thinks I should write a letter to the "boys". Drewdy and Lloyd are sprawled on the floor playing "United States History". Jean, Peggy and Norma have gone to the Episcopal Church to hear a cantata.

I hope the great financial drought is over for a little while. The long awaited appointment came a few days ago, and was ratified by a meeting of the University Regents on Friday, following which there were announcements in the local newspapers that "A. M. Smith was appointed mining engineer for the Bureau of Mines, effective at once."

Carl Stoddard was given a similar appointment, and between us we are the active force of the Bureau, and are surely going to be busy men this year, for much is planned, and it is hoped that with our experience we can make a good showing. We have a fine large office and semi-workroom in the Mackay School building, fitted with numerous cases, work tables, and two desks, a beautiful place to work, and we have the cooperation of all the highly efficient staff of the Mackay School and the perfect laboratory equipment.

Our first work is to go to the new mining camp of Scossa near Lovelock and get out a state bulletin on it as soon as possible, for free distribution.

In the morning I leave for Scossa in the old Dodge which I have had put in good condition for my field car this summer. Carl has been out there nearly every day since the camp was discovered and has a good tent house and I will live for the next two weeks or so with him and his two boys, Mort and Kirby. Mother cannot do without a car so we have been living a sort of hectic life the last few days looking for cars, old and new. One is a 1925 Studebaker in good condition for $150. Another is a 1927 reconditioned Buick for $325. Nothing more tonight.

Much love from

DAD

Mother wrote Wednesday afternoon—April 1. There was a five-cent airmail stamp stuck on the letter for my use, and it's still there.

Dearest Dale,

Just received two nice letters from you—written Sat. and Sun. Glad you were feeling in good spirits again—Sorry we can't be of more comfort to you when your spirits are low but we are confident that you will make the struggle and come out of your year's "imprisonment" and be a credit to yourself and we shall be proud of you. There is no doubt that such discipline is needed to make good soldiers of you boys. Two months more—counting in the 60s now. We shall be glad to have the phone talk with you on the 26th. The charge is $5 for the first three minutes when the call is put in between midnight and 4.30 a.m. Your midnight will be about 9 p.m. here and so even later will be OK with us and perhaps the wires would be less busy. There's a chance that Dad won't be here. He will be in the field very much between now and July.

It was a big effort to get Dad off Monday morning—you remember how it always was. It was noon before he got started. We had the Dodge overhauled and it was running fine. I have been driving every kind on the market. Nearly all the dealers in town have been showing us what they have.

I am glad Ruth has written you again and we will send you some money before you go on the choir trip. We will have to send it in bills, I suppose, and shall I register the letter? A money order would be safest but since we are not supposed to send money that might not be a good way.

This is spring vacation week and Jean and Drew have been enjoying it most of the time. Sometimes Drew doesn't know what to do with himself. Last night Jean went to Moana with the Gills for a swim. . . .

We enjoy your letters so much dear—I will send these on to Dad hoping he will receive them. Mail is taken out to Lovelock by anyone who happens to be going.

Much love from us all—

MOTHER

My next letter home was dated April 2, 1931.

Dear Mother and Dad,

I'm awfully glad to hear that Dad got his appointment and will soon be hitting the trail again. I hope you are all in high spirits and happy— I know I am.

Things are about the same here. It hasn't been very good weather— mostly rainy. Track for me is in a bad way. I did something to my left foot and I can't even run on it now. It's been this way for over a week and is getting worse. Guess I'll go to sick call with it tomorrow after breakfast. It's over a month till the first plebe meet so I still have a chance.

Lost a section in English. We're having Shakespeare's Henry IV and I don't hive it very well. Fact is I don't hive the math or Frog either but neither does anyone else.

I'm doing pretty well in gym again, but I won't rank as high as last term. I've maxed boxing, wrestling and fencing, but have just barely gone pro upstairs.

Well, I must get down to a little studying. Lots of love to you all,

DALE

Mother wrote on Saturday, April 4.

Dearest Daley—

My how I wish we could hear you tomorrow at Columbia. And I hope you have something interesting for the day after Chapel. . . .

We have only had one short note from Dad since he left for Scossa last Mon. I had hoped for him to come home tonite but so far he has not shown up. Carl Stoddard came in from there last Tues. and is still here—will go back tomorrow.

I have had the use of a Nash 1928 Coach for a couple of days. It drives nicely but I do not think we want a coach—the front seat is so low. This one is priced at $350.

No letter from Thor this week. The SP Co. have been giving wonderful excursion rates for weekends—a cent a mile and anywhere. A round trip ticket to SF is only 5.35 and to LA 13.10. I might use them sometime to go see Thor. If we get a dependable car we might drive down in June.

Much love to you dear,

MOTHER

19. On boxing team, winter 1934.
20. Summer 1932, on yearling furlo: left to right, Ken Kenerick, John Hutchison, Dale Smith, Dick Moorman, Bill Gross.

19

20

21

22

23

21. Studying in room.
22. At summer camp, 1933.
23. Yearling year.
24–26. Dale at West Point:
left, with Mother and Drew;
bottom left, with Dad; bottom right, with Thor.

24

25

26

27. Marching up the hill to chapel, 1933. Dale is in center of picture.

28. Hop, Cullum Hall, 1933. Most of the couples are too busy to notice that the photograph is being taken.

29. A Company firstclassmen, 1934. Dale Smith is second from right, top row.

30. Boxing squad, 1934. Dale Smith is at right of front row.

27

28

29

30

31

32

33

31. Dale Smith with Chinese pilot and F-100, Taiwan, 1959.
32. Lieutenant Drew Smith, named for Dale's brother, gets his wings at Big Springs Air Force Base, Texas, 1974.
33. Plebes reporting at West Point, 1970s: some things have changed—*U.S. Army.*
34. Major General Dale O. Smith, Okinawa, 1958.
35. Upon retirement from the U.S. Air Force, Pentagon, 1964: left to right, Dale M. Smith, Drew Smith, Virginia and Dale O. Smith. The award is the Legion of Merit.

34

35

36–37. June Week Parade, West Point: top, 1933; bottom, 1975.—*U.S. Military Academy.*

36

37

I wrote home April 5, 1931.

Dear Mother and Dad,

Mr. & Mrs. Seaborn came to see me today. We rode around the circle in their car talking, and then they took me up to meet some friends of theirs. Major Mumma* and his wife—very nice people. It was a good break for me. He (the Major) is going to have me up to dinner sometime. They have a daughter, I think, but I didn't meet her. The major is the basketball officer in charge, and spent much time trying to get me to come out for it next year. He even asked Mr. Seaborn to work on me. I believe I'll try my luck at that again and if I don't do well, the major said he'd let me know before boxing season starts. There are 3 basketball trips next year.

The Seaborns left early because they had a dinner date. It was good to see them and I enjoyed the afternoon.

I'm glad things are going well at home. I couldn't give any advice about the car purchasing situation. I hardly know one make from another now.

Last night I sat next to Shepardson at the show and we saw Hell's Angels. Shep won't be able to go west for furlo—he hasn't the money. I suppose there isn't a real home for him in the west anyhow—poor devil. But he'll get a good job somewhere here in the east—they all do.

Wally [Wollaston] is a classmate and a good pal. He's from the middle west. I gave him the date with Sue that I broke on the Illinois game. He wasn't disappointed. He is in M Co and lives with Upham,** another good friend of mine. The latter is an Army brat [from an Army family] and his uncle is an Admiral in the Navy.

I haven't been doing so well in my studies lately. Getting pretty low in everything. I'll have to buck up.

---

*Harlan L. Mumma, class of 1916, was quartermaster of the Panama Canal Department during World War II, winning two Legion of Merits. He rose to the rank of brigadier general.

**Hudson H. Upham had a bubbling sense of humor. He convulsed us once in wrestling when he was tangled up with his opponent and won the fall by patting himself on the back. In World War II Hudson commanded the 306th Bomb Group, which was charged with dropping agents into occupied France. His awards included the American Air Medal, the British Distinguished Flying Cross, and the French Croix de Guerre with Palm. After the war, while piloting a B-17 at night from Naples to England, he was killed when it crashed in the Alps.

My foot is better and I'm out for track again. I have hopes of much success this year in the hurdles and high jump. I've been playing with the javelin and find I can throw it nearly as far as those who are out for it.

I believe I'll spend my 4 years in the Army after graduation and then resign. Do all the traveling I can in the service and go to flying school if I can make it. Then I'll go into civilian life—aviation if possible.

Well, I'd better get down to the books. Lots of love to you all.

DALE

P.S. I'm looking forward to our telephone conversation. You must have all the questions written down or something because we must make the most of our 3 minutes. Love,

DALE

Mother wrote Wednesday afternoon, April 8.

Dearest Dale,

Your nice letter of Sunday came so quickly—and it was so newsy—and answered our questions. So glad Mr. and Mrs. Seaborn drove up to see you and took you to meet their friends—Hope the Major remembers you and that you make the BB team if you go out for it. I have written Mrs. Seaborn a letter today.

Sorry you fell down in academics—just for the sake of the rewards you would receive for good grades—I know you will keep on trying but I realize how hard it is to keep up the concerted effort. I don't blame you a bit—I could not keep it up either—so I know that after laying off a week or so you will get in and work all the harder. . . .

I am glad your foot is better—both for the sake of your track and for your comfort. Wish we could see some of the track work. I always enjoyed it more than football because it was more individual work. The hurdles and dashes are so exciting.

Dad is still at Scossa, have been looking for him since Sat. but I think he wants to finish there before coming in—so now I am going to quit looking for him and he will come!

The last car I looked at was a Ford as per Thor's suggestion. It was a 1930 sedan with less than 11000 miles, looks and runs like new—for $600. . . .

I must stop and dress to go to town. It's a fine spring day—Jean said at noon she had spring fever and did not want to go back to school. . . .

I am sending you a pkg. today—probably won't reach you before Monday. I hope the contents will not burn you up and yet answer your purpose. [It was a pair of pajamas that Mother made from some colorful material.]

Lots of love dear from

MOTHER

I wrote home on April 8.

Dearest Mother and Dad—

Well, things are going better this week. We're having gym tests again and I'm doing very well. Upstairs [gymnastics] on the apparatus I didn't do so well, but so far I've maxed it cold in boxing, wrestling and fencing. The two matches in wrestling and fencing are all over, and all I have left to do is fence once more. I hope I can rank high again, I might be a make. I doubt if my academics are high enough for that, but anyhow it's just mainly a matter of luck. I'd like to wear the gold chevrons, but then it's a lot of extra work, too.

I came in third in my first hurdle race. All were plebes and I wasn't far behind, so I might bone that up and become a hurdler. In the high jump (today there were tryouts, we have them twice a week) everyone tied at 5′4″ except Dick Moorman who did 5′6″. Very poor, all of it, but for some reason this life doesn't make or rather hinders high jumpers, which accounts for the low record of only 6′. Even so Army hasn't lost a track meet in about 7 years.

I'm piping the Choir trip. It will be great to have some money to spend, because then I can take Ruth out, but I don't want you to send it unless you can really afford to.

This is about all. I've spent the last 5 minutes trying to think of something interesting but "inutilement."

Lots of love,

DALE

A letter from Dad written in Reno on Monday, April 13.

Dear Dale-boy:

My days are busy now, and happy. I have not written you for 2 weeks. At Camp Scossa, long dinnerless days in the desert hills followed by Gargantuan nocturnal eats, technical talks and some sleeps in our big

16′ × 16′ tent. The tent was heated by a good little laundry stove. Coal costs $1.50 per sack at the so-called store, and we burned much to combat bleak winds that too frequently howled about the camp. Food consisted of sour-dough hotcakes in the morning, and the usual routine of beans, bacon and eggs at other times. Water we hauled from a well at Placeritos 6 miles distant. I found Scossa to have some gold possibilities, but to be vastly over-boomed. Virginia Cities, Goldfields and Tonopahs are glories of the past, "gone glimmering through a dream of things that were". There are many new rich fields in Nevada awaiting development, but capital is needed for the purpose. The great bonanzas that yielded fabulous wealth have vanished. . . .

It is wonderful to be working with the University group. Such fine, happy, hopeful fellows, both students and teachers. We have brought in many rocks for determination, and have help in making microscopic slides, and have been told to help ourselves to the assay labs—do our own work in chem and assaying which is exactly what I wanted.

Two of your good letters reached me at Scossa and I found another here on my return Friday nite, and another came today. You are doing most splendidly, son, and of course we are inordinately proud of you. West Point, the world's greatest, is a hard old school, not so hard perhaps in the daily task, which can always be done with a reasonable amount of work, but hard in the sense of demanding and exacting *sustained* effort to bring out the will and the iron necessary to leaders in any work.

In all reverence I am here to say that an institution that puts *honor* and *duty* and *patriotism* above everything else—above life—is fostering the only thing that makes any real human happiness. . . . Therein is the root and the glamor and the glory of West Point.

The fly in the ointment of course is that we can't see you, but nothing is really perfect, and our best bet is to do our best. And you may find some grains of comfort in the fact that we no doubt miss you more than you miss us. And when your furlo does come—won't we have a grand old reunion—Dale, Thor, Mary, Thornicito or -cita? Jean, Drew, Mom and Dad. Meanwhile we all work and are happy, for happiness is a condition of mind largely induced by earnest work. . . .

Much love from

DAD

I wrote home on Sunday, April 12, 1931.

Dear Folks—

I received lots of nice letters from you this week, and two Sage-brushes. It is less than 2 weeks till the Choir trip. We sing at Columbia University this time and if I stay in York I might sleep at the Sigma Nu house there.

I took my last Gym test yesterday—a saber bout, and made a 3.0. It was a surprise to me. I fought one of the Plebes on the fencing team and beat him 5 to 2.

We had a couple of practice reviews last week in F.D. [full dress]. We have to shine the tarbuckets for S.I. now—the overcoats are getting a rest. Today we have our first P-rade and a formal guard mount—at which D.O. is scheduled to be present, godamit.

Monday we will be reviewed by H.R.H. the Crown Prince of Japan. A funny, queer, almost foolish (but most things in the Army seem like this in peacetime) custom, is to give visiting royalty the privilege of re-leasing all special confinements and tours on the Area. Pretty lucky for some of the men who have been recently slugged.

The instructors here are O.K. They all know what they are teaching and one can seldom stick them, even if they haven't PhDs.

I'm planning on getting my photo taken if I can ever find the time. Only 60 more days of the Great Humiliation and Torture. Then I might be able to get some sleep.

Lots of love to you all,

DALE

A letter from Mother, dated only "Sunday evening," must have been written about April 12. The Depression had struck again.

Dearest Dale—Thor and Mary,

Friday night about 9 Dad and Carl Stoddard returned from Scossa Camp, dirty, weary and heavily loaded with camp equipment—tents, samples and tons of desert dust over everything. It was unfortunate that Dad had to start out the next day with Mr. Howell to see a property north of Fernley—not so long a trip as the day before and in Mr. How-ell's car. They returned about 8 last night and you may know that Dad is some weary from the past two weeks. This morning he started to get the dust off the Dodge and found that something had gone wrong with the gasoline pipe to the generator or some darned thing—anyway he worked on it till 1, got it washed and running. . . .

You will remember that we held four thousand dollars bonds or gold notes which Dad bought some six years ago thru the American Mortgage Co. in LA. They have drawn 8% interest, payable quarterly. The coupon which we cut last month and deposited thru the bank here was returned to the bank with the notation "Interest unpaid". It looks rather serious to us. The bonds were to have matured May 20th next—and we had hoped we would realize that amount to place on our encumbered property here . . . it seems quite certain that they will not redeem the notes. Dad is writing letters to the American Mortgage Co. tonite. . . .

[Mother went on with all the details of the bonds and asked Thor to look into it.]

I made Dale a suit of PJs last week and hope they will reach him about tomorrow. . . . Am sending several letters from him. You'd better be sending back a flock of Dale's letters too—you kids down in LA— the last one we have here on file is dated Jan. 24th. Don't you dare lose any of them—and also how about seeing some of those Pointers which have been coming since Christmas? . . .

Very much love to each of you from all of us,

MOTHER

I wrote a letter to Thor dated April 20, 1931.

Dear Thor,

You can pay for your violent neglect of me by lending me $5 (five) bucks. Can you get this off so that I will have it by Friday? I'm sorry to ask for it, but it is very necessary. I'll pay it back, old horse, never fear. I know you're pinched but it's better to be pinched than penniless. You know the story about "a friend in need. . . ." Unless I get this 'twould be very embarrasing [sic] for me on the choir trip. I have a date and hardly money enough to pay for the taxi. I shouldn't be dating a poor girl!

I'll write you a long letter later, fellow. I must bone some Math now. Thanks much for the anticipated loan. Five will be plenty so don't send more. I'll pay you back this summer.

Yours,

DALE

P.S. Send it in cash—air mail. Never mind registering it.

I wrote home on April 17, 1931.

Dear Folks:

The P.J.s came. They are a great success. When not in use they make good tapistry [sic].

Things are going better. The days are warmer. Leaves are beginning to come out. Days are speeding by. Only 9 days till the Choir trip.

I bought, or rather charged, a very good Kodak. The whole works cost 21 bucks but I believe it's worth it. I'll have some pictures for you soon.

We're reviewing in Frog now. So far I've knocked the lessons for a row and hope to pile up some tenths. The Math is plenty tuff and getting tuffer. I'm still in the 3rd section but will probably drop one soon. Shakespeare in B.S. is a deadbeat. We're reading Antony & Cleopatra. In drills we are still having rifle marksmanship. It's a gripe. We've reviewed it 3 times now and it's very tiresome and boring. I suppose they think it will make us good shots, but to my mind, good shots are made by plenty of shooting, and we have done hardly any.

The Japanese Prince did his good turn, and so no one is walking the Area now. Very, very lucky for the Slugoids. I'll bet they say "God bless the Japanese" every night in their prayers. I got out of two tours on the Area myself. There were about 90 on the Area at the time.

I'm sitting at a very good table now—all interesting and likable fellows. Durfee,* one of the candidates I met at Letterman Hospital in S.F. [when taking the West Point entrance physical exam] is on the table. He's a good dash man.

I'm doing only fairly well in track. I came in 3rd on the Highs, and about second on the High Jump. In gym we're taking the life-saving tests. They are plenty stiff and when I get out of the pool I can hardly walk. One man nearly drowned and had to be pulled out. I feel sorry for some of the poor swimmers—they have a fearful time, but are all game.

---

*Donald Linscott Durfee, from a family of West Pointers, was one of my close friends. Although it was a struggle for him to get through academics, he excelled in almost everything else and was made a cadet lieutenant his first class year. He became a Spanish and Portuguese scholar and spent most of World War II teaching these languages at West Point. When he finally was released for duty with troops, he was given assignments that didn't challenge him and he retired as a colonel in 1962. Nevertheless, he was not embittered by these experiences and he and his charming wife, Thelma, encouraged their two boys to don uniforms. One became a USMA cadet and the other a midshipman at the U.S. Naval Academy.

I get mail regularly from Browny [Frank Brown at Annapolis, my high school friend]. He's doing well there. Ruth seldom writes.

Well, I must dive into some Math. Lots of love,

DALE

This is a letter dated simply "Sunday before reveille." I had finally learned how to spell reveille.

Dear Mother and Dad,

I got your nice long letters yesterday with the cash enclosed. Thanks much.

I was on Guard last nite in the 4th div—first relief. Got inspected twice but didn't get skinned. [At guard inspections we were usually asked to recite our general and special orders.] Afterwards we went to see the last of the movie in the Gym.

I have a date with Ruth for next Saturday afternoon in York. I'll take her to see The New Yorkers and then to dinner, and then put her on a train for home. She's bringing a friend so I'll have to get her a date. We're to meet them in the Astor at 2:00 p.m. I don't know what I'll do in the evening yet.

The Hell Cats are yelling now. Geez they make a lot of unnecessary noise. It's been rumored that we'll have no more reveille soon, but then there's a rumor every month about something. They don't have reveille at Annapolis. [And as I have noted, there is no reveille at West Point today.]

Now it's 6 p.m. This afternoon I went over to M Co and Wally and I wrote for some theater tickets. We also wrote a fellow to get us some dates for the evening. Then there was guard mount and P-rade. That ended the weekend.

Won't be long till the writs start. But I'm not worried, I have plenty of tenths to the good in everything.

I'm doing a bit better in track. Last Sat. I tied for second in the hurdles. All I need is speed—Coach [Leo] Novak says I have good form. Jumped about 5'9"—the standards were at 5'11" but the stick sagged.

I met Duke McEntee's* father yesterday. He's a Colonel and a very wonderful man. Duke is in A Co—a plebe.

*Ducat McEntee was found from our class and turned back to the class of 1935. During World War II he commanded the 541st Parachute Infantry Regiment in the Western Pa-

We get to go to graduation hop. I've signed up for a program and now I'll have to get a date. But where? I've also put in for two Howitzers— one for you and one for me. [Both have been lost.]

Lots of love,

DALE

A letter from Dad was written in Reno, April 22.

Dear Dale—

A little short letter from busy Dad to let you know how happy your two good letters recd today made us, and how we enjoyed the photos you sent. I hope you have a good time in New York on the Choir trip, you will be about ready to go when this reaches you. I don't see though how you can splurge much on the five we sent you. We got another financial shock a few days ago which left us flat except for our houses and an equity in the duplex on Lake St. I had for the past 6 years $4000 invested in real estate bonds of the American Mortgage Co. of Los Angeles. They passed their last interest and now are in the hands of a receiver. I don't expect to get anything out of it at all—they probably were worse than flat when they failed.

But we have our health, a home, a job, many friends, and I am not at all in the dumps. So many worse things can happen than losing some money. I have resolved not to worry any more over finances so long as we keep the main blessings. When we look about us we just can't keep our spirits down!

My work is good and interesting. Yesterday I drove out beyond Yerington to examine a gold mine—worth little as usual—and back home again before 9 p.m. The roads are fine. I am busy writing a State Bulletin on the new Scossa district, a vastly overrated place that will be deserted in a year or two. I have found a mighty good gold prospect to promote, one of real possibilities. I am sending details to Macgregor tonight.

We are having a big snowstorm today. It came on suddenly, and now is about 6 inches deep. What it won't do to all the blossoms now out! Yesterday was like midsummer.

cific Theater and retired as a colonel for disability in 1946. His father, Girard Lindsley McEntee, wrote the lucid and thorough *Military History of The World War*, published in 1937 by Charles Scribner's Sons. It was dedicated to Duke and his brother, Girard Lindsley McEntee III, who graduated from the Naval Academy in 1935.

I hope you have good luck in the writs. As to athletics, your averages in miscellaneous sports are great. Good old Jap prince! I wonder if he knew how glad the area birds were to see him. And now to close and drive down through the snowstorm to get this mailed.

Much love from

DAD

CHAPTER 15 SECOND CHOIR TRIP AND TRACK

The Army loved the cavalry and horses. Throughout history, and particularly after the invention of horseshoes and stirrups, man and horse had been inseparable in war. From the armored knight to the dashing mounted troops of J. E. B. Stuart in the Civil War, the warrior in the saddle was the most romantic of all fighting men. But the handwriting of technology was on the wall even in 1931. The cavalry had shown little usefulness in the Spanish-American War and none on the machine-gun-swept Western Front of World War I.

But traditions die hard. Cavalry officers hypothesized many situations when horses might be useful in modern war. There's a story that when General "Vinegar Joe" Stilwell reported to headquarters after his spectacular retreat from China in World War II, an old cavalry staff officer cleared his throat and asked, "General, did you have any use for horses in China?" "Yes, we did," responded Vinegar Joe, "and mighty tasty, too."

But in my day at West Point it was still the privilege of senior officers to ride horses while the troops marched. In fact, officers were encouraged to keep private mounts and were provided a government allowance to do so. As today, the "horsy set" were people of wealth, and having a good seat in the saddle was the mark of a gentleman.

So it is not surprising that cadets were well drilled in riding. As one of the following letters reveals, that spring we began our training in the Riding Hall and continued it for the next three years until we were all fully capable of taking our places in a cavalry troop. We enjoyed the drill and it's kind of sad that the course has finally been discontinued.

I wrote home April 23, 1931.

Dear Mother and Dad—

Just day-after-tomorrow will be my big day. Things certainly look great.

Last Monday I had a drag. Jimmy Walsh pulled a bunch of us into Wilson's room, as we were coming in from drill, and recruited 4 of us to drag the femmes who came up with his O.A.O. They were nice fems, ranging from about 2.0 to 3.0. I drew about a 2.1, but she was educated and pleasant. We walked up to Delafield Pond and down by the Chapel. By that time first call for supper had sounded and we said goodby.

Night before last, at about 9 p.m. we were startled by a shot in the Area which really was only a firecracker. I looked out my window and saw the O.C. in the guard house rush out onto the poopdeck. In a minute he put on his hat and sword and was off to war. He called out the guard, and they rushed here and there asking who fired the shot. It was big business—the Area was full of running men. Then someone came to our door and said, "The O.C. wants to see the occupants of this room immediately." John and I felt like seasoned criminals as we climbed into our best dress grey and ran over to the Guard House. But the O.C. was jiggered—we didn't do it. So he was left with a baffling mystery. We commented upon the O.C.'s (Joe-Joe was the O.C.) remarkable detection of sound direction.

I visited Ed Weber in D Co. before call to quarters tonite. He keeps a good A book with many of the same pictures that I have sent home. Be sure to save them all.

I have a good (believe it or not) soiree now. Before meal formations I call off the minutes before assembly. They used to ring bells but have discontinued that. Therefore, I don't have to be in ranks till assembly and get out of the inspection by the corporal.

Wednesday we had a track meet with Newburgh High. It was very impromptu—I didn't know about it until I got on the field. They had no high hurdle men so we didn't run them. I took a third in the high jump. Moorman,* Army, jumped 5'10", a Newburgh man jumped 5'9" and I

---

*Richard R. "Dick" Moorman from Kirksville, Missouri, became one of my good friends. He won major "As" in both basketball and track. On yearling furlo I joined a group of classmates from M Company, who with tongue in cheek called themselves "The Virgins." We bought a model B Ford touring car on time to drive to our respective homes across the country. Then we turned it in to the dealer on return from furlo. One of the Virgins was Dick Moorman, and we enjoyed a delightful sojourn with Dick's mother in

Summer camp: the horse cavalry still played a symbolic role in West Point life. From 1934 *Howitzer*.

did 5′8″. I believe I can do a lot better, however. All of these jumps were over the Plebe record of 5′7″.

    Love,

      DALE

Kirksville. Dick chose the Coast Artillery but was transferred to Field Artillery and saw action in the European Theater during World War II. He also saw combat in Korea and was awarded the Legion of Merit and Air Medal. Later he became an expert in missiles and air defense, winning two Commendation Medals.

    William M. "Bill" Gross was from Salina, Kansas. He was the oldest and unofficial leader of The Virgins. Bill captained the fencing team and proudly carried the colors first class year. After graduation we became roommates in Flying School at Kelly Field. A superb pilot and fearless leader, he was the first of The Virgins to see combat in World War II, and as a wing commander in England he was the first classmate to wear the stars of a brigadier general. Bill was decorated with two Silver Stars, three Distinguished Flying Crosses, a Bronze Star, four Air Medals, and a Purple Heart.

    Ken Kenerick, John Hutchison, and Artie Meier were three other Virgins. All but Dick started Flying School at Randolph Field, Texas, but Ken and Artie washed out. Ken's home in Columbus, Ohio, was the first stop on our furlo odyssey, and his mother gave us a memorable welcome. After leaving Flying School, Ken returned to the Infantry and a distinguished career, which was cut short as I've noted by a fatal helicopter crash in Greenland.

    Artie resigned. John M. "Hutch" Hutchison was from Coeur d'Alene, Idaho. He had played varsity tackle for Army. John organized and commanded one of the first air navigation schools during the war and held many important command and staff positions fol-

I wrote Thor April 26, 1931.

Dear Thor,

Thanks for the 5 spot, old man. It got here a day late, but that was my fault, not yours. However, I managed to make out all right and enjoyed the trip pretty much.

I met Ruth and her friend Mary Lou Black about 2:15 at the Woodstock Hotel (where a lot of us stayed) and with them and another Kaydet, went to see The New Yorkers. It was a riot. Not too risqué to be dirty but enough to give it ginger. It was raining all the while, so afterwards we took a cab to a restaurant on 72nd street that Ruth knew of and had dinner. Then we bummed around; went to the new Globe building and saw their huge mechanical world in the lobby. Finally we put the girls on the subway and said goodby. Ruth asked me to come out and stay with her and I'm sorry now that I didn't even though she did have a date for the evening. The rest of my evening went phft. I'd planned to spend it with Wollaston. We went to see Girl Crazy, which was another review not quite as good as The New Yorkers, but plenty entertaining. Then we were broke except for enough to get cockeyed. We could have had a hell of a good time doing this and then riding double decker busses, going up in the high buildings, visiting Arabian restaurants etc. But Wally backed out and so we walked the streets in the rain for hours waiting for something to break. But nothing broke—nothing ever does when you're sober.

The evening was saved by my phone call to Mother and Dad. That was a thrill indeed. I went to bed with pleasant dreams.

Yours,

DALE

Mother typed a letter dated Sunday afternoon, April 26.

Dearest Dale,

It was a wonderful thrill to hear your voice last night—it was clear enough to seem good and natural—but dim and indistinct too—at

---

lowing, including membership on the Military Staff Commission at Panmunjon after the Korean war. He was awarded the Legion of Merit and retired as a brigadier general.

To defray expenses The Virgins took along Joseph O. Killian from Manson, Washington, as a paid passenger. Joe ranked high in our class and joined the Corps of Engineers. He saw combat in Africa, Sicily, and Italy in World War II and was awarded two Legion of Merits and two Bronze Stars.

times— The least little rustle of noise by the side of me was enough for me to lose what you were saying. We were terribly disappointed to have you call so late. There was a big party on at the State Bldg. Jean and I were there. Dad came for us just before 10—and Jean left in the middle of a dance to hurry home to get here by 10 so we would not miss you. Drew had been in all day with a bad cold—but he took a big nap in the aft so he could stay up. Each one of us picked our position, Drew was to be with me downstairs—Dad at the telephone upstairs and Jean was at Hill's telephone, so we could all be on the line at the same time. Jean fell asleep. I was the only one who heard the bell—I called upstairs to waken them and no one wakened but Dad and instead of picking up the phone there he came downstairs. When I turned the phone over to him I went upstairs but Jean was so dead tired she didn't waken. Drew wakened just as we were saying goodby. This morning when Jean realized she had missed hearing you she cried. She had been out the night before to a party and had worked all day and so was very tired—I can understand how you were making the most of every minute but you should have tried to keep your appointment for 1 to 1:30 for the call.

[Mother was so right and should have done more than slap my hand for this negligence. Apparently I was walking the streets aimlessly in the rain with Wally.]

Must stop and go to work. Much love from us all,

MOTHER

I wrote home April 27, 1931.

Dearest Mother and Dad,

Our phone conversation certainly was a big thrill for me. You sounded like you were across the street. I should have phoned earlier, but didn't get the chance. In case you didn't hear all I said, I'll go over my talk again:

I met Ruth. . . . She brought a friend along, and Darrah,* another Kaydet, dragged her.

---

*Relaxed and soft-spoken, John W. Darrah, Jr., was from an Army family. He played football four years at the Academy but didn't quite have the beef to make his letter. During the big war he fought in Indochina and China and became military advisor to Chiang Kaishek. He also fought in the Korean War. He suffered a heart attack in 1954 and was retired later for physical disability, having been awarded three Legion of Merits during his service.

The show was a riot—Warings Pennsylvanians and the three Waring Sisters were in it. Love for Sale, Where Have You Been, and other hits originated there. . . . Ruth looked stunning and was very nice. It looks as if I'm getting back in there.

In the evening Wally and I went to see Girl Crazy. We were too broke to do anything else. Bidin' My Time, I've Got Rhythm [sung by Ethel Merman, whose unbelievably sustained loud note made her famous] and other hits were its attraction. . . .

It rained continually and we were all in raincoats. Many people thought us policemen. But Tony, my bootlegger, recognized me. We went there to get some medicinal whiskey to keep from catching cold. I drank very little, however; only two shots. My great sin was to smoke a few cigarettes—I didn't even get a kiss the whole trip.

While I was in the lobby of the theater in the evening someone asked me how long the intermission was. He thought I was an usher. I heard of a lady asking a Kaydet where the woman's room was. He said, "I don't know, Madame, I've never been there."

New York is truly one hell of a city. 50% unemployed. Next time I'm going out to New Rochelle and stay with Ruth. She's asked me to several times, but I've always thought the bright lights were more important.

I think Ruth will be up for the Graduation Ball. We get to go to that—we'll be recognized then. She's coming up before then, too.

We stayed at the Woodstock right near Times Square on 43rd St. I phoned you from my room. Sorry I had to reverse the charges, but they only gave us $10 this time.

We got up at 11 a.m. (at 2 a.m. the clocks were set ahead because of daylight saving time) and went up to Columbia University. We had a terrible time getting there too. They make no attempt to direct you. We were told to "follow the green lights". We did, but they took a V shape and we followed one branch to a subway platform where the cars would have taken us to the Battery. So we went back and tried the other branch. This took us back to the street. Finally we used our own judgment ("we" was Wally and me) and took an Uptown train, for we knew Columbia was at 116th St. We found out when at 96th St. that we had to change trains. Wally got out but the door shut in my face. I've since learned that it is only necessary to put out your hand to stop the mechanical sliding doors, and then the train won't start—all automatic. Well, I went on to the next station and then came back. I met Wally at the Sigma Nu house where we had planned to go. Before this, however,

I thought I'd try to find the Chapel. I asked not less than 20 people and none knew. The world is going to hell. In my wandering I took a look at General Grant's stone box, which is near the campus.

The Sigma Nus at Columbia are a fine bunch. They treated us like brothers. They had a hop the night before and we kicked ourselves for not going up. We ate free at the Columbia Grill and finally got into the buttons and went to Church. Their's is a very small chapel. We had a hard time finding seats.

We had to rush to get to Wehauken [sic] in time—6:30 was the deadline. We got home at 8 and it was still light because of the new time. [According to tradition we again sang under the clock tower in the Area of Central Barracks before breaking up.]

I got very little studying done and was going to stay up after taps. John said the writ wasn't going to be tuff, so I hit the pillow for some needed sleep.

Today I knocked the writ for at least a 2.7 and would have made a 3.0 if I'd known that the parallel latitudes begin at 0 degrees at the equator instead of at the North Pole.

Then we finished up on the life-saving work. Only a few of us were left (proficient) so it didn't take long. I think I maxed it.

Well, I've spent my only free hour on this and it's about dinner time. Lots of love to you all,

DALE

I wrote to Thor and Mary on April 29, 1931.

Dear Thor and Mary,

These writs every day are a grind unequaled, and on top of them comes the "Spring buck-up". However I have a few minutes now to continue some of the dope about New York.

Let's see; yeah, the subways. They are typical of New York. Gad what a network of tunnels. You go down through one of the unnoticeable doors on the street and immediately find yourself in an underground city. If it wasn't for the dirtiness of everything you would think you were in some futuristic city of Atlantis. But it isn't a bit pretty. The floors were originally concrete, but now they have an almost even layer of chewing gum on them. It would be easy to become lost because some of the downtown stations are huge. In order to get into the station proper you must drop a nickel in one of the lines of turnstiles, and then push your way thru it. You can then travel on every one of the subways in the city, or under the city. Every place is well lighted, even the miles of tunnels have strings of lights thru them. You feel as if you really weren't underground, but only as if it were nighttime. Every ten blocks there are large stations. The express trains boom up to them at a fearful speed and all the doors open as soon as it stops. During the rush hours people cram and push with no consideration for anyone but themselves. The trainmen sometimes have to push them all in so that they can shut the doors. It is worse than a load of cattle, and would be a pick-pocket's paradise if there were any pockets to pick. Truly, it's an awful rabble. Not one out of ten of the passengers would you care to know, and many of them are repulsive. It is easy to see how O. O. McIntire gets all his material for writing.

Well, my time is up and I won't have another minute for at least three days. This place is certainly hard to endure but there are only 43 more days of hell.

Lots of love,
DALE

A letter from Dad was dated April 30.

Dear Dale—
Tomorrow you will begin your last month of Plebe year—the days are passing fast. We enjoyed your last letter so much and the pictures. Your camera has a good lens and before long you will learn how to use it to get best results. . . .

I enjoy my new work very much, and will like it even better as I become accustomed to it. A fellow came in and was calling me "Professor" yesterday, made me feel funny.

We are glad you had a good time in N.Y. with the choir, and are more glad about the nice times you have coming this summer at the Point. Then the military regime will be tempered with much recreation and pleasure. Long ere this the novelty of West Point for you has passed; duties are becoming fixed habits, and as such are easier. Yet the hand of the grim old mother will never leave the shoulder of a cadet while he is there, and she so trains him that few indeed care to leave the service for civilian life.

The desire to come to West Point grows on me. There are very few good Americans who do not wish to see the place. There is something to be said about that cradle of so many of our great men that makes men feel better when they see it and have watched the boys drill. It's the "long grey line" of the past they see. Pickett, Grant, Lee—an endless parade, and the feeling of security and pride about what is best in us and our country.

Well, I am sleepy as usual and must go to bed

Much love from

DAD

I wrote home on May 2, 1931.

Dearest Mother and Dad:

I'm awfully sorry about phoning late last Saturday. I would have loved to say hello to Jean and Bud. I thought it would be best to wait till your midnight because I didn't have enough money to pay for the call and had to reverse the charges. As it is, I understand that by reversing the charges you must pay the full rate. But that was my call and my idea, so I want you to let me know what the bill was and I'll send you the money this summer. Also, will arrange it so that we can talk again next summer. If you phone me it would be legal.

I maxed a math writ this morning. I needed to because I know I went dee on one last week.

I get out of S.I. today. We have a track meet with some high school. I'm going to enter in the high jump, high hurdles and broad jump.

We had our track tests—the whole class, part of the Gym tests—a few days ago and I made 114 points out of a possible 120. One other man in the class got 114, but this is the highest I've heard of. I think it's the highest in the class. Last summer during beast barracks I made 98, so I have improved. I maxed the standing broad-jump at 9′4″ (remember when I did 6′3¾″ in the 6th grade and won a ribbon for first place?) and the running broad on my first jump at 19′ (18′ was the max on points) and I maxed the high jump. I ran the hundred in 11.1 sec and put the shot 39′ which lost me my 6 points. All of these tests, you understand, were taken in tennis shoes, trousers and jersies [sic], no one (except the lucky ones like me) had had any track practice. That's why all the maxes for the different events were so low.

But the running broad jump surprised me and I'm going to take a try at it this afternoon. I might be really good at something.

The writs are a fearful grind. Last night John and I pulled our beds out [of the alcoves] and studied in our beds for an hour after taps, shielding the light from our desk lamps with a blanket. It was the first time we did this but I guess it was worth it.

The tactics class of Saturday morning now is taken up with Cavalry. We march down to the riding hall and saddle, bridle and mount the ponies. We also "stand mount" which is a military way of standing at attention with a horse. I like it; it's all very interesting and sometimes uproariously funny especially when somebody gets policed [thrown].

[One day as we rode around the hall bareback with my wild animal in the lead, he shied and threw me. I lay on my back and kicked frantically as the herd galloped over me. Not a hoof touched me, although I connected with some equine bellies. When the riding instructor finally stopped the charge he carefully examined my horse before asking if I were hurt.

[At the beginning of the riding class all the plebes milled around searching for good mounts, asking the horse handlers about them. The standard reply was, "They're all good horses!" and this became a traditional remark in our class whenever any comparison was asked for.

[I always seemed to end up with "Steamboat," a vicious little gelding remount that had a hatred for cadets and me in particular. But he was fast and sturdy and he taught me how to stay in the saddle, even though we never achieved much mutual affection.]

Artillery is over now except the practice work we will do in the summer. I am a first class gunner, and will be getting a medal for it some day. Pretty nearly everybody got it.

Our weekday drill periods till June will be taken up with just plain close order infantry drill. We have nine of them, and nobody is piping it.

We went to reveille in dress grey coats yesterday morning for the first time. I guess we'll be putting the overcoats away before long, We don't go into white until June 1st.

I think Ruth will be up for the Grad. Ball, but I can fix it up for Elizabeth [Hawkins, who planned to visit West Point] if she comes. I'd be happy to take her myself if Ruth doesn't come. I'll write to her.

I was surely sorry to hear about the tough break with your bond in L.A. I guess everything has gone to smash in this panic. But plenty have lost much more than we have, so we oughtn't to feel too bad.

Did you get the pictures—the big one—that I sent? When it comes, it's supposed to be for May 10th [Mother's Day].

Well, I guess I should catch a little sleep. I have to do my best this aft.

Lots of love,

DALE

An undated portion of a letter to Thor and Mary had this to say:

Last nite Alden Sibley came over and we went to the show together. It was a lousy picture, at least it was made lousy for us because the chumps who run them never can get the sound devices to work so that we can hear the dialogue. But we had a good time B.S.ing about Nevada. Elizabeth Hawkins is going to be up here for June week and we were figuring how to drag her. I guess it won't be much trouble to get drags for her if she's as charming as she used to be in Reno.

[In this letter I also told them how I did at the meet:]

I only got a 3rd in the high jump. They didn't run the high hurdles. I entered the broad jump but because I didn't have my stride markers I hit the mark only once and fouled the other 5 jumps. My one jump gave me a 4th.

I wrote home on May 4, 1931.

Dearest Mother and Dad,

No, I wasn't slamming the loud P.J.s. They are just what I wanted. Everyone tries to outdo the other here in violent colored shorts and P.J.s. They are the only colored things we can have, and it helps to haze the tacs.

P-rades and drills now on weekdays. They are a big soiree, but it's a good sign of spring. Only 8 more drills.

I went 13 tenths pro in the writs last week and am plenty safe. On the last two I got nearly 3.0's. I'm pro in the Frog general reviews too so it looks as if I'll be here another year at least.

The first class is away on an Ordnance trip for about 3 days. The second class are big shots now, and they make a success out of tying everything up royally. One thing, we have a big stack of records from the 1st class room across the hall.

I guess college is just about out and everyone is looking for jobs back home. Well, I won't have to find one this summer. Sib gave me a lot of dope about summer camp. We go on a hike up to Popolopen again, and have a big battle with all the trimmings. It's called "The Battle of the Torn". The Torn is a high mountain near Popolopen Camp.

Well, I'd better get to work on a term theme to be handed in tomorrow. One nice thing, term themes here are only 500 words. They at least realize that we don't have time to write more.

Lots of love,

DALE

Dad wrote on Monday, May 4.

Dear Dale—

Day before yesterday there was an auction sale of cars here by the Coverston Motor Co. and Mother and I went down to it and bid on a Viking 8 sedan for $550, a big very finely finished 8 window car. Our contract for it cost $225 cash and $52 per month. When we get it all paid it will amount to $630. Yesterday we drove up the Geiger grade and around to Carson, 100 miles. It runs nicely but only makes about 9 miles to the gallon and has about 60 miles speed when pushed. Today Mother was out trading again—wants a lighter car that will burn less gas. She found that Coverston refused $750 for the Viking less than a month ago and she can probably sell the contract to the same man if he is around. I rather favor keeping the car, it's such a beauty—but I want her to be satisfied. She is out to Eastern Star tonight—I tried to get her to take the old Dodge and save gas—but *nothing doing!*

The new job goes fine. I also have another mining deal brewing—one never can tell when a better future will come. I haven't lost a minute of sleep or even felt badly about the probable loss of all our savings by the failure of the American Mortgage Co. of L.A. Thousands of wiser men than I lost every cent in some kind of business venture during the past year. Ma and I are really happier than we have been for a good while— we have so many blessings. Our Dale is doing finely at West Point— many a wealthy father would give his all to see his son there—usually a son not worth his salt. Jean and Drew are doing well and happy—so are Thor and Mary. We eat, sleep, work, have many friends and a comfortable home. Now really, if we are happy, can life give us any more than that?

The town is jammed with people all the time, some are just curious sightseers—some come to gamble, some are divorcees—hotels are full, houses in demand again. Wonder if it will last, and if it will do business any real good?

We received your nice picture of the Corps. The glass was broken but twas insured so we'll get it fixed all right. Mother wants a picture of you in uniform. It ought to be easier this summer when you are a Yearling. . . .

Much love from Dad who hopes you'll knock the final writs for a big loop.

I wrote home May 7, 1931.

Dearest Folks,

Message from the firing line to Battery Commanders: "Still pro and firing steadily."

I ranked 20 in gym this time. If it hadn't been for the 77% I got in apparatus I'd have been up in the money. I maxed nearly everything else, including the life-saving. I'll have to take some details as life guard at Delafield pond this summer for those extra 15 points.

Got my white cap today. It won't be long now.

I think I'll deadbeat June week and get my nose fixed. It's so bad now that I can't use it, and I don't know any better time to have the operation. I'll get out of the principle hell and be back in time for recognition.

I'm doing better in track. I have a step measured off with the two checks on it for the broad jump, and I'll surely place in the next meet. We had a tryout in the highs Wednesday and I nearly won. I got a very poor start and could see everyone else go over the first hurdle before I left the ground. Gosh it was fun; after that I ran like the devil and just barely skinned the top of the sticks. When I had passed the first man it gave me such a thrill that I passed them all but the winner and was only about a couple of inches behind him at the finish. I hope I can win the next race we have. This was my third high-hurdle race.

This spring buck-up is giving me a lot of demerits. I have a flock of them already and they count a lot towards a make. I'm not so sure of being a make after all.

Well, goodby. I have to write a thank-you letter for an English theme now.

Lots of love,
DALE

P.S. I got your letter, Dad, telling about the new Viking. I think Mother is right—9 miles to the gallon and only 60 mph are negative qualities. Don't put money into another Chalmers. [When I was in junior high, Dad bought a huge secondhand touring car, a Chalmers, and it hardly ever ran.] The Viking isn't a very standard make—I think the Jameson's Graham Page is the thing. The family is small now—a small car will give you better service in every way. Love, DALE

I wrote home again on May 9.

Dearest Dad and Mother,

Schenectady (I'd better write that down before I forget how to spell it) was the high school we had a meet with today. We won. The A squad beat Boston College also. This last is the school Jimmy Walsh graduated from.

In the highs I was right up in the money, not first, but close in—until the next-to-last stick. We hadn't had much time to warm up, and on about the 7th and 8th hurdle I was kicking splinters off of them with my right spikes. At the 9th I hit it square and nearly fell in the wreckage. But I scrambled around and by a miracle got over the last stick. I finished 4th, I think.

I was feeling pretty low because of this. I'd been counting on some points there. You see, this is my last chance to make a numeral. Not that it amounts to much, but I've been just jiggered out of one twice, in football and in boxing, by a hairs width each time, and I wanted to cinch it in track.

The next event was the high-jump, and I played in the luck. Moorman was a bit off form, and we tied for second at 5′7″. It was won at 5′8″. This gave me 2 points. Not enough. I had to make five points today to bring my average up to 3 points a meet.

Well, I played in the luck in the broad jump too, and hit the mark every time but once, when I went over. I won this event at 19′ 6¾″. I know I can do better than this, too. 5 points plus 2 equals 7, plus one last Saturday equals 8. One point to go for the numeral. I hope I don't break a leg next week, but I probably will.

This is all a lot about nothing, but I haven't anything else to write. Ah yes, I'm still plenty pro, but I'm not gaining any files on my grades. I'll have to do better. 3 more weeks of writs. 33 days till recognition.

Got out of S.I. again today. It's been a month now since I've been to one. I feel like a privileged character. Won't go next Saturday either.

Everything is rosy now. Summer has come and everyone is happy.

Lots of love,

DALE

Dad wrote on Monday, May 11.

Dear Dale:

Your good letter and photos came today and we have greatly enjoyed both. . . . I think your idea of having your proboscis fixed up June week is good, if it doesn't tie you up so long that you will miss Recognition and the Grad Ball. That would be too bad for those are high lights at the Academy. You are surely doing wonderful in all around athletics and that counts for a lot there.

Today was Commencement here. Some 128 grads. I was slated to parade and sit on the platform with the dignitaries and profs, but having no engineer's hood I passed it up. I think I'll have to get a hood—I like the colors—orange and others.

We would have liked to see you run that hurdle race—I'll bet you just scared some of those runts to death. They didn't want to be run down by a big moose on a rampage and so just naturally got out of your way.

A wonderful run to the lake in the new Viking—it just floats along. Made about 12 miles to the gallon, has fast pickup. So far I like it very much. Mother needs a big car. She always fills it up with people and things wherever we go—it was loaded to the guards on the trip to the lake—5 kids, supplies and ourselves! It's a General Motors car and far from dead. For that matter, aren't *all* 1929 cars dead? None are being manufactured anymore.

Much love from

DAD

Mother wrote Tuesday evening, May 12.

Dearest Dale,

We have enjoyed your nice letter with the second batch of pictures. . . .

I am glad you plan to have your nose fixed. How many days will it take you into the hospital? . . . Is Yearling deadbeat between June 11th and

July 1st when the new plebes arrive? . . . How I wish I could have seen you in the high hurdle race. You will win the next one.

What do you mean the "spring buckup is giving you demerits"? What are the demerits for? Won't you have to walk the area to walk them off? [Demerits were never "walked off." You carried them on your record to the grave. But if a cadet acquired over a certain limit he then had to walk the Area as a punishment—one hour for each excess demerit.]

I talked with Mrs. Hawkins this morning. A few days ago she got a telg. saying "Your son Carson was operated on this aft for appendicitis, etc." The teleg. this a.m. said he was doing fine. She thinks he will be able to graduate OK but they are leaving tomorrow morning to drive back there. Elizabeth cannot leave until May 22 and will go on by train. I told her that you had written that you would be glad to see her—hope you have written to her—she is at Stanford University. She is eager to go to West Point—The Lockmans are not going to Annapolis—Frank says they cannot afford it—all their stocks are still dropping. Mrs. L would like to go anyway but it seems Frank won't give her the money. Bill [Parsons] has to report to San Diego June 15th, also Carson, for a month of training in aviation, after which they come home for 6 weeks and after that they report to the USS Nevada.

Yesterday was Commencement Day. I was surprised to see that Jean Hughes, Clarence Jones, Marvin Humphrey, Rose Mahana were all graduated. Just 4 years ago that Thor finished and one more year and you would have finished if you had remained here. . . .

Bob Merriman has brought over all his belongings which he cannot put in a trunk—Tux, overcoats, uniform, ski boots, etc. and we have stored them for him for the summer. He went to Hawthorne yesterday to look for work and says he will be back about June 15th to go to military Summer Camp.

Much love dear and best luck,
   MOTHER

I wrote home on May 16, 1931.

Dear Folks,
   I haven't much to report. The writs are hitting us harder now but I'm still going pro. It's a terrible strain, however, and I'd like to hide somewhere till June. They don't make the writs short enough to finish them in the required time. Sometimes I finish but I rarely have a chance to

check my work and sometimes don't even get the last question started. After each writ I feel like going home and piling into bed. They make us work under fire around here—at everything.

Tomorrow is our last track meet. I must get to bed early tonite. To hell with the writs.

We have "doughboy" drill on the Plain now twice a week. Not a bit fun. [I got crawled unmercifully at these drills, particularly by the upperclassmen from other companies. Some resented the fact that plebes on the corps squads were so often excused.]

Lots of love to you all,

DALE

There must be a letter missing because nothing is said in the next letter about the last plebe track meet on May 16 with New Utrecht High, which would give me a chance to get my numerals. I must have picked up the point I needed, however, for the *Howitzer* notes that I was awarded the coveted numerals.

CHAPTER **16** RECOGNITION

Plebe year was drawing to a close. It was just days away and the long-dreamed-of Recognition dominated our thoughts. Nothing else in life at this time could have seemed important.

My next letter was dated May 24.

Dear Folks,

The writs are over and I'm about one hundred tenths pro on them. But best of all, Allie Povall whom I've been helping is also pro. Pro by about two or three tenths. It was a hard fight for him but worth it. John Lawlor put Neilson* pro also—by one tenth! Pretty close.

Today we had some real fun. Allie and I signed up for a canoe and went paddling on the Hudson. It was windy and rough, but that made it even more fun. We almost swamped several times when the waves from a river craft struck us.

Last week we were thrilled by an Autogyro. It lit on the parade ground and only rolled about ten feet. It can land almost vertically and it takes off at a fearful angle. Sometimes when it's in the air it doesn't seem to move at all. It can come straight [I finally learned how to spell

---

*As I noted earlier, Allie Povall didn't make it through yearling year, but Hank Neilson survived and graduated. Serious and conscientious Henry Neilson, from Alaska, commanded a battalion in World War II and led it from the beaches of Normandy to within sixty miles of Berlin. He also commanded a regiment in the Korean War and later advised the Republic of Korea army. Hank had much to do with the development of the M-16 rifle, now the standard infantry weapon. He was decorated with two Silver Stars, three Bronze Stars, the Legion of Merit, the Purple Heart, and the Commendation Ribbon. After retirement he took up citrus farming near McAllen, Texas.

"straight"] down and land at less speed than a man in a parachute. It's a queer looking thing—like some big insect.

I had some x-rays taken of my nose this morning. I don't know what they will do to it. I haven't much choice in the matter, I guess.

Lots of love,

DALE

Mary typed a letter to me on May 25, 1931.

Dearest Dale:

I like kisses . . . especially great big expressive ones from West Point with you as the sender such as your last letter brought. I am not quite as apt to draw them . . . been out of practice too long I guess . . . but with the typewriter's help perhaps this !!!!%%%%????!!!! will put across what I mean until I can deliver in person.

Had a yen to talk to you today so I am foregoing lunch, washing dishes, making bed and no end of things just to have a little chat with my big brudder way out in Neau Yawk. . . .

You have been DOING THINGS Dale and may I add my congratulations to those which you no doubt have already piled high on your desk. . . .

Sorry the fiver arrived too late for your use in the N. Y. jaunt. It might have helped to brighten the evening after Ruth left you. We certainly are piping a glimpse of that ace high femme. . . .

Right in front of me as I write stands a little pink bed all beflowered with roses and whatnots. In it soon will squirm a little something which will probably rival the pinkness of the bed. If IT'S a boy, Thor predicts that he will chew all the pink paint off the bed. . . . but what could I do, I couldn't buy a navy blue bed, a brown one or even an orange one could I?

And while we're on the subject Pod Sten—my Alpha Chi chum who took my place at the News Pilot sends these clippings . . .

Due to an error, Mr. and Mrs. Ankrum, 104 West Healy Street, are the parents of a girl born Thursday morning at the Mercy Hospital, instead of Mr. and Mrs. Everett Ankin.—Champaign (Ill.) News Gazette.

The comment is: "Must have been sloppy thinking." Pod adds "Thinking up a name like Diane might cause something like that, you

know!" By the way, we think we'll call it "Barbara Diane" if it's a girl.
. . . If a boy "Thor Merritt Smith" has it . . . with a Jr. added, of course.
Here's another of Pod's prize clippings:

James A. Chapin is the proud father of triplets, two sons and a daughter, born to Mrs. T. M. McRay, wife of Thomas McRay. All are reported doing fine. —Uhrichsville (O) Evening Chronicle.

With the comment from Pod: All except possibly Mr. Thomas McRay.
Thor has been whooping it up at the office . . . his boss calls him the "fair haired boy" . . . no doubt he'll be a 30,000 dollar a year man soon. No foolin' I mean it. . . .

Our love to you Dale, we think of you often and are piping the time when we can have some fun together again.

MARY

My next letter home was dated Friday, May 29, 1931.

Dearest Mother and Dad,

It won't be long now. The upperclassmen are certainly making up for lost time. This place is a second beast barracks but we don't care much. Wednesday is our last day of academics and we go to camp on the 6th, Saturday (I think). The first class is all through. They are playing around here all the time and haven't any call-to-quarters. Many trunks are being packed and sent.

The Yearlings are reaching a maximum volume with their yells of "Yea Furlo" which they have been crying ever since Christmas. Sometimes a crowd of them gather around the Area clock to yell it.

"Thanks to You" is the big song hit here now. It's beautiful. Have you heard it?

Ruth isn't coming up for the Grad. Ball. She says her writs will be on then. To hell with her—she shouldn't have consented in the first place. Now I'm left with my hands in my pockets. I hope Elizabeth will come. I've written her.

The Doc doesn't want to fix my nose so I'll continue breathing through my mouth. I'm not so hot about an operation anyhow. It will probably get smashed up a few more times in the next three years.

The air fleet of 500 odd planes flew over here a few days ago. It was a wonderful sight and I took a flock of pictures. Some of them flying high

Report of Delinquencies, Co. "A ," United States Corps of Cadets

For......June 7th..................1934.

NAME	OFFENSE	REPORTING OFFICER	D.	C.	P. T.
	FIRST CLASS				
*Dany	Absent at posting of punishment squad, 1:30 p.m. 7th inst.	Lt. Cole	5		
Smith D.O.	Walking hand in hand with young lady in vicinity of Guard tents, about 11:50 a.m. 6th inst. (Held report of June 6th.)	Lt. Keyes	5	5	
*Stewart, A.J.	Holding hands with young lady while walking in the vicinity of Washington Monument, 12:00 noon, 7th inst.	Lt. Lystad	5	5	
*Walsh, J.E.	Card not accounting for absence at 3:30 p.m. 7th inst.	Lt. Cole,	2		
	SECOND CLASS				
Ellerson	Late at breakfast formation, 8th inst.	Harris	1		
*Glassford	Destroying property, i.e., dropping a chair off the balcony of Cullum Hall during a hop, 7th inst.	Rogers	5		

formed a huge "A" meant for us. Others formed an "AC" for Air Corps. The sky was filled with them and it took eight minutes for all to pass.

We go into white on Monday. It's about time, for it's plenty hot now.

I enjoyed Dad's letter from the field. I'm glad you are all happy. From the pictures you sent I see that Jean has certainly grown up. She is very pretty too, and I know she'll enjoy her three years in Reno High.

Tell me something about Dode. [Another nickname for Drew.] I suppose he's piping vacation.

Lots of love,

DALE

P.S. Tomorrow is a holiday for us [Memorial Day]. We get Saturday night privileges tonite. I got skinned yesterday for "looking out of an Area window in improper uniform, 7.30 a.m." Wouldn't that take a prize? My own window too and I had a shirt on. Evidently we must wear dress coats to look out the window. D.S.

A letter dated May 31, 1931, came from Jean.

Dear Dale,

I received my birthday letter from you and enjoyed it so much. . . .

I have been doing so many things of interest. One thing I think you will be interested in is that I was initiated into the Honor Society last Tuesday. You have to have an average of 90 for two semesters before they will take you in. They had us frightened to death telling us they would feed us red peppers and soap candy. There is nothing to it except the honor of graduating with a badge. . . .

We went on a picnic last Friday. We had so much fun . . . our cooking teacher went too. She is a swell swimmer and we had so much fun diving and ducking each other. Mother came and went in too. . . .

I suppose mother has told you we went to the lake last Sunday. We took Miss Moe, my cooking, sewing and algebra teachers. Mother wanted to take some young people along so I asked my favorites. They took off their "teach manners" and played baseball with us. We had lots of fun, eating, dancing and teaching the teachers how to shoot rubber bands they had taken away from the kids. . . .

With lots of love,

JEAN

A carbon copy arrived of a letter Mother wrote on June 3.

To my dearest All,

A letter from Dale enclosed came yesterday. Everything is OK with him except his nose. I wish he had gone more into detail as to the doctor's opinion. Wonder if we will have to write the doctor. If Dale cannot breathe thru his nose at all why should the doctor say he does not want to operate. . . . [I had exaggerated, something one should never do with concerned parents, for I could breathe easily through one nostril.]

How wonderful it must have been to see that air fleet pass over West Point, Dale—I am sorry you are disappointed in Ruth again, and surely hope Elizabeth gets there. Hope you wrote to her at Annapolis in care of Carson.

Dode went to the park with us yesterday. He found a bird with an injured wing on the river bank and RESCUED it—hero—and kept it in the car all evening and brought it home and is keeping it on the back porch—and the cat's down in the cellar. . . .

Much love to you all—

MOTHER

I wrote home June 3, 1931.

Dearest Folks,

The song for today is, "Just One More Time." Tomorrow is the last day of academics. The departments don't let up a bit even though the writs are over. But we do. The studying I have done this week has been to read 300 pages of the Vicomte de Bragelonne. And yet in math this morning I maxed it. Geez, I'm beginning to think I'm hivy. But we're having solid analytical geometry now and all it is is adding a "z" to the "x" and "y"s of plane analyt—frightfully easy.

The Corps is in white now. The white trou are much cooler and more comfortable but we must be very careful not to get them dirty and have to take them off when we enter our room, for we can't sit down in them. Also we can't take them off alone—spoils them—our roommates must "drag" them.

Friday we go back to company tables and will suffer 6 days of starvation. We will also be barred from the boodlers, so how about sending some cookies to tide me over the drought? [Today the plebes are banished to Camp Buckner and eat comfortably during Graduation Week, which is now the end of May.]

June week has practically begun. Yesterday there was a horse show which was my idea of nothing at all. Just a lot of nags jumping over four fences. . . .

We move to camp Friday. I'm going to room with Thompson, G.C., Cleary, and Fields,* four to a tent. They are three fine fellows and we'll have a great time this summer.

Well, I can't think of anything more. I hope you will have a good summer too, and that Thor gets to come up to Tahoe on his vacation.

Lots of love,

DALE

P.S. Last week at about 9:15 p.m. we were bounced in our chairs by a terrific explosion. In a second the whole south area was cheering—they cheer and yell at the least excuse, probably because we are supposed to be quiet during C.Q. [Call to Quarters]. All we could see in the darkness was the red and green running lights of a plane circling overhead. Soon he cut his motor and there followed another ear-splitting crack accompanied by a brilliant light (2,000,000 candle power) which lit up the

---

*Glenn C. Thompson was found yearling year and turned back to the class of 1935. He served a career in the Air Force and saw action in the China-Burma-India theater and later in Korea. He retired in 1961 with a Legion of Merit and a Bronze Star and lives in Boulder City, Nevada.

I noted Joe Cleary's tragic career earlier. Asbel O. Fields was found and I lost track of him.

earth like a small sun. He was taking flashlight pictures on a large scale. By the time he had let down his third huge flare there were several powerful spotlights focused on him. It looked like a wartime scene from the movies. He immediately took flight—literally. Today I saw one of the pictures posted on the bulletin board. It was exceptionally clear.

25 Yearlings were turned out in math, and 26 of my class were also turned out in math.

Lots of love,
DALE

My next letter was dated simply Sunday but was probably written June 8. It came from Camp Clinton, where we had moved under canvas on the other side of the Plain.

Dearest Mother and Dad,

Well, the big move is over and now we have to grit our teeth for 3 more days.

The moving was a great soiree. We were inspected in the afternoon and it was a rush-all-the-time to get the tent in order. After we had moved, at 11 a.m. we got into a queer uniform and officially marched to camp with the band and all. Just the 2nd and 4th classes, however, the others stayed or moved to central barracks. North barracks are going to be used by the old grads.

The secondclassmen certainly hazed us the first day. It was like beast barracks. "Sitting up" at the table is very uncomfortable for me, too, after having sat at a training table all year.

I like camp. It will be great when we are alone here. [Yearling summer not only promised much free time with swims at Delafield Pond and hops at Cullum, but many days on the rifle and pistol ranges along with a series of field exercises in the nearby hills.]

I saw two movies in the last two nights. Last night it was "City Lights" and everyone enjoyed it.

My tentmates are great fellows. One, Fields, isn't with us yet. He was turned out and is still in barracks. [As I mentioned, poor Fields was found.]

Today is the first day of June Week and it rained. I'm not a bit sorry. Maybe it will keep up till this aft, then no P-rade.

Soiree of all soirees, I'm on guard today. A 24 hour tour beginning at

"At last, Lew, we're recognized."

Cartoon from *The Pointer*.

4:45. I hate to think of walking post—rather dig ditches. But I'll get out of other work and hazing.

These 3 days will be long ones. When P-rade on the 11th (Graduation Parade) is over we will be RECOGNIZED. I know someone who is going to get a "big kick" out of going through the sallyport.

We climbed the steep steps to the Chapel for the last time today. Next time the services will be in the open at Battle Monument. That's where graduation will take place if it doesn't rain. We have two schedules for everything here: Regular and rainy day.

I'd better start to spec [memorize] my General and Special Orders now.

Lots of love,

DALE

P.S. You make too big a fuss over a triviality, my nose. I'm government property now. They do as they please.

My next letter home was dated June 9, 1931, at 9 P.M.

Dearest Mother and Dad,

I received a letter from Dad in Las Vegas today and also a nice one from Mother. Jean did very well in her studies. If I had done as well this year I would have worn stars. Drew did well too—much better than I did in that grade. It looks like I'm the goat of the family.

I'm flat on my back in bed under a mosquito bar (regulations); so you had better excuse this writing, altho I don't suppose it is much worse when done under ideal conditions. Phonographs are playing everywhere. Most every tent has a vic, and they are running all the time. I like to go to sleep with music.

It is raining hard now, and has been off and on for the past week. Too bad for June Week and the visitors. So many well laid plans "gang aft a'glee". And we don't like it either because it doesn't get us out of much. We go to the reviews and P-rades regardless—as yet we haven't had one in a storm greater than a drizzle. And it raises the duce [*sic*] with our brass, guns, and especially uniforms. Everything is a royal mess. I'm "sleeping" on 2 pair of trou tonite. We used to do this during beast barracks when we had just one pair.

My guard tour was a bad one. It rained all night while I was on post and I couldn't stand in the sentry box—it was too small. I amused myself by singing all the songs I knew and making up new ones. We got less than 3 hours sleep in our uniforms. [When the order came to "Turn out the guard!" we had to form in ranks immediately and so we never could get out of our clothes.] The next day we changed uniforms so often we wore everything but overcoats. We were relieved in the morning by some Yearlings in order to attend the 4th class gym exercises which we had been practicing for several weeks. I specialized in boxing. . . . Gym has! [Meaning "Gym has ended."]

This morning we attended the athletic review. Every man in an athletic uniform because "Every man an athlete" is what they strive for here and almost attain. It was wet bitter weather and we weren't sure they would hold it outside until the last few minutes. As a result it was quite a tied up affair. Squad captains were the commanders of the different sport units and they weren't very sure what to do, even though a long poop sheet was printed about the event. Perhaps it was so long that no one read it. We finally got organized and were put into 5 platoons—3 of intramural (we call it intra-murder), one of C squad, and the last of A & B squads. Soon the band started up and it came our turn to move off. The intramural platoons marched off but we in the C squad platoon were left without a commander and stood fast. The lead platoons down the street all halted and no one seemed to know what to do. I was the right guide of our platoon and after a rattled wait I cried "Forward March" and then "Squads right, March." They took my command and then we double timed to get on line. Perhaps I was taking too much authority into my hands but we couldn't tie up the review. When we were along side of the 3rd intramural group I entreated to have some upper-classman take command because I didn't have a very clear idea of how to drive a platoon—especially at a review. No one would do it. They either said they weren't in proper uniform (the corps squads wore regular track uniforms, different from the intramural) or that they didn't have a loud enough sound-off [voice of command]. So there I was with my hands in my pockets [figuratively]. I pulled a man out of the rear rank to take right guide and tried to remember what the lieutenants did at the other reviews I had been in. We managed all right and soon we were halted and dressed on the line. I then fell in the file closers and stayed there until the end of the review. Things went off fairly well. At least it looked all right from the stands and that's all that matters.

All the athletic awards were presented at this review. Glenn Thompson got one for ranking number one in gym. He was the only plebe to get one. It was a long stand for us with the cold wind blowing around our bare legs.

In the afternoon there was the "star" parade and the scholarship awards. It was another long wait even though we were given "Stand at Ease." Andrews* in our company was the only one to get stars. But if I had to file-bone as he does I wouldn't want them. His ambition is intense. I don't think he will rank very high.

10th of June: It has been raining steadily. The alumni review was called off, but the choir sang for them in Cullum Hall. Lots of old grads from way back.

We have been getting hazed quite regularly and unmercifully. Tomorrow is Graduation Parade and RECOGNITION.

13th of June: PLEBE YEAR HAS! This is a new place now—a different world. We are outsiders no longer; just full-fledged West Pointers.

It rained steadily till the day before graduation. But it cleared up enough to have Graduation Parade. Wow, how we were crawled on that P-rade. And we put out too, with all our might. It was an impressive

---

*How wrong I was! Charles L. "Chick" Andrews mellowed in subsequent cadet years and became a coach of deficient cadets. He was made battalion commander his first class year, a cadet rank second only to the first captain. Moreover, he actively participated in sports, winning a minor "A" in fencing. After graduation Chick became a language specialist and taught French, Spanish, and Portuguese at West Point. This led to tours as military attaché, and Chick missed the big war. He did, however, see combat service in Korea and was awarded the Legion of Merit and the Bronze Star.

event. [The Corps marched onto the parade ground to the tune of "The Stars and Stripes Forever," changing to the "The Dashing White Sergeant." This sequence of music is not used for any other parade. The band trooped the line to the tunes of "Home Sweet Home," "The Wedding March," "The Girl I Left Behind Me," and "Auld Lang Syne."] After the band trooped the line the whole first class went front and center with the music of "Army Blue." They kept a perfect line the entire length of the Plain and it was beautiful. Then we passed in review [as the band led playing "The Official West Point March," which is played at every parade] and did "Eyes Right" to the firstclassmen.

During it all we were being hazed to death and just about passing out with exhaustion. But we plebes had grim smiles on our pusses. Before I knew it our column had entered the sallyport and a great commotion began. As soon as I entered I shoved the 2nd classman on my left with a bang against the wall [I think it was Bob Scott], turned around and grabbed the guide, twisted him and gave him a healthy boot. It did my heart good.

[Other plebes were taking similar liberties. The sallyport rang with shouts and curses as plebes shoved and kicked the nearest upperclassmen. It's a wonder there was any semblance left of a military formation but the column straightened out as soon as it left the sallyport and entered the Area of Central Barracks. Then the command was "Column left," and when our company was well into the Area, it was "Squads right." The squads wheeled to the right into a company front and halted with the upperclassmen in the front rank and the plebes in the rear, where they had marched for almost a year. Then the cadet company commander ordered, "Front rank, about face," and the upperclassmen turned, thrusting out their hands to recognize us.]

The south Area was crowded with visitors. *Recognition.* It was all over. A great, smiling and laughing event. Animosities were forgotten on the spot. Everyone was a friend. Since then everything has looked great.

That night I dragged blind to the graduation hop. It was held in the gym for the lower three classes. The decorations were beautiful and everyone enjoyed it. It was much like a formal dance in the Nevada gym. My fem was only about a 2.0 but I had a flock of good hops with other girls.

Thursday, the next day, we went to graduation. You will probably see it in the movies. Directly afterwards we were marched out to the Plain and the "makes" were announced. I'm sorry to say I didn't get made. It was a great disappointment because I was almost certain I would be. I guess I wasn't humble enough and the first classmen ranked me low. I had quite a few demos, too, but still not too many. No one in my tent got made either. Glenn Thompson ranked number one in Gym and wasn't made. Also, the plebe who ranked one in academics didn't get made. It puzzles me. Another thing, I haven't got a good sound-off (low and loud voice). I must bone one up. [Practice helped some but by and large a voice is inherited.] And also a set-up (big chest).

But actually makes don't mean anything really big. Many first captains were never acting corporals. However, it would have been nice to wield a sword and wear a sash at P-rades. There is another make list in August. They are called "Augustinians". I'll get made then or won't know the reason why. I'm staging one hell of a big buck-up. [I wasn't made in August, either. There might have been a tac who didn't like me, because the first class had graduated. Or could it have been one of those former secondclassmen who gave me such a hard time as a plebe?]

The new first class left today for Virginia and Yearling Deadbeat has begun. Monday we start work on the firing range with the afternoons off.

Elizabeth is in the East playing tennis, and will be up soon to see me. I'm going to write her now. [She never came.]

I'm glad Jean and Drew are through school and are enjoying the vacation. Lots of love to you all,

DALE

No one who hasn't gone through it can quite appreciate the exquisite euphoria and deep satisfaction of Recognition at West Point. We plebes had been on trial for eleven months, treated as inferiors by all upperclassmen except those few who had voluntarily shook our hands and thus "recognized" us. We had been crawled unmercifully at every military formation and forced to pull in our chins until our necks ached, pop up our chests with a final painful gasp of breath, throw our shoulders back until the blades almost ground against each other, and suck in our guts until they knotted. This unnatural stance had become almost habitual. Now, after Recognition, we could "fall out," stand naturally, and relax. No longer would we "sir" upperclassmen, for we became upperclassmen ourselves. We became *Yearlings*, thirdclassmen, with a thin black stripe above the cuff of our dress grey jackets and a thin diagonal gold stripe on the cuffs of our full dress coats. We could hardly wait to get our uniforms altered. And in the winter we could casually throw the capes of our overcoats over our shoulders, a privilege only permitted to upperclassmen.

So it was with heart-swelling happiness that we grasped the hands of the upperclassmen in the front ranks and forgot all their abuse. It was all smiles, first names, and congratulations for having made the grade. Truly the upperclassmen were proud of us and showed it. Those we had roughed up a bit in the sallyport were laughing about it. It was all just part of the ancient tradition.

Firstclassmen now became new second lieutenants, and Recognition was for them and us a sort of good-bye. We had grown fond of many of them, and were sorry to see them leave. The secondclassmen became firstclassmen and would shortly embark on a coastal vessel headed for Old Point Comfort, Virginia, where they would be introduced to the Air Corps at Langley Field, the Coast Artillery at Fort Monroe, and the Field Artillery at Fort Bragg, North Carolina.

The yearlings, who now became secondclassmen, left the post in a rush after the graduation exercises. Yearling furlo had begun. There were no cadets left at West Point but new yearlings, and we were very ready for the long anticipated "yearling deadbeat." We rejoiced in our new freedoms and exalted status. Except for those who later suffered as prisoners of war, perhaps none of us ever again had to endure such an ordeal as plebe year.

I received a telegram about five minutes before Graduation Parade and Recognition. It read: CONGRATULATIONS FROM DAD ON YOUR AR-RIVAL AT THIS HIGH POINT IN YOUR CAREER. (signed) ALFRED MERRITT SMITH.

CHAPTER 17 WHERE ARE THEY NOW?

Because this has been a chronicle not only of plebe year at West Point but also of the Alfred Merritt Smith family for the months between July 1930 and June 1931, the reader may be interested in what has happened to them.

The youngest, Drew Merritt Smith, and Drewdy to us along with several other fond nicknames, was the most beloved by all because of his buoyant, lighthearted personality. And, of course, he was the doted "baby" of the family. Drew attended the University of Nevada in Reno for two years, joined the Lambda Chi Alpha fraternity, fell in love with classmate Harriet Hills, and in general enjoyed himself. War clouds were on the horizon, and all at once Drew decided he would seriously try for West Point. The folks sent him to a prep school in San Francisco and he passed the entrance exams.

Since cadets couldn't be married, Drew and Harriet planned to wed after Drew graduated. And so he came east in June of 1941 and spent a wonderful week with us at Langley Field, Virginia. I was able to fly him to Mitchel Field, New York, in a new four-engine B-17 bomber. From there he took a bus to West Point.

Pearl Harbor was attacked that December and life began to accelerate at West Point. The first class was graduated early and a three-year curriculum was established for Drew's class. Moreover, an airfield was carved out of the hills near Newburgh, nine miles north of the Academy, and soon those who chose the Army Air Forces and passed the strict physical exam were learning to fly at Stewart Field. Drew was one of these and graduated in June 1944 with silver pilot wings.

At that time I was commanding a B-17 group in England and Drew implored me to ask for him. But our losses were so heavy that I couldn't bring myself to do it. He stayed in the States for the next year transitioning in B-17s and then huge B-29s. He had orders to Guam, along with the B-29 Superfortresses that were bombing Japan when the war ended. Mother and Dad were happily congratulating themselves that their three sons had survived the long war.

Harriet was now an overseas airline hostess, and Drew convinced her that they should be married by proxy so that she could join him in Guam on government orders. The odd ceremony was completed, but before Harriet could join Drew, he had been killed in a take-off accident.

It was a night training mission to photograph Wake Island and return. There was a double crew aboard. The heavily laden B-29 took off into a low dark cloud, a wing tipped, and the big airplane dove into the Pacific. Only a tire was found. No one knew who was at the controls and one could only speculate on what had caused the crash. Perhaps an engine fire and failure, a not uncommon fault of the B-29s. Perhaps pilot disorientation in the black cloud. Perhaps a combination of both.

Harriet received the word in Rome. It was a cruel blow. Mother and Dad could never accept it, while I could not help but feel responsible for having urged Drew to pursue a career in the Army Air Forces.

But it was done. And we have one thing to be thankful for. Drew will never be old. He will be eternally twenty-four, the young, cheerful, fun-loving, harum-scarum kid we all adored. Every now and then one of Drew's classmates will introduce himself to me. Two did so at my fiftieth class reunion at West Point. They were at their fortieth reunion, in their mid-sixties, retired, baldish, grey, and somewhat thick around the middle. I couldn't picture Drew that way.

And what became of Jean? Jean came east with Mother and Drew to attend my graduation. Dad, who was then the Nevada Director of the Public Works Administration, felt he could not take the time off. The true reason was that the folks simply couldn't afford for all of them to make the trip. Since Dad had visited West Point in the winter of my second class year while he was on a business trip to New York, it was logical that he should stay home.

Jean graduated from the University of Nevada in 1938 with a teaching degree. She held several teaching jobs in Nevada, and when I was stationed in Hawaii she came over and spent a year there, partly with us and partly at Schofield Barracks, where she taught in the dependents' school. A love affair with an infantry officer didn't quite jell and she returned to Reno to marry an earlier love, James Kenneth Dobey.

Jim Dobey, a graduate of the University of California at Berkeley, was a banker and pursued that career clear to the top, retiring as Chairman of the Board of Wells Fargo Bank. During World War II, as an officer of glider troops, he saw action in Europe, while Jean lived with the folks in Reno at 229 Maple Street. During this period she cared for my two children, Kort and Voan, when my marriage to Elise broke up—a casualty of the war.

Jean and Jim raised two fine boys, Jimmy and Peter, who are now married and raising families of their own. Now Jean and I are the only survivors of the Alfred Merritt Smith clan of 229 Maple Street. In fact, even Maple Street has all but vanished, the whole neighborhood having been bulldozed clean for the Interstate 80 highway.

Brother Thor Merritt Smith, who subscribed to the philosophy of "America First" advocated by Charles Lindbergh and others opposed to President Franklin D. Roosevelt's pro-Anglo policy, supported the contention that England was dragging us into the war. Nevertheless, he was one of the first in line at the Army recruiting office in San Francisco after the Japanese struck at Pearl Harbor. But the Army rejected him because of flat feet.

A few weeks later I was assigned a "public relations" officer—a specialty I had never before heard of. But we were at war and the public demanded information about its military units. Providing that information was the job of the PR officer. I asked this new captain how he had obtained his commission. He explained that as a newspaperman he had filled out a certain form and submitted it to the Army. Next thing he knew he was a captain.

"Your first duty," I told him, "is to get me one of those forms." He did so and I sent it to Thor, who had been in the promotion field of the Hearst organization for several years. In no time at all he was commissioned a captain in the Army Air Corps, his flat feet forgotten.

He was ordered to headquarters in Washington, D.C., which was then in the Munitions Building on Constitution Avenue. Thor hurriedly bought himself a ready-made uniform at the Emporium in San Francisco and I sent him a facetious and entirely unauthorized telegram: REPORT IMMEDIATELY TO LANGLEY FIELD FOR BASIC TRAINING IN THE SCHOOL OF THE SOLDIER (signed) LT. COL. DALE O. SMITH. He came and we had a wonderful visit. It was a good thing he did, too, for I was able to teach him how to put insignia on his uniform, how not to wear his cap like a taxi driver on the side of his head, and how not to salute like a chorus girl.

Eventually I flew him to Washington and we went searching in the vast Munitions Building for someone who knew where he was to be assigned. Being shunted from one office to another we encountered an old cavalry retread, who looked at my silver leaves and Thor's captain's bars and said to me, "Oh, so this is your son?" From then on Thor, four years my senior, called me "Pappy."

With the help of my classmate Bill Gross, Thor was eventually assigned to the Eighth Air Force Service Command, which was being sent to England to prepare for the buildup of the mighty Eighth Air Force of heavy bombers and long-range fighters. Off to England he went with the original contingent. His conscientious nature and engaging personality assured his rapid promotion and before long he was a full colonel, a rank it had taken me nine years to achieve.

While I was in England I spent several pleasant forty-eight-hour passes in London visiting him and his roommate, Jack Redding, at their flat in Portsea Hall near Marble Arch.

Thor was one of those who was ready to win the war single-handedly. He worked on the staff for Cossack, the plan to invade the Continent in 1943, and also on the planning staff for Overlord, the actual invasion in 1944. I spent a week with him in a camouflaged tent at General Ike's headquarters not far from Portsmouth just before D-day. We were frequently kept awake listening to the buzz bombs fly overhead as they searched for the invasion forces. Thor was then Ike's advance public relations officer and in charge of war correspondents.

Although a noncombat officer, Thor sought every opportunity to experience the shooting war. He pestered me repeatedly to go on bombing raids but that I could never approve. The possibility of his blood on my hands, as with Drew, was more than I could risk. But I did take him on a practice mission in which my group bombed a rock in the North Sea. With the help of this mission and the stories Bill Gross and I told them, he and Jack Redding wrote a novel, *Wake of Glory*, published in 1945 by the Bobbs-Merrill Company of Indianapolis.

Thor happened to be riding in a jeep near the front when the Remagen Bridge on the Rhine River was seized. Dodging gunfire, he crossed with the troops and managed to return through the carnage before the bridge was blown up by the enemy. Somehow he was one of the first to greet the Russian troops on the Elbe River, and he participated in the surrender ceremonies in the schoolhouse at Reims.

Thor was General Eisenhower's respected friend and confidant and could have used this association to advantage, but he never presumed upon this friendship and returned to work in San Francisco as assistant to the publisher of the *Call-Bulletin* newspaper.

During his long four-year tour overseas, Mary had worked in Reno as a stringer for *Life* magazine and faithfully cared for their three girls, Diane, Suzanne, and Marianne. Thor's return was a grand and happy reunion.

An invitation to attend the year-long course of the Air War College at Maxwell Air Force Base in Alabama kept up Thor's interest as a reserve colonel. Then a promotion to the *New York Journal American* caused the family to move east for a few years. But California pulled them back and Thor ended his career as Vice President for Promotion of Mills College.

Tragedy struck the happy family shortly after their fiftieth wedding anniversary celebration. Thor died of a heart attack and his first daughter, Diane, soon followed him with cancer. A fond granddaughter was struck down with leukemia, and Mary contracted Alzheimer's disease.

While transcribing these letters I came to realize that the principal character in this saga was Dad. It was Dad who suffered the psychic trauma and embarrassment of losing his job and remaining out of work during the depths of the Great Depression. It was Dad who never lost faith in himself, in me, and in his country. It was Dad who believed that if he prevailed, worked like hell, and never lost hope, his lot would eventually improve. It was Dad who was enthralled by my being at West Point, a dream he had always held for himself but had considered impossible to fulfill. It was Dad who encouraged me to stick it out, to behave like a gentleman with the "hickory," as he put it, and to go the route. No boy ever received better guidance and support than I. He fired me with his lore, his spirit, and the glory of West Point.

Exciting news came from Dad in a letter written to me on January 28, 1933, when I was a corporal secondclassman. The Nevada section of the American Institute of Mining Engineers was sending him to a meeting in New York. But hard times still weighed heavily on the family, and although the Institute would reimburse him for travel expenses he would have to pay for meals and lodging. The folks had no savings and were going into the red with their apartments. For a time it looked as if Dad would have to give up this golden opportunity because he didn't have the money. But he managed to borrow $250 and departed Reno on Wednesday morning, February 15.

After three days on the train Dad arrived in New York early Saturday morning and was met at the station by Thor, who was in New York checking out a new job. Just as soon as Dad got settled in Thor's hotel room, they drove to West Point and I met them early that afternoon in the Grant Hall visitors' room. It was an emotional experience for each of us, but we didn't embrace. In our family a warm handshake was our only contact.

I had written a formal letter to the Commandant, Lt. Col. Robert C. "Nellie" Richardson, requesting permission for my father to spend Saturday night in barracks and to eat in the mess hall. Arrangements had been made for my roommate, George "Major" Dany, to sleep in the empty bed of a cadet who was in the hospital. The compassionate "Nellie" approved my request and I was granted a privilege that was so rare that none of my friends had ever heard of it.

I had invited Ruth Marschalk down to meet Dad. She was attending school at Skidmore, a few miles up the Hudson from us, and she planned to visit on Sunday.

Word had reached my friends that my dad and brother would be visiting and soon these gracious cadets appeared at George's and my room to meet the honored guest. Afterward Dad wrote, "I am forever in love with Maj Dany, Ken Kenerick, Dick Moorman, Hutch Hutchison, Bill Gross and Artie Meier, your splendid friends."

Snow was on the ground and it was a blustery, bitterly cold day. So we donned overcoats for a tour of the post. Maj took Thor, while Ken and I took Dad. Thor had visited me two or three times that winter, so West Point was no novelty for him. The bad weather didn't dim Dad's awe of the Academy; he drank in every scene and snapped pictures at every opportunity. He seemed particularly impressed by the stone shield in the Old Chapel; it had once held the name of Benedict Arnold, but it had been carved out.

Assembly for the supper formation that time of year was in the dark, so Maj and I decided to have Dad march with us. We found an extra cadet overcoat that fit fairly well and a cap. When the bugler blew "Assembly" we put Dad in ranks between us and he marched to the mess hall like a cadet. My friends in "A" company went along with this deception. We pulled the same stunt for reveille the next morning. Dad wasn't too enthusiastic about jumping to the Hell Cats and rushing out to form ranks in the dark frigid Area, but Maj and I convinced him it was part of the drill. Upperclassmen usually left their rooms when the

Hell Cats stopped playing and the bugler began the call of "Assembly." Then they sprinted down the stairs and out into ranks, managing to slide into their slots just as the bugler sounded his last drawn-out note. Anyone only a few seconds late to the formation was sure to get skinned. Everyone was amused that Dad made it just like a cadet. Again, he marched with us to the mess hall for breakfast.

On Sunday, with Thor and Ruth, we attended Chapel, where Dad marveled at the tattered battle flags hanging from the gothic ceiling of the nave and the profusion of stained glass windows, several depicting mythical Christian soldiers. We visited frozen Lusk Reservoir, the restored Fort Putnam, built during the Revolutionary War, Michie Stadium, and the new ice skating rink. Too soon it was time to say good-bye.

Dad wrote, "What a grand and perfect day we had, and how much I learned. Henceforth Dad will have an understanding heart. With deepest love from your proud Dad."

Mother was always Dad's loyal lieutenant during the lean years, responding to his many moods, bolstering his waning ego as a steady job eluded him. Dad loved her dearly and their union was the envy of their friends.

In 1935 Governor Richard Kirman asked Dad to be state engineer and Dad readily accepted, holding that position for sixteen years. After retirement from the state engineer post he and Mother came to visit us at Maxwell Air Force Base, Alabama, and spent several months. But the idle life was not for Dad. He had few hobbies and had never played golf. Hearing of openings in a forerunner of the Peace Corps, he applied for a position in Pakistan but, much to the relief of Mother, he was turned down because of his age, then seventy-six. In high indignation he flew to Washington to confer with Senator George Malone of Nevada, who had preceded Dad as state engineer. The senator offered Dad a job as administrative assistant with duties to promote mining ventures in Nevada. He was delighted with the assignment, which was right down his alley. Dad and Mother returned to Reno and spent their declining years in considerable happiness.

In 1962 they came to visit Virginia and me in Washington, D.C., and there Dad broke a hip in a bathtub fall. He was then eighty-seven and healed slowly. Mother visited him faithfully in the hospital until he was well enough to return to Reno. Their fortunes never improved. Dad's hip failed to heal well enough for him to walk, and Mother had a radical

George B. Dany

mastectomy that drained her strength. Jean moved them to Los Gatos, California, near her home, where the folks lived out their few remaining years in a comfortable condo.

Thor once said, "Dad is the complete gentleman," and indeed he was. Soft-spoken, considerate of everyone, I never heard him utter an unkind word, unless it was to condemn the kaiser or Hitler. Sometimes Mother would tear into him for being too "humble" or "timid," but Dad never responded.

Humble he was, but timid he was not. True, he could never drive a hard bargain and might have failed as a businessman, but he responded quickly to injustice, insults, or boorishness. Once a mean pugnacious drunk came to our door and Dad roughly propelled him clear to the curb. When he was a mill manager Dad bested a huge bully who was fomenting trouble and threw him down a tailings dump.

He was a dreamer and a poet. In his years of commuting from Reno to Carson he memorized the whole of *The Rubáiyát of Omar Khayyám* and loved to recite passages of this and other poems. This bored some of the family, but not me, and I still can hear him recite Coleridge's "In Xanadu did Kubla Khan a stately pleasure-dome decree. . . ."

He was a devoted Mason and achieved the high rank of thirty-third degree. This was his religion. He was a deist with an unwavering belief in God and the rightness of all things, but somewhat of a fatalist, too, even though he did believe that hard work would change his lot.

Dad was my closest friend. I loved him dearly and I miss his always wise counsel and example. Any father could take a lesson from him on how to inspire a son. I tried my best to emulate Dad in the raising of my own children, but could never approach his high standards.

Well, what happened to me? My remaining three years at West Point were not marked with any resounding success. I was finally promoted to corporal my second class year, but only achieved the two chevrons of a sergeant my final year. I carried the guidon of "A" Company and at least no longer had to suffer with a rifle. After struggling two years on the scrub "B" squad of football I became disenchanted and gave it up. I tried basketball yearling year and made the varsity but not my letter, and so I returned to boxing the following year. It wasn't until my last year that I won letters in boxing and track. Then it was too late to wear them at the Academy and too late for these honors to appear in the *Howitzer* yearbook.

Why didn't I marry Ruth? The final break came when, after returning early from yearling furlo to spend a planned few days with her, she was not at home. Her mother had insisted that Ruth join her in a visit to friends on Long Island. At least that's what I was told. We continued to see each other from time to time but she was no longer my O.A.O. Ruth married a physician and had two children. In later years she suffered from agoraphobia, and she died in 1981.

I graduated in the upper half of the class of 1934 and was accepted for Flying School at Randolph Field, Texas. So things turned out just about as I had hoped for, and my career in the Air Force was rewarding. But my private life was less successful until I met and married the brilliant and charming Virginia Posvar of Reno. She courageously accepted the task of raising my two children, Kort and Voan, and bore two more, Drew and Dale. After some twenty moves around the world all our children have departed the nest; we have six grandchildren, and are comfortably retired in Reno.

In looking back, my greatest pride and satisfaction comes from having attended West Point. It was an experience I treasure deeply, for there I was taught how to behave with confidence, given training in manners and morals that have never left me, imbued with a self-discipline that I could never have found elsewhere, and provided with endearing and loyal friendships.

No event in my military career can compare in gratification to graduating from the Military Academy—not the winning of silver pilot's wings, nor heady commands of squadrons, groups, and air divisions, nor military decorations, nor V-E or V-J days, nor the pinning on of general's stars. The pinnacle of my career came on that sunny day I received a diploma on Trophy Point from the Secretary of War and threw my white hat into the air.

Oh, while there I cursed West Point, writhed under the harsh and sometimes, it seemed to me, unreasonable discipline, railed against the boredom and confinement, rebelled against the unyielding strictness of the tactical officers and instructors. But perhaps it was all necessary. As Dad so colorfully put it, the Iron Mother knew what she was doing.

In any event, the system has worked and has produced military leaders who, given the authority, have won our country's wars and preserved our lofty principles. In the final analysis that is what it's all about. I would therefore caution "reformers" to be wary about making changes in the program. Recommendations by educators, psychologists, and congressmen are seldom tempered with the understanding of what it takes to create a successful and loyal officer corps.

But perhaps my objections are just the musings of an old man who is confused by the inevitable changes that have grown up all around him. It will take another war to determine whether the changes at West Point have been good ones, and let us pray that we never see that. Whatever the future brings, West Point will continue to produce patriots in the regular Army who extol the military virtues of Duty, Honor, and Country.

Nothing symbolizes West Point so clearly as the lyrics of "The Corps," a hymn sung with much feeling by all cadets and graduates. In his famous farewell address at the Academy in 1962, General Douglas MacArthur concluded by quoting the last line.

THE CORPS

The Corps! Bareheaded salute it,
With eyes up, thanking our God

That we of the Corps are treading
Where they of the Corps have trod—

They are here in ghostly assemblage,
The men of the Corps long dead,

And our hearts are standing attention
While we wait for their passing tread.

We sons of today we salute you—
You sons of an earlier day;

We follow, close order, behind you,
Where you have pointed the way;

The long grey line of us stretches
Through the years of a century told,

And the last man feels to his marrow
The grip of your far off hold.

Grip hands with us now though we see thee not,
Grip hands with us, strengthen our hearts

As the long line stiffens and straightens
With the thrill that your presence imparts.

Grip hands though it be from the shadows—
While we swear as you did of yore,

Or living or dying to honor
The Corps, and the Corps, and the Corps!

APPENDIX I GLOSSARY OF 1930 CADET SLANG

Area—that area enclosed by barracks.
Area bird—a cadet required to walk punishment tours in the Area of Barracks.

B-ache—to bellyache, make excuses; a written explanation required of every skin, usually followed by demerits.
Beast—a new cadet.
B.J.—fresh, lacking in respect.
blasé—fresh, behaving with a world-weary air.
bone—to study up on something; to bone a section meant to move up one section.
boodle—candy, cake, ice cream—anything good to eat.
boodlers—the cadet restaurant.
brace—the exaggerated military posture for a plebe.
B.S.—lots of talk.
buck up—to improve one's behavior, work harder.

cit—civilian.
cits—civilian clothing.
cold—absolutely without error, a max or 3.0 grade.
com—the Commandant of Cadets.
cow—a secondclassman; junior.
crawl—to correct a plebe, make him take an extreme brace, require him to recite "plebe knowledge."

D, De or Dee—deficient.

deadbeat—easy duty or none at all. (Seldom heard today.)
D.P.—dining permit. (Not required today.)
drag—a young lady being escorted by a cadet; to escort a young lady. (Not heard today.)
D.T.—to double time, run.
ducrot—a name applied to all plebes. (Not heard today.)
dukes—fists, hands.
dumbjohn—same as ducrot.

engineer—a cadet ranking high in academics. (Seldom heard today.)

femme—a girl. (Seldom heard at the modern Academy.)
fess—a flunking grade.
file—a cadet, a cadet in ranks, a space in ranks, one step in a rank order of any sort.
file boner—overly conscientious cadet. (Now called a "grey hog.")
flanker—a tall cadet usually assigned to A or M company. (Today cadets are not assigned to companies according to size.)
flock—many.
found—to be found deficient and be dismissed.

gig—a report for a delinquency, a skin.
goat—a cadet ranking low in academics.
gobs—lots.

[256]

grind—a joke. (Not heard today.)
griped—annoyed.
gross—dense, dull, slow.

Hell Cats—the drum and bugle corps that sounds reveille.
hive—to understand, comprehend.
hivy—smart.
hop—dance.

kaydet—cadet.
K.O.—knock out.

limits—the limits on the reservation to which cadets are restricted.
L.P.—an undesirable "drag"; "lady of the post."

make—a cadet officer or noncommissioned officer.
max—to make a perfect grade.

O.A.O.—one and only girlfriend.
O.C.—officer in charge.
O.D.—officer of the day; a cadet in charge of the guard detail.
O.G.—officer of the guard; a cadet assistant to the O.D.
oke—O.K.

P—professor or instructor.
pipe—to anticipate.
plebe—a cadet fourthclassman; freshman.
podunk—a cadet's home town.
police—to be thrown as from a horse; to throw away, discard, clean up; or to be moved out of a section or a team.
poop—information or directions.
poop-deck—a balcony where the O.C. stands to watch cadets. Also the balcony in the mess hall where the O.C. eats and where orders are published by the "Woof-woof."
poop sheet—a paper with instructions of any sort.

pro—proficient, above passing in studies.
P.S.—to escort visitors around the post. (Not heard today.)

recognize—by shaking a plebe's hand, to treat him henceforth as an upperclassman.

set-up—good military posture, big chest.
skin—to be reported for a delinquency usually resulting in demerits, sometimes used as a synonym for demerit; gig and quill have the same meaning.
slug—a special punishment for serious offenses, usually requiring many hours walking the Area and confinement to quarters.
soiree—unpleasant duty or activity. (Seldom heard today.)
sound-off—loud and low voice capable of giving commands.
spec—to memorize verbatim.
spoon up—to put in order, clean up and polish. (Seldom heard today.)
spoony—neat in personal appearance. (Seldom heard today.)
supe—superintendent.

tac—a regular army tactical officer in charge of cadets.
tarbucket—the full dress hat.
tenth—the lowest division of the system of marking.
tie up—to make a gross error.
turnback—a re-admitted cadet.

wife—roommate. (No longer heard.)
Woof-woof—the cadet officer who reads the orders of the day.
writ—a written examination.

yearling—a member of the third class; sophomore.

APPENDIX II "POISON IVY AND HIGHWAYS"

The hike described in Chapter 4 of this book was the subject of an article by the author published in 1930 in The Pointer, *the cadet magazine of the United States Military Academy. The full text is as follows:*

After giving the world the impression for forty-eight days that we were all extremely proud of ourselves, we were given two dollars and a "Squads Right," and the great Plebe Hike had begun. It was thrilling no end to go marching down to the South Gate right behind the band, just like soldiers going off to war or something. It wasn't long, though, before we began wishing that we were going to war—war would have been a pleasure, despite Sherman's assertion to the opposite.

They told us that rests would be given every forty-five minutes, each rest to be of fifteen minutes duration, and for a while, just after the first halt, it looked as if we had been told the truth. It seemed that the further we marched, the fewer were the rests, and we would no sooner get settled than the bugler would blow attention, and off we would go for another walk. On the first halt we became acquainted with poison ivy, in somewhat the following manner.

"You man. Do you know what poison ivy looks like?" (This from one of the detail.)

"No, sir." (This from one of us, sitting quite at ease in the ditch.)

"Well, look right under your left hand. See that funny looking weed? Well, that's poison ivy."

It wasn't so very bad the first day, the marching, that is. Not many feet went under the weather, so when the call for dinner came, we were all ready to eat, at ease, on the banks of the rushing Popolopen. And did we sit at ease, and did we eat? One man, either lazier or more original than the rest, was lying flat on his back, while an adoring wife stuffed steak into his mouth. There were seconds, and thirds, which made the scanty repasts of Beast Barracks seem very far away.

And, oh! that swimming hole at Popolopen! Refreshing to the proverbial nth degree. Someone very quaintly remarked that the good fairies should have left the ice on, so we could have gone skating. There was an excellent chance to bone either mountain goat or polar bear at that swimming hole, as well as high diver.

Some of the more adventurous souls, with ancestry that surely must be Swiss, climbed to the top of the Torn, as tradition demands, and came back to camp filled with stories of how wonderful the Hudson and the Bear Mountain Bridge looked from there. Less fortunate (?) men went to guard mount, which was a splendid affair, with newspaper cameras, and reporters and all that sort of thing. More than one fond mother pointed to the rotogravure section of the *Times* and said "That's my son, there."

The evening bonfire on the first night uncovered much local talent and we were entertained quite royally. The first class orchestra, composed of two torrid banjoes and a hot sax, was the main attraction. Boy, they made that bonfire look like a small iceberg in comparison. Henderson was tried and not found wanting, and we were told many times about that "Man from the south," and his enormous cigar. Webster favored us with a reading somewhat similar to "The Shooting of Dan McGrew," which was well received.

Taps found some of us trying to sleep, while others went to the posts of the guard. There were statements to the effect that walking guard was a pleasure, as in that way one could get warm. There were four posts, and they covered a multitude of sins, I mean ground. One sentinel had to use the North Star as a bearing point to find his way from one end of his post to the other.

After breakfast, there was a mad scamper to get the camp broken, and on our way to the next camp. It was a sorry looking rabble which left Popolopen Creek for Bocky Swamp. Faces were embellished with scratches caused by shaving without a mirror and with mosquito bites. Packs were messes, no less.

It is three miles, as the crow flies, to our next camp, but not being crows, just Plebes out for some good, clean fun, it was fourteen miles. So we were told, but after the third hour, it seemed that there must have been something wrong with the computations. This march taught us that there are 762 ways of carrying a rifle with a sling, and that there are 762 ways which are uncomfortable. Packs showed an unusual tendency to increase in weight, probably due to the fact that they absorbed moisture from the atmosphere.

At last, however, Bocky Swamp hove into view, at least the mess tents and the K. P.'s did, and you may rest assured that the sight was most welcome to the class of 1934. How hard it was to pitch tents with all that food over there in the tents!

Must give something about our swimming hole at Bocky Swamp. The sign said "Fish Pond," and we believed in that sign, after a look around and a dive into the water. You know that stuff people put in the water in goldfish bowls to keep the goldfish amused? Well, this place had that, long and stringy weeds of some unknown species. We were all rather loath to swim much until the sight of some vivid bathing suits on the other side sent the romantic souls over to investigate. Alas and alack, the suits contained some Girl Scouts, averaging fourteen years in age. Picture the effect on our ego when they demanded "Are you Boy Scouts?"

There was the usual bonfire that evening, but many were so tired that the attendance was somewhat small.

The next morning, bright and early in the grey dawn (something is wrong with this, because how can a dawn be both bright and grey?) we were off with tightly rolled packs and some blisters, for Round Pond, eleven miles away. It was swell, that march. We went over the hills without even breathing hard, feeling like seasoned troopers. This, too, must be wrong, because troopers ride, and the amount of riding we did was not enough to make a baby sore. Nevertheless, we cheered at the sight of the camp.

Round Pond Camp was beautiful. The pond itself was very pastoral with ducks and all the requisites. It was a dirty trick to feed those ducks cigarettes, oh, noble Cataline! Especially when they were so easily satisfied with some small pieces of bread.

The Pond promised some excellent swimming, but along in the early afternoon, the sky grew dark, and the tears of the Gods fell thickly upon us. In short, it rained, and, to be common, *and how!* The shelter tents were at a disadvantage that time for sure, and they could hardly live up to their names. But, as the purpose of the hike was to teach us conditions in the field, we were glad (?) to have the rain. It was great fun to attempt sleeping in the middle of a stream which made the Mississippi look small in comparison. But it stopped about morning, and the bonfire became very popular.

During the evening, the rain let up long enough to let us all break into the movies. We sang and gave yells right into the staring eyes of a movie camera and in the midst of the smoke from about ninety magnesium flares. The Engineers gave a boxing match and some coffee and cake, which made some of us happy and others sick. We weren't accustomed to the luxury, you see.

In the morning, we prepared ourselves for another fifteen mile hike, and you can imagine our surprise when we found out that the distance from camp to barracks was extremely short. Even at that many of the boys who came prancing behind the band were awfully tired by the time we got to Central Barracks. There was a "Dismissed" and the hike was over, as snappily as it had begun. Our dismissal meant more to us than just that. It meant that Beast Barracks was over, and that a new period of golden opportunity was in the immediate offing. The Fourth Class had finished its period of training in the field for awhile, the First Class got its practice in commanding troops on the march, and everything was quite as it should have been. And in just a few more years, we'll start it all over again, with a four-pound pack, no rifles, and a large amount of authority. But until then, much water must flow under many bridges, so we'll be good Plebes, Yearlings, and Second-Classmen until duty calls in 1933.

APPENDIX III ROSTER OF THE GRADUATING
CLASS OF 1934
UNITED STATES MILITARY ACADEMY

The names of the members of the entering plebe class in 1930 who sur-
vived the four-year curriculum and graduated in 1934 are given below,
together with present-day address or date, cause, and place of death.
See key for abbreviations.

KEY

(A) Army

(AF) Air Force

(AC) Army Air Corps

(PA) Philippine Army

D: deceased: date (cause; place of
death)

KIA killed in action

MIA missing in action

PI Philippine Islands

POW Cp. prisoner of war Compound

WRAH Walter Reed Army Hospital

Lt. Col. George E. Adams (A) 9744
Sheldon Road, S.E., Olympia, WA
98502.

Maj. Gen. Robert H. Adams (A) D: 12
June 82 (Seattle, WA).

Lt. Gen. Harvey T. Alness (AF) 4917
Ravenswood Road, #1752, San Antonio, TX 78227.

Col. John H. Anderson (A) 1431 W.
Woodard Street, Denison, TX 75020.

Col. Herbert H. Andrae (A) 88 Setauket
Trail, Medford Lakes, NJ 08055.

Col. Charles L. Andrews (A) 475
Heard's Ferry Road, N.W., Atlanta,
GA 30328.

Bey M. Arosemena P.O. Box 7663, Panama 9, Republic of Panama.

Col. Paul C. Ashworth (AF) 6511 Cy-
press Point Drive, Houston, TX 77069.

Col. Robert C. Bahr (A) D: 28 June 87
(Savannah, GA).

1st Lt. Herbert M. Baker, Jr. (AC) D: 10
June 40 (Ft. Shafter, HI).

Col. James O. Baker (A) D: 27 Sept. 63
(McCall, ID).

Col. Robert G. Baker (A) D: 1 Aug. 79
(Naples, FL).

Col. Frederic W. Barnes (AF) 914
Greenway Lane, Vero Beach, FL
32963.

Lt. Col. William G. Barnwell, Jr. (A) D:
10 June 49 (Alexandria, VA).

Col. Joseph E. Barton (AF) D: 24 May
78 (Washington, DC).

Brig. Gen. Paul L. Barton (AF) D: 13
May 85 (Washington, DC).

Maj. Howard M. Batson, Jr. (A) D: 28
Jan. 45 (POW Cp., Fukuoka, Japan).

2nd Lt. Karl W. Bauer (AC) D: 2 Dec. 35 (air accident; CA).

Capt. Lewis K. Beazley (A) D: 26 July 74 (Washington, DC).

Col. John G. Benner (A) D: 28 May 72 (Mexico).

Capt. Robert M. Bennett (A) D: 29 Jan. 41 (Ft. Davis, Panama, Canal Zone).

2nd Lt. Edward F. Benson (A) D: 10 Dec. 34 (Ft. Benning, GA).

Lt. Col. Paul H. Berkowitz (A) D: 26 July 44 (air accident; South Pacific).

Lt. Gen. Austin W. Betts (A) 6414 View Point, San Antonio, TX 78229.

Col. Severin R. Beyma (A) 701 N. Hope Street, Phoebus, VA 23663.

Col. Theodore G. Bilbo (A) D: 29 Aug. 79 (Pompano Beach, FL).

Col. Jerome E. Blair, Jr. (AF) 3316 Mapleton Crescent, Chesapeake, VA 23321.

Lt. Col. Gerhard L. Bolland (A) 306 S. Van Buren Street, Stoughton, WI 53589.

Maj. Gen. Charles J. Bondley, Jr. (AF) D: 13 Oct. 73 (Orlando, FL).

Col. Harold C. Brookhart (A) D: 26 Feb. 84 (Piscataway, NJ).

Col. Charles E. Brown (A) D: 30 Sept. 82 (Reedville, VA).

Rev. P. Stanley Brown (A) 3590 Gleneagles Drive, Silver Spring, MD 20906.

Col. Staunton L. Brown (A) D: 7 Oct. 84 (Mystic, CT).

Brig. Gen. Travis T. Brown (A) 1156 Grizzly Peak, Berkeley, CA 94708.

Col. Harold W. Browning (A) 35 Glen Drive, Mill Valley, CA 94941.

Col. Burton B. Bruce (A) 203 Yoakum Parkway, #312, Alexandria, VA 22304.

Col. Byron E. Brugge (AC) D: 4 Mar. 45 (POW Cp., Fukuoka, Japan).

Ralph E. Bucknam P.O. Box 2151, Halevik, Long Island, NY 11743.

Col. John P. Buehler (A) 820 Greenfield Road, St. Helena, CA 94574.

Lt. Gen. William B. Bunker (A) D: 5 June 69 (Ft. Myer, VA).

Capt. Paul Burlingame, Jr. (AC) D: 17 June 40 (air accident; Mitchel Field, NY).

Maj. Gen. William M. Canterbury (AF) 5821 Box Canyon Road, La Jolla, CA 92037.

Maj. Gen. John B. Cary (AF) D: 10 June 81 (San Antonio, TX).

Brig. Gen. Frank J. Caufield (A) D: 27 July 78 (San Francisco, CA).

Col. Miles B. Chatfield (A) 950 Woodland Avenue, #123, Ojai, CA 92023.

Col. Daniel M. Cheston, III (A) 200 Paddington Road, Baltimore, MD 21212.

Maj. Joseph A. Cleary (A) D: 16 Jan. 42 (KIA; Bataan, PI).

Maj. Eugene H. Cloud (A) D: 29 May 43 (auto accident; Tunisia).

Col. Fredric C. Cook (A) 403 Woodlake Drive East, San Antonio, TX 78229.

Lt. Col. Robert E. Corrigan (A) 2721 S. Hayes Street, Arlington, VA 22202.

Lt. Col. James A. Costain (A) D: 15 June 44 (KIA; Normandy, France).

Col. Jean P. Craig (AF) 1013 Dover Lane, Arlington, TX 76010.

Maj. Gen. William H. Craig (A) 6 East High Point Road, Stuart, FL 33494.

Col. Thomas L. Crystal, Jr. (AF) D: 21 Aug. 71 (Palo Alto, CA).

Lt. Col. Joseph M. Cummings, Jr. (A) D: 1 Mar. 45 (KIA; Rhineland, Germany).

Col. Kenneth A. Cunin (A) 5843 Royal Club, San Antonio, TX 78239.

Maj. Gen. William A. Cunningham, III (A) D: 25 Sept. 83 (WRAH).

Maj. Gen. George B. Dany (AF) 7400 Crestway #727, San Antonio, TX 78239.

Col. John W. Darrah, Jr. (A) D: 26 Mar. 75 (Brownsville, TX).

Col. Harold C. Davall (A) D: 9 Apr. 74 (San Francisco, CA).

Col. Ellis O. Davis (A) Box 6, West Point, NY 10996.

Maj. Gen. Kermit L. Davis (A) 12367 Antelope Trail, Box 156, Parker, CO 80134.

Brig. Gen. Merlin L. DeGuire (A) D: 15 July 83 (Clearwater, FL).

William D. Denson 85 Park View, Cedarhurst, NY 11516.

Lt. Col. John E. Diefendorf, Jr. (A) 3017 Willow Spring Court, Williamsburg, VA 23185.

Col. John H. Donoghue (A) D: 12 Feb. 71 (Hudson, MA).

Lt. Gen. Stanley J. Donovan (AF) APO Box 3009, New York, NY 09283.

Col. Meade J. Dugas (A) D: 26 Sept. 65 (Gulfport, MS).

Col. Donald L. Durfee (A) D: 1 Apr. 84 (Boca Raton, FL).

Col. George L. Eatman (A) D: 25 Dec. 82 (Oxford, MS).

Col. Henry W. Ebel (A) 9836 N. 110th Street, Scottsdale, AZ 85259.

Brig. Gen. Hallett D. Edson (A) 6521 Old Dominion Drive # 360, McLean, VA 22101.

Col. Charles B. Elliott, Jr. (A) D: 15 Mar. 80 (El Paso, TX).

Col. Robert Erlenkotter (A) D: 15 Nov. 83 (Ft. Bragg, CA).

Gen. Tirso G. Fajardo (PA) D: 6 May 86 (Blue Ridge, Queson City, Philippines).

Col. Charles F. Fell (A) 505 Tara Court, Boulder City, NV 89005.

Maj. Gen. Lloyd E. Fellenz (A) D: 21 Aug. 87 (St. Petersburg, FL).

Col. Robert G. Finkenaur (A) 24 Garden Drive, New Windsor, NY 12550.

Lt. Col. Edward Flanick (AC) D: 5 Mar. 42 (MIA; anti-sub patrol off Southeast coast).

Col. Thomas C. Foote (A) 330 Ray's Ford Circle, Earlysville, VA 22936.

Maj. Floyd F. Forte (A) D: May 42 (KIA; Mindoro, PI).

Maj. Gen. John. F. Franklin (A) 10 Lupine Way, Hillsborough, CA 94010.

Lt. Col. Robert W. Fuller, III (A) D: 30 Aug. 85 (Washington, DC).

Col. George H. Gerhart (A) 14130 Rosemary Lane, #3320, Largo, FL 33544.

Col. Seymour I. Gilman (A) Box 26, Quechee, VT 05059.

Col. Stacy W. Gooch (A) 3120 La Ronda Place, N.E., Albuquerque, NM 87110.

Col. Karl. T. Gould (A) 128 Colonial, S.E., Port Charlotte, FL 33950.

2nd Lt. Rudolph Green (A) D: 11 Jan. 36 (Ft. Peck, MT).

Maj. Gen. Perry B. Griffith. (AF) D: 10 Jan. 85 (Redlands, CA).

Brig. Gen. Willaim M. Gross. (AF) D: 2 Feb. 72 (McAllen, TX).

Col. Paul. T. Hanley (AF) 527 Cyprus Court, Lompoc, CA 93436.

2nd Lt. James F. Harris (A) D: 4 Jan. 35 (San Francisco, CA).

Brig. Gen. Thomas M. Hayes (A) D: 1 Oct. 60 (air accident; Oakland, CA).

Lt. Col. Percy T. Hennigar (A) D: 22 Dec. 64 (San Francisco, CA).

Lt. Col. Henry R. Hester (A) D: 30 Oct. 79 (Atlanta, GA).

Col. Daniel H. Heyne (A) D: 28 July 86 (Glen Flora, TX).

Lt. Col. Edwin G. Hickman (A) D: 3 Feb. 78 (Bradenton, FL).

Maj. Gen. Gerald J. Higgins (A) 45-555 Pueblo Road, Indian Wells, CA 92210.

Col. Charles W. Hill (A) 15 Magnolia Gardens Drive, Covington, LA 70433.

John T. Hillis Hillis Bldg., 4th & North Streets, Logansport, IN 46947.

Col. J. deP. Townsend Hills (AF) D: 17 Aug. 75 (Bethesda, MD).

Maj. Gen. Harry L. Hillyard (A) 410 Oakland Avenue, Indialantic, FL 32903.

Col. William J. Himes (A) D: 19 Sep. 86 (Lancaster, WI).

Col. Theodore F. Hoffman (A) 4207 Tarlac Drive, San Antonio, TX 78239.

Lt. Col. David L. Hollingsworth (A) 1345 Stagingwood Court #6, Walnut Creek, CA 94595.

Lt. Col. Stanley Holmes (A) D: 15 Dec. 44 (POW ship).

Col. William J. Holzapfel (AF) D: 26 Feb. 83 (Hurst, TX).

Col. Claude M. Howard (A) 5052 St. Mary's Road, Columbus, GA 31904.

Col. Harry J. Hubbard (A) 8012 Big Bend Drive, El Paso, TX 79904.

Capt. Dale E. Huber (A) 3200 La Rotonda Drive, #504, Ranchos Palos Verdes, CA 90274.

Col. Victor C. Huffsmith (A) D: 4 Aug. 70 (Loveland, CO).

1st Lt. Theodore F. Hurt, Jr. (A) D: 26 Oct. 41 (traffic accident; PI).

Brig. Gen. John M. Hutchison (AF) 7646 Tippit Trail, San Antonio, TX 78240.

Col. Thew J. Ice (AF) D: 8 Aug. 75 (Burlingham, NY).

Col. Louis L. Ingram (A) 1566 Leisure World, Mesa, AZ 85205.

Col. Arthur L. Inman (AF) 220 Corte Del Cerro, Novato, CA 94947.

Maj. Gen. Harvey J. Jablonsky (A) 7400 Crestway #1120, San Antonio, TX 78239.

Col. Russell W. Jenna (A) D: 7 Oct. 69 (Tallahassee, FL).

Maj. Gen. Charles E. Johnson, III (A) D: 14 Oct. 83 (Ft. Ord, CA).

Joseph L. Johnson 816 Erin Lane, Nashville, TN 37221.

Paul E. Johnson, Jr. 723 Indian Trail, Ashland, OH 44805.

Col. Dana W. Johnston (A) D: 19 Apr. 75 (Washington, DC).

Col. Franklin Kemble, Jr. (A) D: 18 Apr. 85 (Greenville, SC).

Col. Kenneth R. Kenerick (A) D: 26 Aug. 59 (Thule, Greenland).

Col. William B. Kern (A) 7624 Midday Lane, Alexandria, VA 22306.

Col. Joseph O. Killian (A) 2052 Shady Lane, Novato, CA 94947.

Col. Peter J. Kopcsak (A) P.O. Box 322, APO New York 09053.

Rev. John S. Kromer D: 25 Nov. 84 (Belmont, MA).

Lt. Col. Gersen L. Kushner (A) 5115 M-36, Stockbridge, MI 49285.

Maj. Gen. Robert C. Kyser (A) P.O. Box 7299, Fort Gordon, GA 30905.

Col. Vincent S. Lamb (AF) 4850 Ocean Beach Blvd., #103, Cocoa Beach, FL 32921.

Col. Harry E. Lardin (A) 1860 Ala Moana, #1703, Honolulu, HI 96815.

Brig. Gen. John D. Lawlor (A) 471 Hill Road, Winnetka, IL 60093.

Col. Richard A. Legg (AF) 1557 Acorn Way, Monument, CO 80132.

Col. Emory A. Lewis (A) D: 10 Mar. 83 (WRAH).

Maj. Gen. Elvin S. Ligon, Jr. (AF) D: 19 Nov. 75 (Washington, DC).

Maj. Gen. Thomas H. Lipscomb (A) 549 Chew's Landing Road, Haddonfield, NJ 08033.

Maj. Gen. Arno H. Luehman (AF) 10108 Donegal Court, Potomac, MD 20854.

1st Lt. Samuel A. Luttrell (A) D: 29 Nov. 51 (shipwreck; off NC).

Col. Clark Lynn, Jr. (A) 216 Mimosa Lane, Lawton, OK 73501.

Maj. Gen. Robert G. MacDonnell (A) D: 26 Aug. 84 (WRAH).

Col. Almon W. Manlove (A) D: 13 June 74 (Noel, MO).

Col. Ronald L. Martin (A) 9309 S. Orange Blossom Trail, Orlando, FL 32821.

Maj. Thompson B. Maury, III (A) D: 15 Dec. 44 (POW ship).

Col. Thomas A. McCrary (A) D: 22 Dec. 86 (Gainesville, GA).

Col. Richard L. McKee (A) D: 29 July 81 (Sun City, AZ).

Col. Ralph D. McKinney (A) Box 209, Marlow, OK 73055.

Col. Robert H. McKinnon (A) D: 29 June 81 (NC).

Col. Donald G. McLennan (A) Given Estates, Wesley Drive, Villa 21-A, Asheville, NC 28803.

Col. Dennis J. McMahon (A) D: 13 Aug. 84 (NY).

Col. Donald A. McPheron (A) D: 4 Feb. 62 (Paris, France).

John E. Mead D: 14 Feb. 78 (San Jose, CA).

Capt. Lawrence K. Meade (A) D: 24 Sept. 42 (POW Cp., Cabanatuan, PI).

Arthur F. Meier D: 1 Nov. 85 (Los Angeles, CA).

Lt. Col. John W. Merrill (A) D: 24 June 44 (KIA; Cherbourg, France).

Maj. James F. Miller, Jr. (A) 8255 Via Escondida, Whittier, CA 90605.

Col. Lee C. Miller (A) D: 5 Mar. 87 (Flagstaff, AZ).

Col. Robert B. Miller (A) D: 22 Nov. 84 (Corpus Christi, TX).

Col. Edward W. Moore (AF) 7312 Choctaw Road, Little Rock, AR 72205.

Maj. Gen. Frank W. Moorman (A) 8 Hunting Ridge Drive, Simsbury, CT 06070.

Col. Richard R. Moorman (A) 614 Bluff Canyon Circle, El Paso, TX 79912.

Brig. Gen. Lawson S. Moseley, Jr. (AF) D: 4 Sept. 68 (Montgomery, AL).

Col. Albert P. Mossman (A) D: 28 Nov. 75 (Ventura, CA).

Col. William J. Mullen (A) D: 19 Feb. 78 (Ft. Bragg, NC).

Col. Wilson H. Neal (AF) 800 Indian Springs Road, Novato, CA 94947.

2nd Lt. Jack J. Neely (AC) D: 22 Sept. 36 (air accident; RI).

Col. Henry Neilson (A) P.O. Box 1347, McAllen, TX 78501.

Col. William F. Northam (A) 229 West Lake Faith Drive, Maitland, FL 32751.

Brig. Gen. Frank C. Norvell (A) 106 East Woodlawn Drive, Harker Heights, TX 76541.

Col. Edward M. O'Connell (A) 3591 Mooney Avenue, Cincinnati, OH 45208.

Col. James O'Hara (A) D: 28 Feb. 85 (Washington, DC).

Col. Thomas A. O'Neil (A) D: 12 Feb. 86 (San Francisco, CA).

Col. Peter S. Peca (A) 123 N. Meadowcroft Drive, Akron, OH 44313.

Col. William S. Penn (A) 900 S. Clairborne Street, Goldsboro, NC 27530.

Col. Travis L. Petty (A) 466 Puncatest Neck Road, Tiverton, RI 02878.

Col. Joseph S. Piram (A) D: 24 June 74 (El Paso, TX).

Col. Mathew V. Pothier (A) D: 28 Feb. 84 (CA).

2nd Lt. Arthur B. Proctor (A) D: 31 Oct. 35 (MD).

Gen. Raymond J. Reeves (AF) 510 L Street, #1006, Anchorage, AK 99501.

Brig. Gen. Walter J. Renfroe, Jr. (A) 17 Inglewood Road, Asheville, NC 28804.

Col. Charles R. Revie (A) D: 8 Apr. 85 (Martinsville, VA).

Col. John B. Richardson, Jr. (A) Box 184, Gibson Island, MD 21056.

Maj. Oliver P. Robinson, Jr. (A) D: 14 Nov. 45 (Honshu, Japan).

Brig. Gen. Thomas DeF. Rogers (A) D: 29 Mar. 68 (San Francisco, CA).

Maj. Gen. William L. Rogers (AF) D: 5 Sept. 68 (Knoxville, TN).

Col. David B. Routh (A) Hampton Convalescent Center, 414 Algonquin Road, Hampton, VA 23661.

Col. Edwin Rusteberg (A) 4880 E. 14th Street, Brownsville, TX 78521.

Brig. Gen. Horace L. Sanders (A) 7522 Stonegate Drive, Lawton, OK 73505.

Lt. Col. Robert H. Sanders (A) D: 24 Feb. 45 (KIA; Heel, Holland).

Lt. Col. Lawrence B. Savage (AF) 147 Summertime Drive, San Antonio, TX 78216.

Col. John L. Schaefer (A) Box 3747, Boles Rural Station, Alamogordo, NM 88310.

Maj. Charles W. Schnabel (A) D: 24 July 48 (Pittsburgh, PA).

Lt. Gen. Jonathan O. Seaman (A) D: 18 Feb. 86 (Beaufort, SC).

Col. Henry A. Sebastian (AF) 5118 Lake Shore Drive, Waco, TX 76710.

Col. Leo W. H. Shaughnessey (A) D: 18 Sept. 83 (Phoenix, AZ).

Col. Jack E. Shuck (AF) D: 16 Aug. 72 (Mountain View, CA).

Lt. Col. Richard M. Sieg (A) D: 1 Dec. 55.

Col. Clifford G. Simenson (A) 1315 Old Tale Road, Boulder, CO 80303.

Col. Curtis D. Sluman (AF) RD #2, Box 31, Lovers Lane, Oriskany, NY 13424.

Maj. Gen. Dale O. Smith (AF) 3055 Heatheridge Lane, Reno, NV 89509.

Capt. Richard A. Smith (A) D: 27 Jan. 45 (from wounds; POW ship).

Col. Stilson H. Smith, Jr. (A) 20935 Coastview Lane, Huntington Beach, CA 92548.

Maj. Gen. John F. Smoller (A) D: 5 Mar. 70 (Denver, CO).

Col. Craig Smyser (A) 4013 Miramar, Dallas, TX 75205.

Col. James W. Snee (A) 185 Country Club Drive, Melbourne, FL 32940.

Gen. Berton E. Spivy (A) 921 Bywater Road, "Dickery Dock," Annapolis, MD 21401.

John H. Squier D: 9 Oct. 63 (Monterey, CA).

Col. John B. Stanley (A) 430 Lewers Street, #19-A, Honolulu, HI 96815.

Col. John J. Stark (AF) D: 25 Sept. 69 (LaMesa, CA).

Brig. Gen. John D. Stevens (A) 6313 Villa Lane, Falls Church, VA 22044.

Col. Daniel E. Still (A) 615 N. Washington Street, Council Grove, KS 66846.

Gen. William S. Stone (AF) D: 2 Dec. 68 (Brussels, Belgium).

Col. Alexander J. Stuart (A) 4635 Leeds Avenue, El Paso, TX 79903.

Col. Joe F. Surratt (A) D: 9 Nov. 75 (Indianapolis, IN).

Brig. Gen. Charles F. Tank (A) D: 31 July 85 (Newport News, VA).

Charles C. Tarbutton 1804 Manzanita, N.E., Salem, OR 97303.

Col. Ferdinand J. Tate (A) 500 W. Ash Avenue, Eunice, LA 70535.

Lt. Col. Sidney T. Telford (A) D: 14 Sept. 44 (KIA; Langfeld, Germany).

Col. Gene H. Tibbets (AF) D: 4 Feb. 66 (Washington, DC).

Col. Harrison F. Turner (A) G-14 Dover Country Club Apts., Dover, DE 19901.

Col. Paul L. Turner, Jr. (A) 1631 Blue Ridge Drive, Gainesville, GA 30501.

Brig. Gen. Robert N. Tyson (A) Lucy's Find, Box 977, White Stone, VA 22578.

Col. Hudson H. Upham (AC) D: 1 Nov. 46 (air crash; between Naples and London).

Edmundo Valdez Apartado de Correo 9152, Guayaquil, Ecuador.

Col. William S. Van Nostrand (A) D: 9 Jan 45 (KIA; POW ship).

Lt. Col. Donald O. Vars (A) D: 29 Jan. 68 (Ft. Knox, KY).

Col. Wilford E. H. Voehl (A) D: 26 July 70 (Davis, OK).

Brig. Gen. Russell W. Volckmann (A) D: 30 June 82 (Clinton, IA).

Lt. Col. John C. Walker, Jr. (A) P.O. Box 84, Oxford, MD 21654.

Col. James E. Walsh (A) D: 14 Dec. 60 (Vicksburg, MS).

Maj. Gen. Louis A. Walsh, Jr. (A) D: 17 May 87 (Bethesda, MD).

Lt. Col. George R. Walton (A) D: 16 Sept. 76 (Chicago, IL).

Col. Nathaniel P. Ward, III (A) 54 Allegheny Road, Hampton, VA 23661.

Col. Gordon G. Warner (A) 2769 Donna Drive, Columbus, OH 43220.

Brig. Gen. Robert B. Warren (A) D: 8 June 76 (Hampton, VA).

Col. William H. Waugh, Jr. (A) 9916 Eastridge Drive, El Paso, TX 79925.

Lt. Col. Edward E. B. Weber (A) D: 30 May 44 (KIA; Velletri, Italy).

Col. Richard E. Weber, Jr. (A) 3022 West 82nd Street, Leawood, KS 66206.

Col. George J. Weitzel (A) D: 24 Mar. 59 (Aiken, SC).

1st Lt. George F. Wells (A) D: 11 Feb. 40 (Washington, DC).

Col. James B. Wells (A) Contentment Island, Darien, CT 06820.

Brig. Gen. Charles H. White, Jr. (A) 7619 Quail Run, San Antonio, TX 78209.

Maj. Gen. John W. White (AF) 419 Lazy Bluff, San Antonio, TX 78216.

Maj. Edmund W. Wilkes (A) D: 26 June 42 (POW Cp., Cabanatuan, PI).

Col. Urquhart P. Williams (A) 3938 Far West Boulevard, Austin, TX 78731.

Col. James D. Wilmeth (A) 8501 Heron

Drive, "Happy Daze," Fort Worth, TX 76108.

Maj. Gen. Albert T. Wilson, Jr. (AF) D: 26 Feb. 70 (McDill AFB, FL).

Col. Charles B. Winkle (AF) P.O. Box 6416, San Antonio, TX 78209.

Maj. Gen. James R. Winn (A) D: 18 Apr. 76 (El Paso, TX).

Maj. Gen. William H. Wise (AF) 24 Dekker Drive, Golden, CO 80401.

Col. Yale H. Wolfe (A) 9 Royal Crest Drive, #8, North Andover, MA 01845.

Lt. Col. Carl D. Womack (A) 2316 Calle Halcon, Santa Fe, NM 87501.

Col. Charles H. Wood (A) Partridge Hill Lane, Greenwich, CT 06830.

Col. Thomas E. Wood (A) 122 Calumet Place, San Antonio, TX 78209.

Col. Samuel K. Yarbrough, Jr. (A) 515 Eleuthra Lane, Indian Harbour Beach, FL 32937.